Ladies' Day
at the Capitol

Ladies' Day at the Capitol

New York's Women Legislators, 1919–1992

Lauren Kozakiewicz

SUNY PRESS

Cover image editorial credit: Cheri Alguire / Shutterstock.com.

Published by State University of New York Press, Albany

© 2022 State University of New York

All rights reserved

Printed in the United States of America

No part of this book may be used or reproduced in any manner whatsoever without written permission. No part of this book may be stored in a retrieval system or transmitted in any form or by any means including electronic, electrostatic, magnetic tape, mechanical, photocopying, recording, or otherwise without the prior permission in writing of the publisher.

For information, contact State University of New York Press, Albany, NY
www.sunypress.edu

Library of Congress Cataloging-in-Publication Data

Name: Kozakiewicz, Lauren, author.
Title: Ladies' day at the capitol : New York's women legislators, 1919–1992 / Lauren Kozakiewicz.
Description: Albany : State University of New York Press, [2022] | Includes bibliographical references and index.
Identifiers: LCCN 2022013435 | ISBN 9781438490977 (hardcover : alk. paper) | ISBN 9781438490984 (ebook) | ISBN 9781438490960 (pbk. : alk. paper)
Subjects: LCSH: Women legislators—New York (State)—Biography. | New York (State)—Politics and government—20th century.
Classification: LCC JK3466 .K69 2022 | DDC 328.747092/52—dc23/eng/20220803
LC record available at https://lccn.loc.gov/2022013435

10 9 8 7 6 5 4 3 2 1

Ladies' Day at the Capitol

New York's Women Legislators, 1919–1992

Lauren Kozakiewicz

Cover image editorial credit: Cheri Alguire / Shutterstock.com.

Published by State University of New York Press, Albany

© 2022 State University of New York

All rights reserved

Printed in the United States of America

No part of this book may be used or reproduced in any manner whatsoever without written permission. No part of this book may be stored in a retrieval system or transmitted in any form or by any means including electronic, electrostatic, magnetic tape, mechanical, photocopying, recording, or otherwise without the prior permission in writing of the publisher.

For information, contact State University of New York Press, Albany, NY
www.sunypress.edu

Library of Congress Cataloging-in-Publication Data

Name: Kozakiewicz, Lauren, author.
Title: Ladies' day at the capitol : New York's women legislators, 1919–1992 / Lauren Kozakiewicz.
Description: Albany : State University of New York Press, [2022] | Includes bibliographical references and index.
Identifiers: LCCN 2022013435 | ISBN 9781438490977 (hardcover : alk. paper) | ISBN 9781438490984 (ebook) | ISBN 9781438490960 (pbk. : alk. paper)
Subjects: LCSH: Women legislators—New York (State)—Biography. | New York (State)—Politics and government—20th century.
Classification: LCC JK3466 .K69 2022 | DDC 328.747092/52—dc23/eng/20220803
LC record available at https://lccn.loc.gov/2022013435

10 9 8 7 6 5 4 3 2 1

Contents

Acknowledgments	vii
Introduction	1
Chapter 1 Politics: The New York Story	7
Chapter 2 Women and the New York Story	21
Chapter 3 Pioneers and Placeholders: Legislators from 1919 through 1964	33
Chapter 4 Activism and the Woman Legislator, 1965–1980	63
Chapter 5 Activist-Era Profiles: Contrasting Career Paths	93
Chapter 6 Women Organize as Women: Maximizing Leverage in the Office	109
Chapter 7 Advocates for Women's Issues	121
Chapter 8 New York's "Year of the Woman": Gender and Politics in the 1992 Legislative Elections	145
Conclusion	163
Notes	169
Bibliography	213
Index	225

Acknowledgments

This book has been a long time coming. Its origins go back to my dissertation, begun in the mid-1990s and finished in the early 2000s. The ideas from that work evolved over time and reemerged as the seeds for this study. None of that would have happened without the support of the University at Albany, State University of New York, for which I am thankful. Institutional support is important. But even more significant than the grant I received to start the project has been the individuals within the institutions who encouraged me along the way. Sue Faerman and Dina Refki of the Center for Women in Government and Civil Society helped me initially develop a project plan. They remained interested in the work and had me speak about pieces of it at center program events over the next several years. *New York History* published a piece drawn from my research in the journal. The editors there helped me visualize and act on the shift from pure research to writing. I want to thank SUNY Press for its support of the project and for understanding that the writing portion always takes longer than expected. Finally, the two anonymous peer reviewers contracted by the press gave invaluable advice about sharpening the organization and presentation of my work. This book is better because of all these influences.

There are several colleagues and friends whose fingerprints are all over this book. I cannot thank Richard Hamm enough. First as my mentor in graduate school and now as my colleague, he pointed me in this scholarly direction and helped me find my voice as a historian. Susan McCormick has been a dear friend throughout, endlessly listening to my ideas and offering suggestions. Her direction of the Albany-based conference Researching New York gave me a venue for presenting pieces of my work. It was at one of those conferences that SUNY Press first heard about and liked the project framework. It is also where I first met Robert Chiles of the University of Maryland. He has been a consistent supporter and copresenter at a number of different conferences. Both Richard and Rob, along with Laura Wittern-Keller of Albany's History Department, read all or parts of the manuscript and offered excellent feedback.

I owe a debt to all those who keep the records that made my research possible. Each facility was welcoming and helpful. I owe special thanks to Brian Keogh, head archivist at the M. E. Grenander Department of Special Collections & Archives at Albany. His herculean effort literally carried the papers of key early legislator Rhoda Fox Graves to Albany from less-than-ideal attic storage at the museum in Gouverneur, New York. These papers are now organized, cataloged, and available for research as part of the archive's modern political collection.

Throughout everything, though, my family has been my most consistent cheering squad, even though they admit not knowing exactly what I do all the time at my desk and computer. A special thank you to my husband, who agreed with my decision to quit my full-time job in my forties to go back to school. Not a blink on that one. Last, I am grateful for the unquestioning love from a series of family dogs who slept at my feet, under that desk, as I wrote. No matter what, they were always there, full of love.

Introduction

On March 11, 1954, the New York State Assembly officially celebrated *Ladies' Day*, "when male legislators gallantly step aside to let the seven members of the fairer sex run the show." But the author of this *New York Times* piece then noted, "Their moment of glory was short lived. When the section of the calendar involving final votes on bills was reached, the men took over again."[1] Aside from the patronizing tone, the short article showed that New York's women, despite having begun serving in the legislature in 1919, were still a rarity thirty-five years later, so much so that political leaders singled them out for special notice. It was also apparent that these women were very much outside the circle of power and thus figuratively invisible.

This faux-celebration of the woman politician was marginally better than the presuffrage days when to be a woman meant literal invisibility with respect to the political system. There was no place for them in formal politics at all. To illustrate, I point to the death of New York City Tammany machine stalwart Murray Hall in January 1901. The death received multiple days of newspaper coverage. Fellow party members were shocked to find Hall was actually a woman.[2] For over a quarter of a century, Hall had dressed and behaved as a man, including the activities and rituals of partisan politics. Hall had been a member of the Iroquois Political Club and an election district leader. The price Hall paid for that participation was hiding her sex to everyone. Then current State Senator Barney Martin of Lower Manhattan had trouble accepting the deception once it was revealed. "He was at the polls every election day, voted once anyway as they say, and helped get out the vote."[3] Senator Martin concluded by observing, "His place will be a hard one to fill, but he won't be a her again if I can help it."[4]

By 1954 women had made a place for themselves in the legislature but significant power still eluded them. They also remained largely absent from broader discussions of New York politics. Their history and contributions are rarely part of the secondary literature even though eighty-eight women served between 1919 and the 1992 elections. These are the years that bookend this study. The year 1918 was the first time New York's women could both vote and run for legislative office. As a result of that election, two women began their terms in the New York State Assembly in January 1919. At the other end, 1992 was considered a wave election for women in congressional races, and one that many hoped signaled a broad breakthrough for women candidates at all levels going forward. Fourteen women won election to New York's legislature in 1992, the most in any single cycle to date, doubling the previous high of seven, ten years earlier.

It is all the more important that we examine these women legislators given that scholars agree women had their earliest and largest success as candidates at the state level. By 1933, 320 women had served in state legislatures across the nation, with Louisiana the only holdout.[5] But as late as 1973, Albert Abrams, then secretary of the New York State Senate, considered the arrival of three new female senators the equivalent of "culture shock" for that body.[6] That was a year after former State Assemblywoman and then Congresswoman Shirley Chisholm became the first black female to seek the presidential nomination. The first goal of this study is to restore these New York women legislators to our political narrative by showing how their actions influenced lawmaking. The second goal is more subtle, for it involves the cultural elements of attitude and behavior. What kind of impact did these women have on the way the legislature conducted its business and how legislators behaved among themselves and appeared to the public?

Realizing these goals requires understanding the political environment of New York State and the position of the legislature within it. Through a series of twenty-two interviews with influential and knowledgeable government figures, two editors—Gerald Benjamin and Robert Nakamura—studied the workings of the New York State Legislature in the mid-twentieth century. In their book, *The Modern New York State Legislature*, they argued that the legislature had professionalized itself and, in doing so, reasserted its authority and influence vis-à-vis the executive. The subtitle of their book—*Redressing the Balance*—highlights the legislature's renewed importance. The book also makes the case that New York, like every state, is the product of a unique set of factors: geography, demography, economics, as well as the accumulated weight of its political party and institutional histories. We can only understand New York's politics by looking at the whole framework. And what is true about the whole is also true about the course of women legislators.

Anne Marie Cammisa and Beth Reingold, two scholars of women state legislators, say "to explain women's behavior and role in state legislatures more fully, we must do so in the context of variations in state political culture, legislative norms and structures, and the continuing process of legislative professionalization."[7] My study documents New York women's actions as elected officials and integrates those actions into both the history of New York State politics and the story of the emerging woman politician.

This study builds off a first generation of scholars interested in women state legislators. In the 1970s, they examined the concept of the woman legislator writ broadly. Jeane Kirkpatrick's *Political Woman* from 1974 sketched out the background and characteristics of women currently entering electoral politics.[8] The typology she laid out reflected women's unique path to politics as well as the gendered social expectations that impacted their time in politics. While her analysis was aimed at women in state legislatures, her conclusions remained generic. Irene Diamond's *Sex Roles in the State House* from 1977 also focused on women state legislators. She looked at the impact of sex differences on women's quest for political office. Diamond acknowledged the impact of local conditions on women's electoral chances, so, at least intuitively, she understood that state circumstances had a role to play. But, again, her analysis was broadly constructed.[9] A next generation of scholars began producing state-centered studies of women legislators in the 1990s. Individual works on women from Iowa, Texas, Arizona, and California, respectively, place the subjects squarely within the context of those states' political histories and unique institutional frameworks. These state-centered studies also consider the social and cultural heritage of the state's residents.[10] This study of the New York woman legislator is consistent with these efforts in that the history of the women is deeply embedded within the broader New York story.

Chapters 1 and 2 provide the contextual background for understanding New York women's political history. Chapter 1 gives a brief overview of New York's development and the effect that development had on the state's politics and governance. The focus there is on where and how developments bred the environment that elected women encountered. Women legislators had to negotiate New York–specific elements if they were to succeed, just as their male colleagues had to do. But the women faced an added adjustment that men did not. They had experienced a political apprenticeship that was unique to their gender. Chapter 2 shifts to the history of women's separate political experiences presuffrage and sketches out the suffrage fight in New York. The history of women's earlier exclusion from partisan politics would affect their identity as politicians going forward. New York's women had to reconcile women's separate political history both with the unique aspects of their state and the gendered nature of partisan politics and with the political institutions within which partisan activities occurred. The suffrage campaign gives us a first glimpse into how well women did in understanding the politics of the state and in developing strategies to succeed in the world as it was and not as they wished it to be.

Chapters 3 and 4 focus on the specific attributes and histories of exemplary women legislators from 1919 through 1980. Presenting all the women's individual stories is neither feasible nor the best way to write the history. Instead, I identified patterns to their service that showed common elements or experiences, or both, at a given time. The chapter names reflect key characteristics of those eras. The title in chapter 3 uses the terms *pioneer* and *placeholder* as shorthand for the first group of women legislators studied. They were pioneers by entering an environment that was truly new for them. They broke new ground that subsequent women built on. They marked and held places for them. It is equally important to notice the points at which the existing pattern changed in a significant way. In the critical years around 1965 and again around 1980, the model of what a woman legislator ought to be shifted. Chapter 4 refers to the woman legislator as an *activist*. The women who ran embraced the idea that activism was challenging and changing old norms. But they divided over the role of the legislature as the best vehicle to effect that change.

Within these chapters, I profile broadly the *archetypical woman legislator* of each era using various parts of the histories of the individual women who were there at that time.[11] The chapters thus group the women together as representative of periods I believe warrant that designation. The periodization framework allows me to make sense of the details in a way that I hope captures the essence of these women politicians' experiences. But throughout, I want to be clear that these women were individuals with their own stories. As Nancy Baker Jones and Ruth Winegarten concluded in their own study of Texas women legislators: there is no one typical female legislative type, though that does not mean there was not an archetype that each existed in tension with.[12] Chapter 5 provides several examples of how important it is to not rely solely on composite profiles. This chapter looks more deeply at the legislative careers of a few women from the activist era.

A key assumption about the woman legislator has been that she would bring more attention to issues women cared about. Chapter 6 follows women's efforts to leverage their influence by building unifying organizations among fellow women legislators. Even as women grappled with how best to maximize the impact of their small numbers in office, they homed in on particular issues. For the first four decades of legislative service, women were most strongly associated with issues of home, family, and community. But in the 1960s, women added a second track: their own societal disadvantage. Some of the expansionist impulse fed off the women's movement's success at getting the public's attention. Some of it reflected an expectation, or maybe a hope, that the timing was right for a nucleus of inspired women officeholders to successfully challenge older, cultural traditions. Chapter 7 looks at how women politicians pursued both a more traditional women's agenda focused on family and community as well as one that focused on women's own position in that community. The chapter takes a deeper look at women's leadership in the 1960s and 1970s on education reform and reproductive rights, specifically the fight for abortion reform.

Chapter 8 uses a microstudy of Westchester County in the lower Hudson Valley to examine what was happening to New York's women politically as the twentieth century ended. In 1992, more women than ever before won seats in the legislature. It was also a banner year for women candidates at the national level. The media dubbed the phenomena "The Year of the Woman" and presumed an outsized influence for gender on electoral outcomes everywhere. I assess the relative weight of that belief against other factors in play in New York that may better explain women's state-level success that year.

In sum, the story of New York's women legislators, a story which has not been told, shows the evolution of the woman politician in New York as the complex interaction of many factors. Gender has been and remains important to how women conceive of themselves as politicians, how they deal with the political environment they enter, and how they make their contributions once there. But while I can sketch out this story, evidentiary matters keep the full details somewhat elusive. Much of what cannot be recovered has to do with the way historical records were previously developed and saved. And those record-keeping decisions had a gendered component. An important impediment to knowing more about these women is that the paper trail is thin, extremely so for the earliest legislators. The default position early on was not to save one's records from the time in office. Nor were there many legislative records, such as legislative bill jackets, for the first years when women served. Jackets were and are collections of supplementary material that are forwarded with passed legislation to the governor to provide background information on the bill. For the earliest women legislators, we are left mostly with what has been said about the women in the media; the biographical information they submitted on themselves to the annual legislative summary, *The New York Red Book*; lists of the laws they introduced; and a few mentions in other sources. These sources, when woven with limited secondary material that take a broad look at women entering politics immediately after suffrage and women in individual state legislatures in this period, are what allow for an understanding of a first generation of New York's women legislators.

Sometimes, however, the absence of something can be meaningful in and of itself. In *Silencing the Past: Power and the Production of History*, Michel-Rolph Trouillot argues that certain voices have been silenced and thus marginalized at key points in the process of creating the historical narrative.[13] The lack of archival materials on the majority of early- and even many mid-twentieth-century women legislators may say something about how hard it was for women to find their own voice in this political arena. There may also have been a social element at work here that traced back to past cultural assumptions about women's selfless nature preventing them from promoting their own political profiles. The way in which the women's movement of the mid-twentieth century broke those traditional taboos has had a positive impact on women taking more control of their own history.

Thankfully, the maturation of the woman politician as a distinct entity has included the recognition that her own story is important. Going forward, more women in politics have saved their records and donated them to archives and libraries. In the early 1990s, the New York State Legislative Women's Caucus, a bipartisan organization of women legislators, began an oral history project whose goal was to interview all the women who were serving or had served in that body. While the project did not prove sustainable, it did capture the reminiscences of a small group, and those voices have proven invaluable to this project. And I am grateful for the ability to have personally interviewed a small group of retired legislators. Still, as I write this introduction, I admit up front that the chapters to follow represent only the start of documenting the collective history of New York's women legislators rather than its end point.

Chapter 1

Politics

The New York Story

Overview

Figure 1.1. New York Map: Counties and Regions.

No one factor explains New York politics. The state's political identity comes from the interplay of geographic, economic, and cultural factors. Woven together, these elements give New York its distinctive character. New York's political leaders then put their stamp on the state through their use of certain forms of political organizing and by their broad interpretation of the role of government in people's lives. The result is that the state is best understood as the product of a set of key elements. First, New York's geography and growth patterns created significant divides within the state, often referred to as "Upstate" versus "Downstate," which in turn generated fights over political power and policy priorities. Figure 2.1 illustrates the common understanding of the state's division into geographic regions. Second, by the early twentieth century, New York's leaders committed to a vision of social liberalism that justified pursing an expansive, activist government. Leadership in this area gave the state outsized national influence through the first six decades of the century. But New York's activist vision was only as good as the state's economic prospects, which had been historically robust. Beginning around 1970, New York instead became a cautionary tale of decline as the state struggled to deal with the effects of post–World War II deindustrialization and changing demographics. Most significantly, the costs of social liberalism now exceeded the capacity of the state to support such policies. Finally, the challenges of mid-century incentivized the legislature to reassert itself as a counterweight to the state's very strong executive. Over time, New York's governor had amassed more power than counterparts in most other states. In response, the legislature modernized and bureaucratized in ways that strengthened its influence.

Geography as a Defining Political Feature: Upstate versus Downstate

In their introduction to *New York Politics: A Tale of Two States*, Edward Schneier and John Murtaugh lay out what is to New Yorkers pretty obvious. "Social and economic cleavages in New York reinforce and confound each other. There are two New Yorks, both socially and politically; and the political system has become increasingly unwilling and unable to bridge the gap."[1] Today, New York's status as one of the most urbanized states in the union overshadows how thinly populated much of remaining state is. More than 50,000 people live within a square mile in Manhattan, yet there are just 3.1 per square mile in Hamilton County, an hour outside the city of Albany.

New York has always had clashing identities. From its seventeenth-century Dutch colonial days, Manhattan's urban commercial diversity competed against an agricultural vision grounded in an interior rich in land. Completion of the Erie Canal in 1825, and construction of peripheral feeder canals ignited the state's economy, catapulting it to a national dominance in the nineteenth century.[2] The 363-mile-long canal moved goods from Buffalo to Albany, making Upstate a powerful economic engine.

At the same time, mid-nineteenth century industrialization supported urban development not just in New York City but around the state. Immigrants made the state their home as that industrialization created jobs. A first wave from Ireland and Northern Europe provided a new labor source pre–Civil War. At the end of the century, first New York's Castle Garden and then Ellis Island were the main points of entry into the country for millions of additional immigrants, many from Eastern and Southern Europe. Railroads were built alongside the old Erie Canal route. People and product flowed to and from cities like Buffalo, Rochester, Syracuse, Utica, and Albany. The census of 1880 showed that New York was first state with an urban majority population; the country only became majority urban in 1920. One-third of America's millionaires lived in New York City in 1892. At the same time, New York had the most farms in the country and 25 percent of its workforce was farmers, which represented the largest single occupational group in the state.[3]

Political competition in the late nineteenth century reflected the growing urban/rural divide. Revisions to the state constitution in 1821 extend suffrage to virtually all white men. Parties actively competed for those voters and developed strongholds within the state that mirrored the economic/demographic divide. Democrats were strongest in New York City, Queens, Bronx, and Richmond Counties. With few exceptions, Republicans maintained legislative control through the middle of the twentieth century by continuing to dominate Upstate and also winning a large percentage of the emerging suburban vote. But as the twentieth century ended, Democrats showed themselves increasingly capable of winning seats outside the New York City metropolitan area. Statewide, Republicans began the twentieth century with a two-to-one lead in registrations. That disappeared by mid-century, when the two parties enjoyed parity. After 1960, the balance swung toward Democrats, who had a five-to-one ratio of registrants over Republicans as the century ended.[4]

In the nineteenth century, partisan loyalties were fashioned around religious and ethnic divisions. The geographic concentration of specific groups around the state further reinforced the sense of a divided state. Immigrants clustered in cities that were more often Democrat. Upstate rural areas and suburbs were peopled by descendants of earlier generations of Northern–European, Protestant settlers who supported the Republican Party. Beginning in the 1960s, racial differences began to supersede ethnic and religious ones. Post–World War II outmigration of whites from cities and the immigration of Blacks and Hispanics to urban areas saw minority populations climb appreciably in cities. By 1990 minorities made up half of New York City's population and nearly 40 percent of the populations of Buffalo and Rochester.[5]

Control of the legislature lagged behind population and party registration shifts that favored Downstate and New York City. Republicans had used the 1894 Constitutional Convention to cap the number of possible seats there to no more than one-third of the total in the State Assembly. Those rules neutralized the power of lopsided victories by Democrats in New York City. Despite Democrats winning upward of 80 percent of the seats from New York City, Republicans still held the majority in the Assembly. But a series of mid-twentieth century court cases finally equalized population and representation by mandating one-person-one-vote districts. Democrats won control of the Assembly in 1965, lost it again in 1968, but regained it for good in 1974. Democrat majorities after that became increasingly lopsided. Republicans held on to the Senate longer, albeit with shrinking majorities as Democrats increasingly won more seats outside New York City.[6]

Political Systems and Party Dynamics in New York

Within the overall party structure, political organizations maximized group allegiances and physical concentrations to wield power. New York's urban politicians operated what we call machine politics. Machines were tightly organized political units that relied on strong leadership and loyalty made possible by patronage. Cities like New York, Albany, and Buffalo all had machines that provided systematic and relatively effective, though often corrupt, governance at the local level. But accepting political corruption as a cost of doing business generated opposition, both from the opposing party as well as reform elements within the dominant machine party. Machines found their control challenged by reform coalitions made up of intraparty and opposing party members. At its broadest then, New York produced a series of power brokers that reflected these very wide-ranging contours of influence. These "bosses," of party, of urban location, or both, controlled access to and shaped the agendas of their respective power centers. Increasingly, those fights revolved around a reform agenda.

Some examples will illustrate the complexity of New York State politics. Between the 1850s and 1930s, New York City's politics were dominated by the political organization known as the Tammany Hall machine. This Manhattan Democratic organization relied on controlling city services and patronage jobs as the way to enroll and secure Democratic voters, particularly members of the working class and new immigrants. This quid pro quo approach to politics generated a great deal of loyalty, both among the many political appointees within the Tammany system and among the population served by the Tammany appointees. Nonetheless, by the end of the nineteenth century, the name Tammany had become synonymous with graft, corruption, and political scandal. Coalitions of reform Democrats and Republicans successfully elected reform mayors in 1894 and 1901. But they did not stay in power or have much real impact beyond a single election cycle, given the dominance of that machine. Republican Theodore Roosevelt tried to reform the New York City Police Department and crack down on vice during the term of fusion mayor William Strong, 1895–1897. Fusion candidates enjoyed the support of the opposing party, here Republican, and the antimachine reform-minded segment of Democratic Party. Strong appointed Roosevelt as one of three police commissioners. But neither Roosevelt nor the Strong administration could change the way the City did business.[7]

Democrats outside the City fought to limit the machine's influence statewide. While serving in the New York State Senate from 1910 to 1913, anti-Tammany Democrat Franklin Roosevelt of the mid-Hudson Valley clashed with the machine, even as he grew to respect rising Tammany stars like Al Smith and Robert Wagner. While Smith and Wagner amassed strong and sincere records as reformers, other Tammany figures remained wedded to a model of power based on corrupt bargaining. Two decades later, in 1932, then Governor Franklin Roosevelt again clashed with Tammany Hall when he personally involved himself in the corruption investigation of New York City Mayor Jimmy Walker. FDR's presidential hopes required he take strong action against corruption within his party and his state.[8] Republican Fiorello La Guardia leveraged the ousting of Mayor Walker into his own election as mayor in 1933, again on a fusion ticket. He served three terms (1934–1945)—an indication of a weakened Tammany and the decline of political clubs in general from the mid-twentieth century on.

There were stirrings of women's interest in reforming politics going back to the New York City elections of 1894, but it was constrained by women's exclusion from politics. That year, Mrs. Josephine Shaw Lowell reached out to women and organized what became the Woman's Municipal League to campaign for reform. Lowell was a social reforming pioneer herself, having been appointed by New York's Governor Samuel Tilden in 1876 to head the New York State Board of Charities. Her Municipal League was not affiliated with either party but was a group focused only on good government.[9] It also remained separate from the male-led reform groups of the period, organizations with more clout since their members could vote. The Municipal League is an early example of how outside the political system women were, even as they sought to improve it. That exclusion will be discussed in detail in chapter 2.

The urban and county-led machine system persisted throughout the twentieth century. But machine leaders faced more and stronger challenges by mid-century, particularly from growing minority populations. Yet opponents mostly all acknowledged that the existing power structure was likely to continue. Shirley Chisholm and other frustrated minority Democrats attacked the 17th Assembly District Democratic Club of Brooklyn in 1960. They created the rival Unity Democratic Club to wrest power from the older organization, as opposed to destroying the system.[10] J. Raymond Jones was a New York City political figure from the 1920s through the 1960s. Elected Tammany Hall's first Black leader in 1964, Jones tried but largely failed to revive the organization's influence. Like Chisholm, Jones made the calculation that working within the system gave Blacks the best chance to advance politically. In his memoirs he was clear, however, that he supported the system and not necessarily the current leadership at any given time.[11]

Political reform was just one cause championed by New Yorkers. In the nineteenth century New York produced leaders in the areas of abolition, temperance, and, yes, women's rights. Many of those New Yorkers were women. However, such causes struggled and failed to translate into effective political organizations. Third parties dedicated specifically to reform issues had little success in the state, much like their counterparts across the nation. Minor party candidates could not win elections. Third parties had better luck in New York cross-endorsing major party candidates, something the state's election law permits. Minor parties frequently claimed they provided the margin of victory for mainstream candidates in close elections.[12] Still, for legislative races between 1950 and 1988, third parties determined the outcome in only 3 percent of them.[13] Third parties have tried to use their cross-endorsement ability to influence the policy agendas of major parties. The Liberal Party, Conservative Party, and Working Families Party are all examples of mid- to late-twentieth-century third-party efforts. The Liberal Party was created in 1944 by labor leaders in an effort to counter what they saw as too much political influence from bossism and special interests, particularly in the Democratic Party. The Liberal Party issues agenda had roots in the socialist labor movement in New York City. The Conservative Party, organized in 1962, aimed to push Republicans toward greater fiscal conservatism and a reversal of expansive administrative growth. Finally, created in 1988, the Working Families Party, also a labor-based initiative, ultimately displaced the Liberal Party (which disbanded in 2003) as New York's main political entity on the left.

New York's Activist Model of Government

One policy effect of New York's early urban/industrial dominance was the state's embrace of expanded government intervention to deal with the social and economic problems associated with urban development and a market economy. Many progressive policies regarding labor conditions, housing, health, and safety began in New York and then spread nationally. For example, the state broke new ground with its Factory Investigating Commission (FIC) following the horrific Triangle Shirtwaist Factory Fire of 1911, in which 146 workers, mostly young women, died. The FIC represented a new model of public/private partnership wherein reformers, including some women, and lawmakers joined forces to identify needed industrial changes. The legislature passed thirty-two new laws based on FIC recommendations.

New York's forward-looking vision influenced what other states and the nation would do. In 1933, former New York Governor and then President Franklin Roosevelt brought the ideology of social liberalism to the national stage. Back in New York, Herbert Lehman assumed the governorship and continued to add new programs to combat the effects of the Great Depression. He implemented a welfare apparatus that included emergency relief, unemployment insurance, and support for marginalized groups like orphans and the mentally ill. Social Justice was at the center of Lehman's political philosophy.[14] To stay competitive, Republicans campaigned on their own version of the expanded state, one that supported a large social agenda combined with a nod to some fiscal restraint. Republican Governor Thomas E.

Dewey (1942–1954) came into office emphasizing economy and efficiency as the way to maintain social programs.[15]

By the 1960s, however, the locus of industrial production had moved away from the northeast to the south, west, and overseas. The resulting deindustrialization of New York ultimately forced a rethinking about what the state needed and could afford to do in terms of programs. Revenue declined along with overall population. The state faced an aging urban and industrial infrastructure and the concentration of poorer citizens in urban areas. Still, political leaders were slow to give up their vision of New York as a place of expansive investment in liberal ideas. Republican Governor Nelson Rockefeller (1958–1973) continued to believe that government spending could cure economic ills; he saw it as his job "to take risks for the people."[16] Rockefeller continued to present budgets that asked for more resources from state residents than they were willing to approve. When voters rejected a $165 million bond issue in 1964, Rockefeller asked for more in next year's budget and proposed the state's first-ever sales tax.[17] By the mid-1970s, the state's financial problems came to a head. Democratic Governor Hugh Carey (1974–1982) had to deal with near-death financial spirals in New York City, Yonkers, Buffalo and Rochester. He announced an end to "the days of wine and roses" in his 1976 State of the State message.[18]

Democrats still continued to promote what political scientist Edward Schneier called a more "muted" liberalism.[19] But increasing numbers of Republicans were pushed by the Conservative Party to embrace the rightward trends that were becoming visible at the national level. Though Rockefeller refused the cross-endorsement of the Conservative Party in his 1970 reelection campaign, it was clear he was borrowing from the party's more conservative positions on both finances and social issues in order to stay in office.[20]

New York's leadership on policy had transformed her politicians into de facto national figures, especially her governors. Between 1900 and 1992 the country elected two former governors to the presidency: Theodore Roosevelt and Franklin Roosevelt. But New York also produced five of the losing nominees: Alton Parker, Charles Evans Hughes, Al Smith, Wendell Wilkie, and Thomas E. Dewey (twice).[21] Three of the five had been elected governor. In addition, Gerald Ford appointed Governor Rockefeller as his vice president from 1974 to 1976, though not as his running mate in 1976. Democratic presidential candidate Walter Mondale chose Queens Congresswoman Geraldine Ferraro as his running mate in 1984, making her the first woman on a major party presidential ticket.

Compared to other states, New York's governorship is among the strongest in the nation.[22] Governors got outsized attention in part because of those expansive powers. Since 1938, New York's governor is one of eleven in the country who can run for an unlimited number of four-year terms.[23] The governor sets the policy agenda, drafts the executive budget and submits it to the legislature, can veto bills or line items of appropriation, and has extensive appointive power. Between 1870 and 1976, the legislature failed to override any gubernatorial veto; since then, overrides have become more common. These extensive powers and the fact that the state legislature was essentially part time into the 1960s allowed the governor to dominate the branch. In sum, governors had more power than most states when it came to advancing the liberal agenda.[24]

That is not to say that all parts of New York embraced an activist state equally. The urban/rural dichotomy yielded differences regarding the scope of government. Republicans, stronger outside the cities, tempered their commitment to expanded government. New York's Republicans, exemplified by governors Dewey and Rockefeller, accepted the idea of more government services and protections for citizens. At the same time, they expressed concern about the state's fiscal health, though that concern rarely translated into policy action. And the Upstate/Downstate divide generated very different priorities when it came to what New Yorkers wanted their money spent on. Political scientist Jeffrey Stonecash suggests that because of the different regional party bases, policy proposals for much of the twentieth century were seen as benefiting either just the larger cities (New York, Buffalo, and Rochester) or the remainder of the state.[25] For example, the extent of the socioeconomic problems experienced by cities led Democrats to demand greater expenditures on social welfare.[26] While the ideological differences between the two parties appeared smaller at mid-century, the urban/rural divide remained. Both Democrats and Republicans were "almost impregnable in their respective strongholds."[27] Even today, Stonecash sees that "the majority parties in each house in New York clearly have electoral bases that differ by region, race, and income."[28]

The Education Policy Example

Fights over education policy illustrate both the urban/rural dichotomy in action, and give a glimpse into the challenges emerging for the activist state in the second half of the twentieth century. The very aspects of education that people cared about differed, depending on whether you were in the country or the city. Fights over resources escalated, especially in urban areas. Education has also been traditionally seen as of special interest to women. Women's path to political activism before suffrage cut through education, and women legislators became some of the strongest voices on education policy going forward.

In the early nineteenth century, the York State Legislature passed bills encouraging the establishment of local schools. Local property taxes would support locally run schools, making public education available regardless of a parent's ability to pay.[29] The state systematized education through the establishment of school districts with elected rather than appointed commissioners. It passed requirements for teacher training and compulsory education for students. Even as the state increased its oversight, the belief that education was mostly a local matter persisted. For rural districts, the biggest concern was limiting forced consolidations. Rural schools were sometimes the only or strongest community builder in an area. For urban districts, New York City in particular, fights were waged over the proper degree of centralized control, how to limit local political involvement in running schools, and how to create a curriculum that could "Americanize" the immigrant student.[30] By the late 1960s, the politics of education encountered new controversies around racial composition, local control, and finances.

In many areas of the City, school boards of the 1960s became sites of confrontation over education policy and resources. The City was committed to supporting the civil rights movement, but real obstacles made it hard to live up to the promise of an equal education for every student regardless of background. Upon taking office in 1966, new mayor John Lindsay inherited a problem with no good solution. It was numerically impossible to engineer racial balance in the public schools because that population was now majority minority. City finances were fragile. The administration used accounting gimmickry just to keep services running. At the same time, minority parents were becoming adamant about having input into the schools they did have. They wanted more resources, new teachers, and new curriculum. Lindsay commissioned a study that recommended creating a federation of five borough school districts connected through a weak central agency. Local school boards elected by each community would have real decision-making power.

Lindsay authorized an externally funded experiment in decentralized control for three districts in 1967–1968. Most of the attention centered on the Ocean-Hill Brownsville district in Brooklyn. This was a heavily minority district with much poverty. The experiment failed on all levels. It took three teachers strikes, the appointment of a state trustee to oversee the district, and ongoing negotiation between Lindsay, the school board, and the teacher's union to get the students back in school permanently. The government's relations with the minority community remained fractured.[31] The following year, 1969, the state legislature formally revised New York City's system. The Decentralization Act broke the City into thirty-two districts. There would be a central, elected Board of Education that would hire a chancellor who would report to the board. Local school boards continued, but areas of control were defined and more limited than under the Ocean Hill Brownsville experiment. Tension over the wisdom of too much decentralized power versus more central oversight prevented education officials and local boards from improving the actual delivery of education to students. The legislature tweaked the system again in 1973, when it approved changing the central board from mainly elected to fully appointive.[32] Despite, their diminished authority, school boards remained an attractive starting point for the politically ambitious. It became common for local politicians to have served or still be serving on school boards while holding other elective offices.

Once revived, the idea of neighborhood-level involvement in government proved resilient. The concept was reimagined as community boards. New York City created fifty-nine district community boards in 1975. Sociocultural anthropologist Roger Sanjek sees the boards as mediators between the "inherently politically powerless street neighborhoods and the inherently powerful city as a whole."[33] Community board members make recommendations on land use and the city budget as well as monitor the delivery of local services. These boards, both community and school, were in addition to other city or town or county government posts. To a degree they have replaced the older tradition of looking to the local party official or county leader for assistance with neighborhood matters.[34]

Modernizing the Legislature

The above example shows how the turmoil at mid-century bred more political activism at the local level as a challenge to New York's tradition of centralized authority. At the opposite end of the institutional spectrum, the state legislature pushed back against what it saw as executive efforts to dominate policy and financial decision-making. The legislature "reinvented" itself as a more modern, professionalized counterweight to the executive. A first step was taken in 1938, when legislative terms were lengthened from one to two years. Then, in the 1960s, leaders in both chambers created professional legislative staffs, especially in the areas of research, budget, bill drafting, and constituent service. Members stayed in the legislature longer, amassing process and issue expertise.[35] While the legislature technically remained part-time, sessions lengthened and more members presented themselves as essentially full-time legislators. In 1988, fully two-thirds of the legislature listed their primary occupation as legislator.[36] Each party benefited from increased legislative power, since divided control of the legislature became the norm after 1974.[37]

Republican loss of the Assembly was accelerated by court decisions that required the legislature reapportion seats to meet the one-person-one-vote threshold mandated by the Supreme Court in its 1962 *Baker v. Carr* decision and the follow-up *Reynolds v. Simms* case in 1964. The first case set the standard and the second mandated reapportionment of noncompliant districts. A third case, *WMCA v. Lomenzo*, decided in 1964, specifically struck down New York's apportionment rules. That case ended the 1894 limits on legislative seats from New York City. It was the WMCA representing several New York City registered voters that challenged the constitutionality of article III, sections 2–5, which mandated weighting rural areas over urban centers.[38] The reapportionment effort increased the number of New York City legislators.

Two other representation adjustments revitalized and accelerated the shift in political power from Upstate to Downstate and Republican to Democrat. A state constitutional amendment approved in 1969 now mandated that noncitizen residents be included in the population base for purposes of apportionment. This change increased New York City's electoral influence. Finally, a 1974 Justice Department–brokered reapportionment decision led to an increase in the number of New York majority-minority districts in the city.[39] The result was a number of new, open seats where minority candidates were expected to win. After 1974, Democrat control of the Assembly was assured.

When it came to running for office, by the 1980s the leaders of both the State Assembly and Senate had centralized election resources under their direct control, which further contributed to the decline of local party organizations as sources of power. The leadership had its own campaign committees to vet candidates, which generally favored incumbents.[40] Reelection became virtually automatic. In 1996, 97 percent of senators returned to office as did 98 percent of Assembly members; two years later every legislator running for reelection won.[41]

New York's unique and complicated political system opened up to women in 1918. Their acculturation to the system would in some ways resemble the experiences of their male counterparts. Geography and party affiliation affected everyone's political opportunities and influenced the issues legislators would care most about. The legislature as a whole contested with the power of the executive. However, in other ways, women had added adjustments to make that stemmed from their historic separation from formal politics and governance. We turn now to how that earlier exclusion influenced the development of a distinct presuffrage women's political consciousness. Women would have to reconcile this identity with the dictates of politics as practiced in New York if they wanted to be successful. Complicating things further were traditional social and cultural expectations about gender attributes and roles that made it harder for women to embrace a political identity.

Chapter 2

Women and the New York Story

Overview

By the end of the nineteenth century, women's concern for issues had brought them to the edge of partisan politics. But women had been forced to find influence along a completely separate track from their male partisans. Many women found success by grounding their politicization in their authority as mothers. In the late nineteenth century, concern for family and community had legitimized women's influence on policy. While this approach afforded them a connection to politics it was as political outsiders. These women could claim a purity on issues validated precisely by that political exclusion. Women entered electoral politics with a background whose rationale for influence seemed to preclude an easy adjustment.

But it would be a mistake to see New York's women as a monolithic group. Women have been no less affected by the existence of "two New Yorks" than have men. Even when big issues like suffrage exerted a global reach, how women approached the issue and the forms of organizing women engaged in reflected where in the state they lived, the politics associated with those locations, as well as their own sociocultural profiles. For example, rural women, like rural men, tended to be more conservative and skeptical of the expanded power of the state. Much of these women's activism would have been centered on local organizations associated with farm and church. Urban women as a cohort were more diverse demographically; they ran the gamut from elite to immigrant, college-educated professionals to working class. Urban women were more accepting of an expanded state, albeit for different reasons. Still, New York's women combined forces convinced voters to approve suffrage in a 1917 referendum. Historians of women's suffrage Susan Goodier and Karen Pastorello acknowledge the diversity of the movement. In their recent study of suffrage in New York, *Women Will Vote*, they take as their theme the need to tell not one woman's story but the "struggles and issues surrounding attainment of women's suffrage in New York State by diverse groups of women and men. . . . They did not form a single coalition but created a fluid, responsive movement of sometimes incongruent alliances."[1]

Women's Gendered Path into Politics

The women who then entered electoral politics in 1918 had to negotiate the parties and power centers around them.[2] Their first task would be to adapt to the political environment as opposed to reenvisioning it. Here is where women as women faced a hurdle that men did not. Women had to reimagine themselves as partisans, for electoral success depended on securing the nomination to run where their party was strong and exhibiting sufficient loyalty to political leadership while in office so as to be reelected. Nineteenth-century partisanship developed in tandem with the rise of the two-party system and universal white, male suffrage. A number of historians have connected nineteenth-century partisanship directly to the formation of a masculine identity. Richard McCormick describes a political environment where parties functioned as fraternal organizations that reinforced shared values.[3] Paula Baker believes "partisan politics characterized the male political environment . . . united all white men, regardless of class or other differences, provided entertainment, a definition of manhood, and the basis for male ritual . . . The right to vote was something important that men held in common."[4] Michael McGerr contends that since it was part of men's identity, "partisanship had to be paraded and asserted in public."[5] Demonstrations of partisan political allegiance flourished and tied men together as citizens of the United States. The unity derived from political rituals and spectacles overcame, at least for a while, entrenched regional or local differences among men. The result was an extraordinarily high level of voter turnout through the end of the nineteenth century. Party leaders benefited from this outpouring of partisan loyalty at elections and rewarded supporters accordingly.[6]

Women's path into party politics was different. While men easily equated public activism with enrolling in a political party and declaring one's partisanship, women saw activism as a commitment to an improved, more moral society made possible through personal and group action. Women's embrace of partisan politics meant they had to conquer not only male skepticism about their suitability for politics but also women's distrust of behaviors that seemingly contradicted deeply held ideas about womanhood. In her history of women's early involvement with the Republican Party, Melanie Gustafson found "one of the most remarkable things I encountered in my research was the consistent difficulty people had, and still seem to have, with women taking on political roles."[7]

Excluded from politics proper, women organized themselves around ideas of home, motherhood, and family. Paula Baker has shown that women learned to wield their motherhood as a powerful tool. At first, it was used to justify women's private organizations providing social services that existing governments were not prepared to offer. Later, women used maternal arguments to pressure governments to assume those responsibilities. Baker argues that women's organizations offered new, effective models for government action.[8] Political Scientist Theda Skocpol goes further, concluding that women's organizations convinced the state to develop certain social welfare policies and pass laws supporting mothers and children. She suggests that women came tantalizingly close to achieving something like a maternalist welfare state in the Progressive Era.[9] Skocpol cites as evidence the passage of mothers' pension laws in forty states by 1920, growing support for women's protective labor laws between 1891 and 1920, and the establishment of two new federal agencies controlled by women and focused on women's concerns: the Children's Bureau in 1911 and the Women's Bureau of the Department of Labor in 1918. Yet even when these activities seemed political, women scrupulously insisted what they were doing should not be called political.[10]

The Women's Christian Temperance Union (WCTU) illustrates just how women's home-centered concerns evolved into public action that bordered on the political. Established nationally in 1874, the WCTU started the year before in Freedonia, New York, as a series of spontaneous demonstrations against alcohol. Groups of women were inspired by a speech given by noted author, physician, and educator Diocletian Lewis. They publicly demonstrated in front of local saloons to convince patrons to stay out and owners to shut their doors.[11] These "women's crusades" developed into a formal organization that offered reform-minded, home-centered women a way to actively campaign for social change.[12] Its membership and leadership was completely female. The WCTU dominated the social reform landscape and had the largest single membership of any organization of the late nineteenth century, about 150,000 by 1900 and nearly a quarter of a million by 1910. At first, the organization emphasized personal moral suasion aimed at getting individual men to abandon drink and the violence associated with it. Later, under the "Do Everything Policy" of its national leader, Frances Willard, the WCTU pursued a broad reform agenda that ranged from prohibition to judicial reform to education law.[13] Willard convinced the national leadership to endorse suffrage, which the WCTU called the "home protection ballot."[14] By the start of the twentieth century, a number of other women's organizations, such as the National Congress of Mothers, the General Federation of Women's Clubs, and the National Consumers League were also using gendered strategies to press for new public policy initiatives.[15] In the first two decades of the twentieth century these organizations, along with a WCTU that increasingly focused on prohibition, further honed a separate women's political culture.

This culture, while segregated, edged closer to the regular business of politics. Within New York specifically, in 1880 women used maternalist ideas to secure the right to vote for school district officials and hold school board positions. After 1892, women could also vote for county school commissioners. Women argued education was a local issue, one that was supported by local taxes and focused on their own children. The teachers themselves, increasingly seen as professionals, were disproportionately young New York women trained at the state teacher normal schools.[16] Even after the New York Court of Appeals struck down women's ability to vote for county school commissioners in 1894, women were still allowed to run for the office. Women ran as third-party candidates, emphasizing their nonpartisanship, and several were elected over the next decade.[17]

Women's development of a separate political ideology was the pragmatic adaptation to their exclusion from party and government. Still, this pragmatism had been leavened with sincerity. The maternalist political culture responded to women's sincere, intense self-identification as mothers, wives, helpmates. Most women understood their identity in those terms. They added a political component to that identity as a way to influence public affairs, and to acknowledge that society's growth had complicated American family life and the roles of its members. Even when the existence of a distinctly separate political identity is disputed, historians usually acknowledge that women did demonstrate what one historian has called a distinct "female consciousness."[18]

These women had refashioned exclusion from the party system and from government into a badge of honor and form of influence. Nonpartisanship implied women were more virtuous than male politicians because they could not be corrupted by that system. It meant they were more interested in the well-being of society than in personal gain. Nonpartisanship held women's presuffrage political culture together just as partisanship defined the male political culture.[19] As Melanie Gustafson observes, "Prominent women of the time argued that if principle and party loyalty were unbalanced, it was principle that had to be protected."[20]

Women, Politics, and Suffrage

This "female consciousness" increasingly connected women to the vote, politics itself, or both, though ostensibly in nonpartisan ways. In the nineteenth century, women's rights activists in New York had advanced an agenda broader than just the vote. After the Civil War, however, that focus narrowed to suffrage. In 1869, Matilda Joslyn Gage, a leading figure in the women's movement at the national level as well as within the state, called for the establishment of the New York State Woman Suffrage Association (NYSWSA). Its grassroots efforts led to the formation of local suffrage groups, often called political equality clubs, in most counties.[21] These suffrage clubs complimented the WCTU and granges in rural areas and reinforced the importance of suffrage as an issue.[22] As historian Lisa Tetrault notes, the 1870s was a time of intense debate over whether suffrage stood or should stand at the pinnacle of a woman's rights agenda.[23] The existence of suffrage-specific groups became increasingly important as the WCTU retreated from aspects of overt politics after the death of Frances Willard in 1898. Many of its deeply religious members had gravitated to suffrage mainly because of her influence.[24] Filling the void, the NYSWSA ultimately became the largest suffrage association in the nation, aided by the relocation of the movement's national headquarters to New York City in 1909.[25]

By the twentieth century, women's domestic authority turned its attention to corrupt political systems. This shift added weight to the call for women's suffrage[26] Second-generation suffrage leaders adopted these arguments. A fracturing of the national effort between 1869 and 1890 was healed when leaders of the National Woman Suffrage Association merged with the American Woman Suffrage Association to become in the National American Woman Suffrage Association (NAWSA). Many of the arguments keyed to the single issue of suffrage fit with gendered expectations about women.[27] Suffragists downplayed the idea that giving women the vote would undermine conventional gender roles. This approach reduced resistance to suffrage among women and men.²⁸ Domestic arguments assuaged fears that extension of the vote to women would lead to a full-blown challenge to patriarchal control in other areas. This was no idle fear on men's part, given the degree to which partisan politics before 1920 was so closely associated with definitions of manhood.

New York City women already had some history of organizing into nonpartisan reform vehicles like the Women's Municipal League mentioned earlier.²⁹ But class divisions complicated suffrage activism in industrialized, urban areas. The NYSWSA made only sporadic efforts to reach working-class and immigrant women before the end of the nineteenth century. The generally elite leadership did not regularly interact with working women. When they did, suffrage women found that working-class women prioritized economic concerns, though they came to see that political rights could be a useful tool.³⁰ Some suffragists such as Harriet Stanton Blatch, Mary Dreier, and Margaret Dreier Robins tried to reach out to working-class, immigrant women by supporting those women's efforts to address economic disenfranchisement. In 1907 Blatch created the Equality League of Self-Supporting Women as a bridge to the working class. Dreier and Robins organized the Women's Trade Union League (WTUL) for the same purpose. WTUL women joined picket lines with the working girls during the 1909–1910 garment strikes in New York City, partly to prevent police brutality against the demonstrators. Still, historian Jo-Ann Argersinger concludes that the WTUL membership "divided by class and ethnicity did not always understand each other's positions or priorities."³¹ As noted above, New York's Factory Investigating Commission following the 1911 Triangle Fire represented the state's fulsome embrace of social responsibility. The investigation brought together the power of the state and that of nonpartisan women's reformism. Here women could and did work politically. Suffrage activists like Blatch hoped such crossover efforts would spill over into support for the 1915 women's suffrage referendum. They did not.

During the 1915 referendum campaign suffragists showed themselves more politically savvy than ever before. Blatch's biographer, Ellen Carol Dubois, notes Blatch was special in "her talent and taste for partisan politics."³² In 1910 Blatch had rechristened her organization the Women's Political Union in recognition that the organization was moving beyond the traditional club framework to pursue an overt political agenda. Other groups followed that lead. In 1915, a number of the political equality clubs around the state replaced "club" in the title with "party."³³ New York City suffragists had earlier created the Woman's Suffrage Party of Greater New York in 1909. The shift was more than just changing group names. Of necessity, women learned how to operate as political insiders. In 1914, Harriet Laidlaw produced *Organizing to Win by the Political District Plan* for the City organization, a document that historian Elizabeth Israels Perry has called "thirty-five pages of precise instructions for how to win legislative approval for woman suffrage."[34] The document was a how-to guide for getting the referendum through the legislature. Women lobbied legislators to support referendum legislation. But in 1915, the referendum failed at the polls. It lost by almost 200 thousand out of some 1.2 million votes cast. Failure was partly due to the two major parties either objecting or standing officially silent on the question. While the parties coveted the cohorts of potential voters should the referendum succeed, they were still unsure of how women could be folded into the organization. For it appeared some women were absorbing the information on politics without considering that they would have to adopt the partisanship practiced by parties. In her manual, Laidlaw had included specific and bold-type instructions for the women *not* to ally themselves with a specific party.[35]

Politicians' skepticism of women as potential partisans was reinforced in 1916. There were still influential women reformers who denounced partisanship during the presidential contest. They clung to the idea of pure issues advocacy. Perhaps the best-known effort that year was Frances Kellor's national nonpartisan Women's Committee for Charles Evans Hughes, the former governor of the New York, former Supreme Court Justice, and the 1916 Republican nominee for president. Kellor was a lawyer, sociologist, and veteran of the 1912 Progressive Party. For 1916, the Committee's key initiative was a Hughes Campaign Train meant to draw attention and support to Hughes's reform record.[36] It failed spectacularly. The train left Grand Central Station in New York City on October 2, 1916, following a breakfast attended by 1,000 women supporters at the Plaza Hotel.[37] Over the next thirty-three days, the train traveled 11,075 miles and visited some 100 cities in an effort to get Hughes elected. Since it was completely self-funded by women and featured only women speakers, the train was regarded as a women-only initiative. Kellor lost her bet that nonpartisanship would prove women could wield a different kind of political influence. Twenty-five women were onboard when the train left; fewer completed the entire journey.[38] Nonpartisanship meant the women had to ignore all state and local races, including the congressional campaign of Jeannette Rankin in Montana, who would go on to become the first woman elected to Congress.[39] The decision also meant avoiding the suffrage issue, even though Hughes had endorsed a suffrage amendment personally and Wilson had not. Speakers were limited to Hughes's record as a New York reformer.[40] Some women on the train felt constrained by these limitations; some broke the rules while others just left in disgust.[41] Following Democrat Woodrow Wilson's successful reelection, Kellor admitted, "We need parties," though she continued to criticize what she saw as "hide-bound loyalty to a formal organization or machine."[42]

Still, the parties could not ignore that over four million women in twelve states were able to vote in the 1916 election. Given the numbers, Democrat and Republican organizations were forced to get serious about incorporating women within the parties. Now party leaders wanted women brought into the fold officially. And not all women abhorred party politics. Since the 1880s, parties had forged unofficial relationships with such women, usually temporary and for specific campaign seasons. Judith Ellen Foster of Iowa got Republican Party endorsement for a network of women's groups she started to support Republican Party interests. She created the Women's National Republican Association (WNRA), located in New York City, and remained president of it till her death in 1911. After that, her protégé Helen Varick Boswell of New York City led the WNRA from 1911 to 1916.[43] In 1916, Boswell's association was renamed the National Women's Campaign Committee of the Republican National Committee. Its sole purpose was to get Republican candidates elected to office nationwide. It operated within the party system, albeit only for the election cycle.

After the 1916 election, both parties formalized roles for women as party members. Each party first created a Women's Bureau of its national committee; that was changed to a Women's Division within each party by the mid-1920s.[44] Party leaders appointed a woman to head the divisions; these Democrat and Republican women became vice chairs of their national committees. Both the full national committees and the smaller executive committees expanded to add women. The norm became one man and woman member from each state on the national committee. The national committee thus doubled in size, effectively making it unwieldy, and less than useful. The national executive committees, as appointed subsets, simply added some spots for women though not enough to give them an equal number of seats.[45]

For the second New York State referendum effort in 1917 Carrie Chapman Catt, who had become leader of NYSWSA in 1915, reorganized it into the New York State Woman Suffrage Party. The rebranding signified the group's commitment to overt political pressure tactics and tighter unity of action.[46] It was recognition that success in politics was, as George Washington Plunkitt of Tammany Hall was credited as saying, "As much a regular business as the grocery or dry-goods or the drug business. You've got to be trained up to it or you're sure to fail."[47] In 1917, the referendum succeeded.

Both parties inside New York quickly created structures to incorporate women. For once, politicians and suffrage leaders offered the same advice to the new woman voter: join a party. Such figures as Carrie Catt of NAWSA, Mary Garrett Hay of the New York City Suffrage Party, and Harriet Stanton Blatch the Political Union called on America's women to enroll in a political party now that suffrage was won.[48] Educational materials prepared by their organizations showered America's women with flowery messages about how "political parties give (government) its life."[49] But, as with the national organization, women entering the Democratic and Republican parties in New York faced segregation and limited influence once inside. Each party appointed a woman as vice chair for the state party committee; other women were named county vice chairs. In all cases the vice chair was responsible for only the women members of the party at the levels below them. Party leaders controlled the women through their power to appoint them to these positions.[50] It was not until 1938, when the state's constitution was amended, that New York's women were elected to the state committees as the men were. State and county committees also added women, again diluting the value of that membership. The New York County Republican Committee, for example, now had over 1,000 members.[51]

More informally, women's political clubs had existed and continued to exist outside the party organizations proper. These clubs copied the political map, most typically organized by state assembly district. As early as the 1880s, women with an interest in politics could only create their own sex-segregated clubs that lacked any overlap with the party proper. Two politically interested New York City residents, Helen Boswell and Corrine Roosevelt Robinson, sister of Theodore Roosevelt, established one of the earliest Republican women's clubs in 1896, the Women's West End Republican Association of New York City.[52] But the party did not recognize women's club efforts. After suffrage, men's clubs made their own decisions about women's access. Some clubs refused to add women; others added women but gave them no meaningful role or influence. Women's reaction was equally varied. Some joined if allowed and tried to effect change from within. Others disdained second-class citizenship and created new, all-women's political clubs. But either inside or outside the men's clubs, women with the vote found they had little influence in choosing candidates for local and state office, which was the main reason such clubs existed.

Nonetheless these newly enrolled party members diligently went about registering their fellow women to vote. For the 1918 elections, the New York State Legislature set up a special registration day on May 25, specifically for women. Normally, registration for the following year took place on the prior Election Day. Without the adjustment women would have had to wait until 1919 to cast ballots. The papers reported an initial number of 387,676 women registered in twenty of New York State's counties: 184,002 Democrat, 178,590 Republican, 14,997 Socialist, and 10,087 Prohibition Party. This number was less than one-half of the total number of eligible women.[53] The final tally of 279,566 was even lower.[54]

Expectations Postsuffrage

Newly enrolled women were being called on to be partisan. Using New York in the period 1917–1932 as her test case, historian Anna Harvey argues that the male leadership intended these women to get their behavioral cues from women leaders in the parties who would supplant the influence of traditional women's clubs.[55] Harvey's larger point is that parties outplayed women's organizations by aggressively moving women voters into their tightly controlled system. The result was woman failed to develop and support their own policy agenda. In many cases, suffrage had been promoted as the first step toward other policy achievements. Instead, the parties acculturated women to their brand of organizational loyalty and rewards.[56] This was not a seamless process. Parties promoted a number of women only to find they would not or could not adapt to the existing partisan system. The suffrage movement had diversified its appeal to so many different constituencies that party leaders had to experiment with different kinds of women as potential leaders: young, old, professional, homemaker. Early on, parties realized that unity on the issue of suffrage masked a host of differences among women. Harvey says the parties started off by courting suffrage leaders but ultimately went after "more docile party functionaries."[57]

Some early women candidates in New York may have fit that description but others did not. Yet it seems all of these women, to one degree or another, had the challenge of how to balance this nonpartisan heritage with the partisan legislative culture they entered. Scholars of women candidates and politicians agree that women's entry into politics was hindered by traditional expectations of women's gender roles. Even as women challenged those expectations, vestiges still remained.[58] Women who behaved like male politicians by following the dictates of party leaders on voting or who took support from the party in recognition of service felt vulnerable to charges they were abandoning their womanhood and causes. Prominent New York women with associations to politics such as Eleanor Roosevelt, Frances Perkins, and Belle Moskowitz all denied interest in party politics for themselves, drawing a distinction between that and "getting things done."[59] Even now we presume women to be more interested in issues of home and family than men; we express concern over women balancing home and legislative obligations; and we presume that women are less politically and personally ambitious than men. If they are too ambitious, then that must reflect badly on them as women. Until recently, it was more acceptable for women to wait until their children were grown to run at all.

Harvey's women as "voters without leverage (on issues)" were further disadvantaged by the small number of women elected to office. And scholars mostly agree that numbers matter. There is a sense that women must reach a critical mass in the legislative body before they can exert clout on policy issues considered important to women. Today in New York, women make up 28 percent of the legislature. That is slightly above the national average of 25 percent.[60] As of August 24, 2021, Lieutenant Governor Kathy Hochul became the state's first female governor, after Andrew Cuomo resigned. Hochul started her career in local and county government in the 1990s, represented Western New York in Congress from 2011 to 2013, and served as Lieutenant Governor from 2014 on. This is progress, especially when New York's first two elected female legislators represented 1 percent of a combined chamber of 201 officials in 1919. Harvey's women did not have a block of supporters who could pressure leaders into supporting more women in winnable races. Emily Newell Blair, the first National vice chair of the Democrats, believed women could not command respect in politics unless they had a following.[61] Women who did win seats in the decade after suffrage exhibited characteristics of what political scientist Michelle Saint Germain has called "tokenism." They were too few to challenge the status quo on their own so they fell back on what she terms "invisibility."[62] This often took the form of avoiding the idea of gender at all; the goal was to be seen as just another legislator. That was a problematic choice since women had argued for the vote so they could make women's voices heard on issues. Invisibility could also mean following the direction of the party's leader on voting. It almost surely meant that stereotypes about women would not be challenged. In sum, succeeding as a politician would be harder for women. One scholar of political women rather politely acknowledged women's very limited political progress up to the 1970s. The assessment was that women followed "a rather passive path to office," in that they were less likely to plan for a political career or undertake preparations that would help them succeed.[63]

This was the landscape facing the newly enfranchised New York woman. Women running for office emerged from the female world of nonpartisanship and stepped into the male world of party politics. Male political leaders might welcome them, but only because they presumed to control them. At the same time, women were dogged by assumptions about character and interests that put limits on their options once elected, even as expectations rose about what women should accomplish in office. All of these political considerations lay atop a New York landscape divided by more than gender. Women, like men, were reflections of the part of the state they represented. Women, like men, had to operate within the long-standing party framework that expected certain types of partisan behavior. In many ways the next step was daunting.

Chapter 3

Pioneers and Placeholders

Legislators from 1919 through 1964

Pioneer and Placeholder Legislators

	Party	Body/Year Elected	through Year	Body/Year Elected	through Year	Region Represented
Mary Lilly	D	A/1918	1919			New York City
Ida B. Sammis	R	A/1918	1919			Long Island
Elizabeth Gillette	D	A/1919	1920			Capital District
Marguerite Smith	R	A/1919	1921			New York City
Rhoda Fox Graves	R	A/1924	1932	S/1934	1948	North Country
Doris Byrne	D	A/1933	1937			New York City
Jane Todd	R	A/1934	1944			Mid-Hudson
Edith Cheney	R	A/1940	1944			Southern Tier
Mary Gillen	D	A/1942	1956			New York City
Gladys Banks	R	A/1944	1950	A/1952	1954	New York City
Genesta Strong	R	A/1944	1959	S/1959*		Long Island
Janet Gordon	R	A/1946	1958	S/1958	1962	Southern Tier
Elizabeth Hanniford	R	A/1946	1950			New York City
Mildred Taylor	R	A/1946	1960			Finger Lakes
Maude Ten Eyck	R	A/1946	1954			New York City
Frances Marlatt	R	A/1953	1960			Mid-Hudson
Bessie Buchanan	D	A/1954	1962			New York City
Dorothy Lawrence	R	A/1958	1962			New York City
Aileen Ryan	D	A/1958	1965			New York City

Assembly = A, Senate = S.
*Genesta Strong was elected to the Senate but resigned prior to taking the oath of office in January due to ill health.

Pioneer-Era Legislators

Gladys Banks • Bessie Buchanan • Doris Byrne • Edith Cheney

Mary Gillen • Elizabeth Gillette • Janet Gordon • Rhoda Fox Graves

Elizabeth Hanniford • Dorothy Lawrence • Mary Lilly • Frances Marlatt

Aileen Ryan • Ida B. Sammis • Marguerite Smith • Genesta Strong

Mildred Taylor • Maude Ten Eyck • Jane Todd

Overview

In January 1919, the first two women elected to the state legislature took their seats in the Assembly. Democrat leaders welcomed Mary Lilly (A1919) and the Republicans Ida B. Sammis (A1919). Some male colleagues resisted seeing the end of the all-male legislative environment. Well into the 1960s, women legislators would find themselves still referred to as "Assemblyman so and so."[1] Others, and much of the public, hoped the women would have a calming, uplifting influence on a rough and combative political environment. The press speculated on whether Sammis and Lilly "may turn down the boisterous last days" of session that had previously seen a fistfight break out among male legislators.[2] For quite a while, male legislators and the public were not sure how exactly to relate to female legislators. Male colleagues responded inconsistently. They sometimes refused to make accommodations for the women, but at other times appeared eager to give women special treatment. As that 1919 session opened, Democrats gave Lilly a choice seat near the front of the chamber in recognition of her gender. The Republican Sammis was at the back of the room and stayed there. Republican Gordon Peck in the front row had been asked to give up his seat "to show the lady member kindness" but had responded, "I don't give it up to no woman."[3] Each "lady" served only for the 1919 legislative session.[4]

Fast-forward forty-five years to the 1964 legislative session and you again see just two women members, both in the Assembly: Democrat Aileen Ryan (A1958–1966) and Republican Constance Cook (A1962–1974).[5] By the numbers, women appeared stuck. But these modest bookends surround a period where women regularized their presence in the legislature and achieved some "first-time" accomplishments. In her 1974 study of elected women legislators, political scientist Jeane Kirkpatrick argued that the years since women's suffrage had seen the arrival of an important new category, the political woman.

> *If* we define political women as members of the female sex who *desire* significant influence in the process of determining public policy, acquire the *skills* necessary to achieved influence, *wield* the influence in institutions where decisions are made, and seek to preserve influence through continued participation in power processes, then there is no question that political woman exists.[6]

There would be a total of nineteen such political women in the pioneer and placeholder era that ran from 1919 through the 1964 legislative session.

New York's females started slowly; between 1919 and 1934 they averaged less than one seat a year. In 1922 and 1923 there were no women elected to the legislature. Their high-water mark of eight was achieved following the 1946 election before leveling off to an average of six per year throughout the 1950s. This is the time when their integration into electoral politics took shape, sometimes in ways that would last well beyond this era. Theirs is a story of firsts and limits, of women entering the house of government as one political scientist wrote "a room at a time."[7]

As discussed in chapter 2, these women's acculturation into the political world meant reconciling women's unique presuffrage history of activism with institutional politics. In particular, they had to learn how to work effectively within parties and with political leaders. Women had to learn how to campaign and govern at an accelerated pace. Until 1938, legislative terms were for one year, not two as they are now, so new legislators had a single-session record on which to seek reelection. Sessions in the 1920s were also shorter, running from January through April, and not through the end of June as they do now. Once elected, women dealt with the normal political considerations about which party held power and whether each woman had the support of the leadership. These women politicians also wrestled with cultural expectations about what was or was not acceptable behavior for female officeholders. Finally, these women struggled with how to represent women's interests, given that so few were elected to office during this period and that the interests of the state were anything but homogeneous. The political tumult of the 1920s resulted in redrawing of boundaries regarding male and female roles in the political arena. Women gained access to new areas such as holding office and party appointments. However, all too often male party leaders determined the limits of those opportunities.[8] The parties did not set women candidates up to fail per se, but their small numbers meant these women effected only incremental changes in how the parties and legislatures operated. Their voices on certain issues may not have been as strong as they liked, but they made the woman elected official a regular, though definitely minority, part of the legislature.

These women's histories are just that, women bringing their experience and interests to politics. In key areas the women's experience remained their own. The very way that women of the time prepared themselves to enter politics differed from the men. That does not mean they were ill-suited to run. It means that most did not justify nominations as men did, through professional credentials or paid work coupled with long party service. The majority of pioneer women were better educated than the general population. But these women emphasized their many volunteer activities with the women's organizations active in the late nineteenth and early twentieth centuries. These organizations gave women entrée to political action at a time when the normative expectation for women was marriage and family, and for husbands the financial security for that family. Yet, family obligations often meant pioneer women waited until they were older to enter regular politics. Whether or not a woman had children and what their ages were colored the decision to run for office and the public's acceptance of the woman as a candidate. Balancing family and a career in politics continued to be more difficult for women than men and would remain so through the end of the twentieth century.

Yet, somewhat inconsistently, party leaders twice cajoled the widows of legislators to run. There was a sense the public would support the widow as an extension of her husband, taking his views to be hers. On one level this idea flew in the face of the belief that men and women had different natures. But, apparently in these cases, the equally old legacy of *femme covert* won out. Literally meaning "woman covered," *femme covert* described a legal system with roots in common law going back to the Middle Ages. It presumed women ceded their independence to their husbands at the time of marriage. Women had no property of their own; the male headed and represented the household in all public ways. The women's rights movement of the nineteenth century had attacked and forced the dismantling of many restrictive laws associated with *femme covert*. Suffragists had attacked the concept as wrongheaded when it came to voting because they argued women would have their own views. Still, many politicians preferred to believe women would vote as their husbands did. Remnants of the doctrine of *femme covert* influenced the entry in to politics of Edith Cheney (R) (A1939–1944) and Mary Gillen (D) (A1942–1956). Gillen's Republican opponent actually withdrew before the special election to replace her husband and the Republicans cross-endorsed Gillen.[9] Upon accepting the nomination, the *Brooklyn Daily Eagle* reported, "She has made no plans for making her mark as a legislator but intends to listen and learn."[10] Still, the woman described as "a sweet-faced lady known for her calm" stayed in the legislature for seven additional terms through 1956. In all that time Gillen missed just one roll-call vote, somewhat of an attendance record.[11]

Cheney and Gillen were initially recruited by party leaders as stand-ins for their husbands. Going forward, widowhood as a status shifted, allowing some women to act on political interests of their own that had existed during their marriages but had no connection to their husbands. Over time widows came to be seen as independent actors and not just substitutes. The last two assemblywomen from the pioneer generation, Dorothy Bell Lawrence (R) (A1953–1963) and Aileen Ryan also ran as widows. But they differed from Cheney and Gillen in that it was they and not their husbands who had the political interest and ambition.[12] Lawrence said she had left her home state of Georgia because women there did not have equal rights.[13] During her failed run for Manhattan Borough president in 1961, the *New York Times* observed, "Mrs. Lawrence campaigns as if she believes that being a woman is an asset rather than a liability."[14] In her freshmen term in 1959, Ryan was credited for using canny political skills to secure passage of a veteran's scholarship. To do so, Ryan left her seat in the Assembly and directly confronted Governor Rockefeller who was passing through the chamber, asking him for a message of necessity to get the bill voted on before the legislature adjourned. She got the scholarships through and was dubbed a "hero" by the press.[15] Here she made skillful use of her gender, for it was unlikely that a male Democrat would have been as effective with the tactic.

The pioneer cohort's greatest contribution was to make themselves a permanent presence in both chambers of the state house, albeit mainly in the Assembly. Several had legislative careers equal to those of well-respected male colleagues. They joined the party organization, supported the ticket at election time and helped pass legislation proposed by the party. The women showed themselves to be party stalwarts but not necessarily party lackeys. There are examples where women legislators broke with their party on issues or even challenged leadership, sometimes successfully and sometimes not. In short, these nineteen women for the most part entered and acclimated to New York politics and legislating as practiced in the middle of the twentieth century. In doing so the women normalized the idea of the woman politician. Each time a pioneer achieved a notable "first" it meant those who followed would have a place waiting.

Running for Office

The women who entered electoral politics realized their success largely rested on their pledging loyalty to their party and its leaders. Establishment help was essential to women winning election to the legislature just as it was for men. The "bargain," if there could be called one, was that women would put their reputations with the public (especially other women) at the service of the leadership. Leaders expected women legislators to attract women voters to the party and thereby increase support for party positions and legislation. At first leaders struggled to figure out which women had the requisite influence and respectability to make good candidates. Leaders found it hard to identify which women would be strong candidates, in part because they tended to see women as a block of voters rather than individuals with varied interests. Some of the women promoted in the first decade after suffrage found the accompanying glare of publicity unpleasant. The women found themselves judged by the public and other women in ways neither they nor party leaders anticipated or appreciated.

Ida Sammis seemed a good nomination choice to Republicans in 1918, as did Marguerite Smith (R) (Assembly 1920–1921) of Manhattan a year later. Smith won a seat in the Assembly for both the 1920 and 1921 sessions, making her the first woman to win reelection to office. On paper they were very different kinds of women. Sammis, about fifty, was well-known for her suffrage advocacy, having started the Huntington Political Equality League in 1911, served as the Franchise Department chair of her local Women's Christian Temperance Union chapter, and authored articles on suffrage for the *Long Islander*, a local paper.[16] Suffolk County's support for the 1917 suffrage referendum suggested Sammis had influence there. Sammis also made it known in 1918 that she wanted to run for office, though not necessarily as a Republican.[17] Smith was only twenty-five, having just graduated Teachers College at Columbia in 1918 with her master's and begun teaching hygiene and physical training at the Horace Mann School.[18] Smith got her offer of the nomination via "surprise" telegram while she was in Vermont during the summer. It was said the Republicans wanted her because she was well known through her work as a hostess at dances arranged for servicemen.[19] During the primary, the *New York Times* had little else to report on other than her school activities, where she captained the baseball team and was president of the Athletic Association of Teachers College, and her work at the summer camp for girls in Vermont.[20] The *Times* profile of her following her election in 1919 began with her skill as a tennis player and only later in the article reported her views on issues. She was called a "progressive" but not a "suffragette," but no further information was provided on what these terms meant. Smith did receive praise for her work during World War I raising funds for the United War Relief Fund, but, again, the article stressed even more her success at organizing dances for the soldiers, "for if there is anything in this world which she likes more than anything in the way of athletics it is the art terpsichorean [love of dance]."[21] Over and over within the *Times* article Smith's youthfulness seemed to be her most prominent feature.

Women candidates like these continued to find themselves judged by two conflicting standards—one for politicians and one for women—which often meant they alienated one constituency or another. In 1918, Sammis ran with the endorsement of both the Republican and Prohibition Parties for a seat in a heavily Republican district.[22] But she lost the backing of her party during her 1919 reelection bid. Leaders suddenly withdrew their endorsement and gave it to her male Democratic opponent.[23] Sammis accused the party of betraying her because she refused to "supinely carry out the wishes of the men leaders."[24] The record, however, shows that she had followed the party's lead. Ten of the fifteen bills she introduced became law, the best record for this early period. During one contentious vote the press noted she "joined [the Speaker], recognizing party obligation above any other."[25] Sammis did grow more critical of party politics after she fell out of political favor and, by the 1930s, was calling for women to "be freed from the dictates of party bosses and to have a voice of their own in the working out of policies."[26] But that does not answer the question of why the party not only abandoned her but supported her opponent in 1919. Sammis was the only Republican running in Suffolk County to lose her race.[27] One possibility is that her personal life impacted her political career. Though nothing was made public at the time, her past played out in the papers in the 1930s when she married for the second and third times.[28] Sammis had run for office in 1918 as a widow with one grown child. But rumors began to emerge that challenged her image as a well-respected former wife and mother. At one point it was suggested Sammis's child from her first marriage might really have been fathered by the man who became her second husband in 1923. Both her second and third marriages generated accusations of gold digging. These stories all appeared after her time in the legislature; there is no evidence that conclusively proves this was the cause of her political downfall. But something pushed Republicans to back away from Sammis so late in the 1919 election cycle that she remained on the ballot as the Republican nominee. At the very least, Sammis's time in the legislature thrust her into the public eye in ways not beneficial for her. She never held elective or appointive public office again but remained someone worthy of newspaper coverage more than a decade after she left office, coverage that showed how gendered ideas about behavior persisted and became the basis for the harsh treatment she received from the press.[29]

Marguerite Smith worked well with fellow Republicans, which may account for her becoming the first woman legislator to win reelection. During her first term she won praise for her parliamentary skills when she briefly took over as speaker and successfully mediated a heated dispute between two members.[30] However, she angered some women's groups in her second term by entering into a public conflict with the Women's Trade Union League (WTUL), an organization of mainly middle-class women focused on supporting protective legislation for women in the industrial workforce. Smith had sponsored legislation to revise the Fifty-Four-Hour Law so women could work more and later hours.[31] The WTUL accused Smith of selling out to political leaders and abandoning women.[32] Here Smith got caught in the crossfire stemming from a division within the ranks of reform-minded women in the 1920s.[33] Like many reform organizations of the Progressive Era, the WTUL saw restricting women's work as a way to prevent their exploitation. But the National Women's Party (NWP) formed by Alice Paul in 1916 favored a strictly equal rights approach that would eliminate any gender-based distinctions in the workplace. To that end, the NWP sought an Equal Rights Amendment to the U.S. Constitution, introduced in Congress in 1923. However, in 1921 the more traditional protectionist viewpoint still dominated. Sammis authored a law in the 1919 session to limit the hours elevator operators could work, most of whom were women, at the request of the Women's Joint Legislative Conference (WJLC) of New York State. It stipulated that no woman under eighteen could work as an operator and that every operator had to receive one day off out of seven worked.[34]

Sammis's bill was one of three introduced that session to limit women's working hours; the other two focused on women office workers and women transportation workers. The WJLC lobbied for all three bills, with Mary Dreier, social reformer and member of the New York WTUL, testifying before a legislative hearing. Yet, women also organized in opposition and by the time supporters of Dreier got to the chamber on the day of her testimony, the room was already full of women belonging to the opposing Women's League for Equal Opportunity, an organization demanding the legislature reject the bills in the name of "industrial equality." Nora Stanton Blatch, granddaughter of Elizabeth Cady Stanton, was present as part of that opposition.[35] Even after the transportation bill was signed into law, women employed by the Brooklyn Transit system unsuccessfully lobbied Governor Al Smith to call a special session and repeal the measure claiming it would harm them economically.[36] In Marguerite Smith's case, newspaper coverage of divisions among women on issues and the vocal criticism leveled against her by a significant organization like the WTUL may have contributed to Smith losing her bid for a third term in 1921. All told, Ida Sammis Woodruff Satchwell came across as the opposite of pure womanhood, something that Republican leaders may have realized. Smith, faced with vocal female critics could not hold her seat.

It was also a world complicated by the state's geography and demographics. These women were as much a reflection of where in the state they lived as they were of their party's strength. Upstate legislators differed on issues from Downstaters in what was labeled a rural/suburban versus urban divide. At the start of the pioneer era, Republicans wielded the most power. By its end, demographic changes coupled with court cases mandating one-person one-vote were shifting power downstate toward democratic strongholds.[37] Until the 1960s, Republicans almost always held both houses of the legislature.[38] From the 1960s on, Democratic enrollment has consistently outpaced the Republicans such that by 2000 Democrats would have a five-to-one enrollment edge, a majority of seats in the Assembly, and growing numbers in the Senate.[39]

It is no surprise that Republican women tended to have longer tenures and more robust legislative records in this era. Rhoda Fox Graves (R) (A1925–1932 and S1934–1948), Jane Todd (R) (A1934–1944), Genesta Strong (R) (A1944–1958), and Janet Gordon (R) (A1946–1958 and S1958–1962) combined length of term with significant influence on legislation. Graves and Gordon represented rural areas, St. Lawrence and Chenango Counties, respectively, while Todd and Strong came from the Republican suburban counties of Westchester and Nassau. Graves, Todd, and Strong were active in traditional women's club activities. Gordon stood apart in that she was a lawyer. All three showed a more conservative outlook on social issues reflective of their nonurban environments. Graves was an ardent prohibitionist and expressed tempered support for book censorship and banning the teaching of evolution in schools.[40] While in the Assembly, Todd chose to focus on reaffirming traditional marriage by pushing a seventy-two-hour waiting period between obtaining a marriage license and the ceremony, rather than push for divorce reform.[41] Gordon would revive divorce reform in the 1950s and make it her signature issue. At the time, New York had the most restrictive divorce laws in the nation. Still, Gordon had her conservative side. She opposed lifting the Sunday blue laws that kept businesses closed.[42] Strong voted twice against the legalization of bingo, even though it was a Republican-sponsored measure.[43]

Graves and Gordon were the only women to serve in the Senate in the pioneer era. Graves's professional experience was as the owner-operator of a dairy farm with her husband, Perle. Many legislators had farming backgrounds but that was changing. Between 1931 and 1965 the percentage of legislators who farmed went from 30 percent to zero.[44] The *New York Times* noted the downward trend in a story on the incoming 1934 legislature when it reported there would be seventy-two lawyers and only fourteen farmers.[45] Gordon, the daughter of a lawyer from the Chenango County seat of Norwich, symbolized the growing presence of lawyers in the legislature, among even legislators from more rural areas.

Equally to be expected, five of the six women Democrats in the pioneer era were from New York City. Lilly was from Manhattan as was Bessie Buchanan (A1954–1962), Gillen from Brooklyn, while Doris Byrne (A1933–1937) and Ryan came from the Bronx. Elizabeth Gillette (A1920) was the exception; she represented the city of Schenectady for a single term. Urban political organizations and leaders played a role these women's candidacies and careers. For example, Byrne and Ryan would hold other positions in government and the judiciary that reflected their loyalty to the establishment. In 1937 Byrne resigned her Assembly seat to accept the position of deputy secretary of State offered by then Secretary of State and Bronx County Chair Edward Flynn. Governor Lehman later appointed her to a vacancy on the New York City Council (1942) and New York City Mayor William O'Dwyer elevated her to a magistracy on the Court of Special Sessions (1950). You see, Byrne was not just any Democrat. For most of the 1940s Byrne served as the vice chair of the State Democratic Committee, which meant she was the de facto leader of women Democrats around the state. Still, the rewards of party loyalty did not come without risk. Ryan withstood a primary challenge in her 1964 reelection campaign that was engineered by Mayor Wagner in an effort to weaken the influence of the Bronx County Democratic Leader, Charles Buckley, whom she supported. Ryan was considered the "organization candidate" both here and when she shifted her focus to the New York City Council in 1965 and ran for and won the at-large seat from the Bronx.[46]

Gender Differences Remain

These women remained distinct as a cohort in many ways, whether they wanted that status or not. Despite a growing number of women in the workforce and the professions, common wisdom still dictated that women ought not to mix marriage, family, and career. In particular, women with small children were not expected to be candidates. The two youngest women elected, Republican Smith and Democrat Byrne, married and started families only after leaving the Assembly. Dorothy Bell Lawrence, another widow, took great pains to justify running, explaining her mother lived with her and watched her nine-year-old son. Gillen, the widow with young children prevailed upon to run, was an exception. She had four children still at home, ages sixteen, fifteen, twelve, and nine when she first took office in 1942. The advice she offered to other women interested in running for office: "First go out and find a good housekeeper, then go after some votes."⁴⁷ Having been drawn into politics rather than seeking it out, Gillen was not so vulnerable to criticism that she was abandoning her family. It was more acceptable for women legislators to have no children or grown children before entering politics. Sammis, Lilly, Graves, Cheney, Strong, Elizabeth Hanniford (R) (A1946–1950), and Maude Ten Eyck (R) (A1946–1954) all ran for office only after their children were older. When she got to Albany in 1919, Sammis pointedly talked about her grown son, Alden, then a student at Albany Law School. Gladys Banks (R) (A1944–1950 and 1952–1954) and Bessie Buchanan were married but childless. There were several women with careers, though the norm there was for those women to be unmarried. Gillette, Todd, and Frances Marlatt (R) (A1953–1960) were all single; Gillette was a physician and Marlatt a lawyer. Todd had no specific profession; throughout her adult life financial stability was always a concern. Janet Gordon, also a lawyer, was the lone woman legislator to defy tradition by giving birth to a daughter in 1950 while serving in the Assembly, the first woman legislator to do so.⁴⁸

Teaching remained one of the few areas where women were not forced to make the binary career or family choice. Five of the nineteen women in the pioneer era said they were teachers or had taught at some point in the past. The pioneers as a whole were well educated. Twelve went to college, though college did not lead to paid careers for all. The more common denominator in women's background was their club work. Lilly, Sammis, Todd, Cheney, Strong, Lawrence, and Ten Eyck all had résumés full of activities. As noted above, Sammis established the first suffrage club on Long Island and was active with the WCTU. Cheney was president of the New York State Federation of Women's Clubs in the 1940s, while Lilly had been the recording secretary of the Federation in the 1910s. When she ran for the legislature, Lilly had tried to get the State General Federation's endorsement, but was rebuked and reminded that these women's organizations were strictly nonpartisan.⁴⁹ Lawrence credited her organizing skills as a politician to having led a Girl Scout troop when she moved to Manhattan from Georgia in 1934. There she met the mothers and fathers of her neighborhood, "and pretty soon she became co-leader of the district

[Republican Club]. Almost as soon, Lawrence became the first female in the City to head an election district."[50]

Bessie Buchanan was the first Black female member in the legislature. She had one of the more colorful résumés of the pioneer women. Like the others, Buchanan was regarded as a civic leader in her Harlem community. But her celebrity had its basis in a career as a singer and actress on Broadway and in silent films. She retired from the theater in 1929 to marry Charles Buchanan, owner and operator of the Savoy Ballroom in Harlem and a civic leader in his own right. Buchanan stayed before the public eye in the 1930s and 1940s, with a column in her husband's weekly, *The Political Voice*, and through the media's coverage of her association with the singer Josephine Baker. That social prominence and popularity had a great deal to do with why Democrats supported her as their first Black female nominee. Earlier, in 1934, Eunice Hunton Carter had run for the Assembly from Harlem but as a Republican. A Black female graduate of Smith and a lawyer, Carter ran against four-term Democratic Assemblyman James Stephens, also Black. Carter won 45 percent of the vote, though she lost the election. That total suggested women's votes were a growing source of power in Harlem. There were just too few Republicans in the district to explain Carter's strong showing otherwise.[51] From 1944 on, Black women were a majority of Harlem's registered Democratic voters. Buchanan used her name recognition and sway with women in the community to pressure Tammany Hall to endorse her for the Assembly in 1954.[52]

Gendered expectations also affected the women officeholders. Once in the legislature itself the women hoped to be seen as capable as the men. Lilly set the tone in 1919 when she asserted, "There is no sex in work. We are all working together."[53] Unfortunately, leadership put up some barriers. At times they specifically emphasized women's differences if it helped advance an agenda. In 1942 it was Senator Graves who introduced a resolution to establish a temporary economy commission to "study and investigate the affairs of the state government and to recommend economies . . . [to] keep the state sound during war.[54] Her name on the proposal neutralized cries that the idea was a partisan action by Republicans against a Democratic administration during wartime. Two decades later, Governor Nelson Rockefeller asked Assemblywoman Lawrence to introduce legislation to create a state arts council (1960) and for construction of a tribute to UN Secretary General Dag Hammarskjold (1962). Both ideas had faced opposition even within the Republican Party. Lawrence rounded up votes by framing the initiates as community uplift projects.[55]

At other times the leadership marginalized women when they clustered them in committees considered best suited to their feminine nature and abilities. Sammis and Lilly, the only two women in the 1919 legislature, were both sent to the Social Welfare and Education committees.[56] Of the nineteen pioneers, eight sat on the Social Welfare and Public Health Committees, seven on Education, but only one on the powerful Ways and Means Committee. Mildred Frick Taylor (R) (A1946–1960) became the first appointee to Ways and Means at the start of the 1953 session. Even as the number and names of committees shifted over time, the pattern continued. For example, Social Welfare became Public Relief and Welfare and both Health and Education had the word *public* inserted into their titles. These changes reflected New York's commitment to an activist government agenda. If you consider these changes and the seeming similarities across various committees' areas of responsibility, the clustering of women legislators is further reinforced. For example, the Committees on Public Institutions, Charitable and Religious Societies, and Penal Institutions all dealt with reform and social concerns. Twelve pioneers collectively served on these committees. Marguerite Smith, the first woman to head a committee, led Social Welfare in 1921. To be fair, clustering women on such committees persisted in part because there was some truth to the idea that this is where women's interests lay. Women who had entered electoral politics citing their social reform credentials should not have been too surprised to be assigned committees that focused on those areas. In 1926, when Assemblywoman Graves was offered the vacant chair of Public Institutions, the *Buffalo Evening News* reported she had really wanted Social Welfare.[57]

Still, these women did take opportunities to secure other committee assignments that broke new ground as with Taylor serving on Ways and Mean. All bills requiring expenditure of state funds must first pass through this committee. No bill reaches the floor for a vote without prior approval from Ways and Means. Yet it would take until 2017 before Helene Weinstein would become the first woman chair of that body. During her time in the legislature, Taylor chaired the standing committee on Affairs of Villages.

Graves headed the Senate Agriculture Committee from 1939 through 1948. Graves had broken enormous ground as the first woman elected to the Senate. The Senate committee honor was not as special as it might seem since every Senator in the majority party that year chaired a committee. Still, Graves became head of Agriculture even after she had publicly criticized party leadership over milk production. She crashed a 1936 conference on a milk-pricing bill organized by then Assembly Agriculture Committee Chair

Howard Allen. She accused lawmakers of giving dealers power to lower the price paid to farmers for their milk. She likened the action to enslaving dairymen to the dealers when she declared the farmers were "being sold on the block."[58] Given the importance of dairying to New York's economy, Graves's actions made her a central figure in rural New York's concerns.

The Most Powerful Women Legislator of the Era

Rhoda Graves's career illustrates several important aspects of the pioneer era. Early on, parties recognized the need to have some women in the legislature. But there was a ceiling; the parties did not rush to support women as State Senate candidates. Graves began her political career in the Assembly as the choice of the party; she advanced it through dint of her own efforts. Of all the early women legislators, she was the most adept at balancing demands for party loyalty, constituent concerns, and the representational burden of being one of the first women in the legislature (and the first in the Senate). Republican leaders encouraged Graves to run for a vacant Assembly seat in

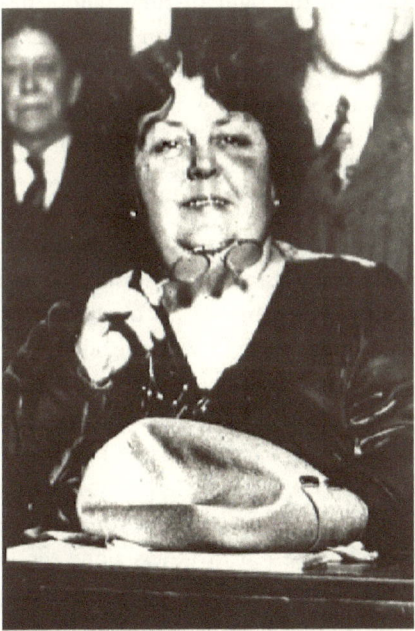

Figure 3.1. Rhoda Fox Graves, 1932.

1924.[59] With party backing she beat two other candidates in the primary, which in the North Country was tantamount to being elected.[60] Once in office, Graves advanced her district's interests even if they brought her into conflict with leadership and the party. In 1928 she broke with her party by refusing to help kill Governor Smith's water-power bills. The Democratic governor wanted to create a State Power Authority to bring hydroelectric power to the region.[61] She continued to support that initiative throughout her career. In 1940, she forced a slow roll call vote on a Senate resolution to Congress *against* construction of the St. Lawrence Seaway, until enough senators who wanted the Seaway could get to the floor to cast their votes. She was tipped off that the Republican majority in the Assembly had already passed the resolution and the Senate would try to sneak it through when members thought no business was taking place.[62] In 1944 she finally succeeded in having a resolution passed in favor of developing water power on the St. Lawrence.[63] The difference in 1944 appeared to be that the state now had a Republican governor. Earlier votes had been designed to deny Democrats the power to move forward. Graves believed the issue was too important to her region to play politics. Graves championed numerous rural issues, including the creation of a commission to plan for a bridge over the St. Lawrence into Canada, the right of rural school districts to have their votes counted when it came to decisions on district consolidations, and the creation of a junior license for rural teens to drive at a younger age.[64] Her bill on rural licenses was so popular with constituents she had to fight off colleagues who wanted to take away the privilege of introducing it.

Her challenges to the party over issues were minor compared to her challenge to party leadership when she ran for the Senate in 1932. Republicans in St. Lawrence and Franklin Counties had agreed, no one remembered just when, that if the area's congressman came from one county then the state senator must be from the other. In 1932, Congressman H. B. Snell lived in St. Lawrence County. Yet declaring "I will not blindly follow the dictates of party bosses when . . . [that] works hardship on the taxpayers of the State," Graves of St. Lawrence County challenged Warren Thayer, the incumbent Republican state senator who lived in Franklin County. Her press release declared, "I am a firm believer in party regularity, but I cannot guarantee the right to hold public office in 1933 should be foreclosed against me by some ancient political deal. . . . The test of fitness alone should be the yard stick by which the candidate is measured."[65] With organization support Thayer knocked Graves out in the primary. But he had to resign the seat in June 1934, after an investigation revealed he had misused his office for personal gain. Thayer had taken money from parties that represented a conflict of interest.[66] Graves immediately declared her candidacy and easily took the seat in the fall election. She both benefited from Thayer's indiscretion as well as the recognition she had gained from challenging him the year before.

Graves is best remembered for her defense of the independent dairy farmer against what can be termed the "big milk" interests. Those interests included the milk dealers who bought and prepared the milk for sale, the cheese producers who resented her advocacy for higher tariffs, and certain dairy farm cooperatives, which she believed were controlled by the dealers.[67] All told, "big milk" aimed to buy low and sell high, thereby hurting the small folk at both ends of the spectrum: the independent dairymen and the consumer. As early as her first Assembly reelection campaign, Graves had identified these elements as seeking to unseat her. On the issue of milk pricing Graves concluded that she would have to act virtually alone since "the Republican Party is so tied up with the milk corporations that they cannot refuse them anything."[68] Graves saw a crisis developing over milk as the Depression deepened. In 1931, she said the price paid to farmers was at a sixteen-year low of four and a half cents a quart, while the consumer was seeing the price in the store rise by thirteen and a half cents.[69] She unsuccessfully called for an official inquiry by the legislature in 1931 and 1932. By middle of the 1930s, her concerns shifted to the question of whether or not to sunset or amend the Milk Control Act of 1933. That law had responded to the crisis in milk prices by guaranteeing dairy farmers a floor below which the price of milk might not go, and laid out rules for purchase from the farmer and marketing of the product so farmers' livelihood would not be jeopardized. In a 1936 speech delivered on the Senate floor, Graves spoke for "demoralized farmers who have been unable to help themselves in their desperate fight to avoid the pitfall of bankruptcy . . . so that the middlemen in the world's most unusual big business press neither [the farmer nor the consumer] too hard." Graves advocated the extension of milk control regulations for another year to give time for a review of dealer practices and the development of new classification and pricing schedules for milk.[70] Graves called for farmers to be given the purchase price of milk up front before dealers took control of the product.

The issue continued unresolved through the 1938 and 1939 sessions. In those years she introduced some twenty-three bills dealing with milk production, pricing, regulations on cooperatives, and health inspections of milk. None became law. However, in 1938 the legislature did commission an audit of fourteen milk companies operating in metropolitan New York

City. But both she and a coalition of five American Labor Party representatives from the City called the final report "a whitewash of the huge milk distributors which comprise the all-powerful milk trust."[71] The audit, sadly, verified the plight of the farmer when it reported that the price paid to the farmer never rose above his cost.

Graves did bow to party pressure in 1948 when she sponsored a bill to allow oleo margarine, also called butterine, to be used in state institutions in place of butter.[72] It was called a cost-saving measure as a way to placate the dairy interests who saw oleo as a threat.[73] Graves's support on this issue added weight in two ways. First, she was a known and trusted advocate for farmers, which would have calmed concerns about dairy industry abuse. Second, she conveyed the support of women for the bill. The ability to use oleo margarine more conveniently became a huge issue to women in the late 1940s and early 1950s around the country.[74] New York was no exception. Governor Dewey supported the Graves bill and a second initiative to allow *colored* oleo to be sold at retail. Until now, oleo and food coloring to turn it yellow remained separate by law. Women had to knead the oleo at home to spread the dye, a task that took some strength and seemed a foolish waste of time. The prohibition on colored oleo existed because of pressure from the dairy industry. It feared butter losing pride of place and sales if the substitute was so similar and less expensive.

Hostility between dairy farmers and oleo manufacturers dates back to the 1880s, when oleo first appeared in large quantities on the American market. Then US Senator Warner Miller from New York sponsored the first federal oleo legislation in 1886 that imposed a tax on its manufacture and sale. Subsequent legislation drew a formal distinction between natural-colored or white oleo offered for sale and oleo colored yellow to mimic butter. Taxes on the latter were increased in 1902. Oleo then fell under the 1906 Pure Food and Drug Act prohibition on the sale of mislabeled products. By the 1940s, however, pro-margarine sentiment was growing. Advances in production had improved the nutritional value of the product, and more of the animal fat and vegetable oils used to make it came from American farms. Finally, wartime shortages of butter led Americans to more readily accept the substitute. Nationally, there was pressure to repeal discriminatory taxes on oleo.[75]

Graves left the legislature just as the second part of the oleo battle, the demand for colored oleo, was heating up. It would have been interesting to see what position Graves as a woman and a farmer would have taken on the question, but the record on that is silent. It fell to Genesta Strong, a Long Island Republican housewife from Nassau, to lead that fight.

Representing Women's Interests

By 1949, two opposing interests pressed on the legislature. On one side were the dairy interests and the State Department of Agriculture and Markets. On the other were New York's women. Assemblywoman Genesta Strong had introduced a bill to allow the sale of colored oleo, but it stayed bottled up in the Agriculture Committee despite strong backing by the New York City Federation of Women's Clubs, the State Federation of Women's Clubs, and various consumer organizations.[76] To be sure, farmers were not totally foolish in their concerns. The heaviest component of the formula governing the price paid to farmers for raw milk was the price of butter.[77] Strong countered with arguments about the unfairness of burdening women with extra work and household budgets with costs they could not handle.[78] Strong, previously described as the "battling housewife legislator," tried again in 1950.[79] She reintroduced her measures along with similar proposals being made by several other legislators. Because she was part of the Republican majority the press reported only her measures had a chance of passing.[80] But again the Agriculture Committee refused to act on them even as the governor and Republican leaders were won over to the repeal side.[81] There were efforts at some kind of compromise such as using a color other than yellow or mandating the margarine be sold in triangular shapes only. These were not serious compromise proposals. One of the colors suggested was purple and it was pointed out that the machinery used to package oleo was not able to produce triangular pieces.[82]

The oleo controversy also had all the earmarks of an Upstate/Downstate issue. Opposition centered in Upstate, rural areas that were Republican strongholds while sentiment in the growing suburbs on Long Island emboldened Strong to act. But Republican leaders balked at joining with Democrats as the way to free the oleo bills from committee.[83] Instead, in 1951 Republicans tried to win support by proposing a special tax of two cents per pound on oleo.[84] That tactic, too, failed to win sufficient support for passage. Donning a yellow apron on the Assembly floor, Strong began the quest for passage in 1952 by "demonstrating the 'messy job' at which housewives of the state spent 6,000,000 hours last year."[85] The *New York Times* credited women, the loudest voices for repeal of the ban, with enough clout to force the bill out of the Assembly Agriculture Committee on onto the floor for a vote.[86] Strong's bill passed but only because of Democratic votes. Republicans split forty supporting and forty-one opposed. Assemblywoman Gordon, one of just two female legislators from a rural area, voted against the bill. Overwhelmed, the farmers did manage to extract a provision that required restaurants to pay an annual fee of ten dollars and post a notice on the wall saying they were serving the substitute. Individual servings were required to have "margarine" imprinted on the wrapper.[87] The four-year saga ended with the *New York Times* headline "Oleo War Heroine Is Still 'Grinning.'"[88]

While the fight for margarine might not seem like the most pressing issue for women, it was one area where a woman legislator achieved unambiguous success. Women worked on other women's issues but never achieved the degree of closure that Strong did. Early on, because they were so few in number, women legislators tried to avoid behaving in ways that would make them stick out. Early pioneer women tended to downplay being seen as the "women's voice" on issues in favor of being just another member. But as the era progressed and more women served, they began to embrace that role, hesitantly at first and later more aggressively.

It should be remembered that not every issue divided along gender lines and not all women thought alike. Differences emerged where women legislators disagreed with each other or where a segment of womanhood in the public disagreed with a woman legislator. Gender solidarity, then as now, had its limits. In 1958 then Assemblywoman Janet Gordon led a successful fight against a bill to mandate babysitting licenses for high school–age students. Her Republican colleague Frances Marlatt had introduced it.[89] In 1959, the six women in the Assembly split four-to-two in favor of a bill that authorized teachers to use "reasonable force in a moderate degree" to restrain students acting out in the classroom. Dorothy Lawrence and Bessie Buchanan opposed what was dubbed "the spanking bill." Lawrence doubted the need for physical force at all and Buchanan worried that white teachers might abuse their authority in Harlem schools. But Aileen Ryan cited her previous experience as a teacher as the reason she supported the "spanking law," declaring it would be "a step toward restoring order in the schools."[90] Governor Rockefeller ultimately vetoed the proposed legislation.[91]

It was even possible for women legislators to agree with each other on an issue but to disagree over details. When the 1919 legislature went into special session to ratify the federal woman suffrage amendment, Lilly caused a stir by injecting a partisan statement that her party, the Democrats, deserved the most credit since the amendment passed during a Democratic administration. Sammis and the Republicans challenged her interpretation.[92] Later, during a crucial vote on a set of bills considered to be a "feminist welfare program," Lilly took shots at Sammis's abandonment of proposals for the eight-hour day, minimum wage, and health insurance for workers. Democrats failed by a single vote to discharge the minimum wage bill from the Rules Committee, which would have allowed a floor vote on the proposal. Sammis was not among the ten Republicans who broke with their party to support the bill that made the vote so close. In her remarks Lilly held the majority up to ridicule and identified Sammis in all but name. "You have passed bills here conserving ducks, skunks and scallops," she said. "But you refuse to pass bills conserving the working power of the state." Sammis's first two pieces of legislation had dealt with water fowl and scallops.[93]

Still, as women developed their legislative skills they more frequently seized opportunities for progress on women's issues despite their small numbers. Doris Byrne and Jane Todd spent a total of four years in the 1930s working to secure women's right to serve on juries. They won, but only the right to "opt in" or what is called permissive service.[94] Women had to affirm their willingness to serve or they would be presumed exempt from jury duty. These battles reveal women struggled to advance issues on which women were not fully united and for which there were organized, powerful interests resisting the women's efforts. These more complicated issues also reveal the limits of what women could accomplish in the pioneer generation, given their small numbers. Their most effective tactic, as had been the case with oleo, was to persist. Because they were in the legislature, the women could introduce proposals each year, tweaking them to make them more acceptable and trying to build support for their passage. Time and the women's growing political sophistication were their best weapons.

Democrat Assemblywoman Byrne introduced a women's juror bill in each of her first three years in office, 1934–1936. Her 1934 proposal called for absolute sex equity in the treatment of men and women as jurors. It never reached the floor for a vote. That was as much due to Byrne being in the chamber's minority as it was to opposition on the issue itself. In 1935, Byrne amended her proposal to exempt married women with minor children from jury service, and it passed the Assembly 105-to-33.[95] Todd, the only other woman and a Republican, sat next to Byrne during the floor debate. Senator Graves, also a Republican, came over to the House to lend her support to Byrne.[96] Graves's support mattered, for women's jury service died in the 1935 Republican-controlled Senate. For 1936, anticipating the same problem, Byrne allowed the Assembly to vote on bills submitted not by her but by her Republican colleague Todd. The bills were identical to Byrne's and had a better chance of support in the Senate.[97] That did not happen, though the two women received praise for having risen above party interest to work on this women's issue.

By the start of the 1937 session, a coalition of organized women's groups put their weight behind Byrne and Todd's leadership on jury service.[98] Again, the women's bills called for mandatory service with the exception for women caring for minor children. But there was a third bill competing with theirs. Senator Philip Kleinfeld, representing the Lower East Side of Manhattan, authored a permissive bill that would exempt women unless they affirmed their desire to serve. It is not clear whether the Kleinfeld version signified growing support for the issue of women's jury service or if it was a political tactic to divide support between multiple bills and thereby kill the initiative. It was thought that neither Byrne nor Todd would accept the Kleinfeld position. Todd used that "assumption" to her advantage and surprised fellow legislators. "Just to let you in on a secret," Todd recalled in an article for the *Woman Republican*, the official publication of that party's women. "The men thought they had us beaten because we had always said we wanted a mandatory bill or nothing. The Todd mandatory bill was dead—oh so dead—and our only hope was the Republican-led Assembly Rules Committee, and so Doris Byrne and I joined in signing the request to have Senator Kleinfeld's bill reported (out of committee for a vote)."[99] One reason for agreeing to a compromise was the realization that women remained divided on the question of jury service. The call for mandatory service came largely from middle-class, urban-based, well-educated women. They were the best organized and got more attention. But cohorts of women remained for whom mandatory service represented a potential hardship, in particular rural women and women who could not afford to take off work. The few surveys of women taken on the issue in the 1920s showed women preferred the permissive type of service.[100]

At the time the two women optimistically hoped that mandatory service could be secured in a few years. Thirteen years later, Assemblywoman Ten Eyck of Manhattan introduced bills to eliminate the blanket exemption for women in both 1950 and 1951.[101] But each time the bills failed to get a vote in the Senate. Full jury service for women would have to wait until 1975, when the legislature repealed the exemption in order to comply with the Supreme Court's decision in *Taylor v. Louisiana* from earlier that year. The Court there ruled that a defendant at trial was denied "equal protection" under the Sixth Amendment because the jury did not include women.[102]

Perhaps the most frustrating battle waged by a female legislator was Janet Gordon's fight to reform New York State's divorce laws. The state's laws were the most restrictive in the nation, allowing divorce only in cases of documented adultery. The *New York Times* reported more than a dozen legislators had fallen on their sword in the first half of the twentieth century in unsuccessful efforts to change those laws.[103] New York State remained "wedded" to this very narrow vision, even as the rest of the country began accepting more reasons for divorce and to award ever larger numbers of divorces. Critics observed that "New York's one-ground divorce law had the effect, not of preventing divorces, but of corrupting the whole machinery of justice."[104] New Yorkers developed ingenious schemes to circumvent the law. There were periodic exposes of divorce fraud rings, where people (usually women) were hired to falsify adulterous liaisons and testify to that effect in court.

One of the main obstacles to reform in New York State was fear of the Catholic Church and its ability to withhold votes from anyone who supported liberalizing the law. Such fear prompted many New Yorkers to try to annul their marriages rather than divorce their spouses. Annulments seemed like divorces in the sense that the marriage was legally dissolved. But annulments legally invalidated the legitimacy of the marriage contract, denying that a valid marriage had ever taken place. Divorces dissolved existing marriages. As of 1827, New York State recognized five annulment criteria: underage participants, bigamy, one participant being mentally incapacitated, one party physically unable to participate in the marriage, or the marriage itself being the consequence of fraud or force.[105] By the 1930s, numerous creative uses of the fraud justification appeared in annulment actions. Suits initiated in the courts argued that partners had misrepresented their ages, professions, education, and emotional attachment. One complainant claimed fraud because her husband had failed to tell her he ran a poolroom.[106]

From 1949 through 1955, Gordon unsuccessfully pursued legislation to simply study the issue of divorce reform. She repeatedly introduced bills in the Assembly and in some years found a Senate sponsor in Reverend Dutton Peterson.[107] She tried to soften resistance by seeking only to create a commission to study and recommend reforms of documented abuses. In each of the years opposition to her bills crossed party lines and was driven, Gordon believed, by lobbying from the State Catholic Welfare Committee.[108] The Assembly held a public hearing in 1953, where Gordon secured supportive statements from both Protestant leaders and sitting judges, all of whom argued that the current laws "were in a deplorable condition," with widespread perjury, collusion, and flouting of the law.[109] Finally, in 1956, Gordon and Peterson succeeded in getting a 25,000-dollar appropriation, but they had to agree to limit their study and any recommendations to procedural rather and substantive changes. It could only recommend changes to rules of procedure, jurisdiction, operation, and practices that might improve the administration of the law.[110] Governor Harriman then vetoed the first piece of substantive legislation produced by the committee, which would have set a higher standard for fraud allegations in annulment cases than in is generally applied in other types of fraud cases.[111]

The fight for divorce reform in New York continued into the twenty-first century. In 2006 a blue-ribbon commission recommended the state approve so-called no-fault divorces. Again, opposition from the Catholic Church prevented action.[112] Finally, in 2010 the state both expanded the list of at-fault categories for divorce along with permitting divorce on a no-fault basis. Couples who affirmed the marriage had irretrievably broken down and who lived apart for six months could now file. New York was the last state in the nation to approve a no-fault category.[113]

Along with pursuing these bigger issues, women focused on constituent needs and in doing so made a lasting impact on legislative culture. At first, they seemed most interested in areas traditionally important to women: family, children, education, and health. Examples include a proposal to amend divorce law to guarantee equal guardianship of children (Graves), expanded education for the handicapped (Strong), money for child care facilities in New York City (Ten Eyck), and development of a system to oversee private, foreign adoptions (Gordon). But these pioneers acquired a broader reputation for themselves as fighters for all their constituents. "I work with my constituents morning, noon and night," Assemblywoman Buchanan explained in a 1961 interview. "I'm not one of those who campaigns just at election time. I campaign all during the year."[114] The association of women with constituent service would continue and male legislators would be pushed to do more of the same type of hands-on problem solving. Good constituent service could overcome a member's thin list of legislative achievements or it could serve as a springboard to other offices. Buchanan, first elected to represent Harlem in 1954, won three more contests before retiring in 1962. Over those eight years she had only three bills become law.[115] Here Buchanan was dealing with being a minority woman in a minority party in the Assembly. But her Harlem district appreciated that she advocated for Black concerns. Many of her bills sought to ban discriminatory language in state laws governing education, banking, and mortgages. The bills consistently died in committee. In commenting on the larger issue of the erosion of party discipline, A *New York Times* piece from 1960 cited both Buchanan and her Democratic colleague from the Bronx, Aileen Ryan, as examples of Assembly members who crossed party lines in their voting because of issues.[116] Ryan made subway safety her key issue. She repeatedly called for improvements, including better equipment, improved exhaust systems, the implementation of a communications system, and a larger police presence.[117] The concentrated focus on this key local issue may have played a part on Ryan leaving the Assembly in 1965 to run for and win a Council-at-large seat on the New York City Council.

In her analysis of political woman that began this chapter, Kirkpatrick argued that women legislators came from a background that predisposed them to be problem solvers for their constituents. Women's traditional roles focused their attention "on people, on duty, service, and the 'higher' aspects of life."[118] Benjamin and Nakamura evaluated the New York legislature's mid-twentieth century modernization efforts and noted one innovation that seemed to stand apart the general focus on increased professionalization and bureaucratization. It was the opening of district offices beginning around 1966. Such offices increased constituent access and elevated constituent concerns. Studies done of women legislators around the country reaffirm that women still spend more time with constituents and help with problems more often than male legislators, even after state differences get factored in.[119] Women frequently framed challenges to party as being in the service of their constituents. As Republican Assemblywoman Gordon noted when she participated in an open revolt in 1947 against a package of taxes promoted by Republican Governor Dewey, "There are times when loyalty to the people back home must transcend other loyalties."[120]

Women's focus on constituent service, even at the expense of party loyalty, enabled two legislators, Gladys Banks and Elizabeth Hanniford, to hold their seats in the face of demographic changes that would ultimately make it almost impossible for Republican candidates in much of New York City to win elections. The women represented parts of the Bronx when the majority of voters in that borough were now registered Democrats. Republican leaders in the Bronx had stated as early as 1940 that their candidates going forward were increasingly doomed to fail there. More so than Hanniford, Banks had been actively involved in Republican politics before running for office. She was elected to the Republican State Committee in 1944, the same year she first ran for office.[121] But it was her willingness to break with the party to support City concerns over education funding, reapportionment, and rent control that got Banks reelected.[122] This may have accounted for the Democrats cross-endorsing Banks in 1948.[123] Nonetheless, Banks and

Hanniford lost their seats in a Democratic sweep of the Bronx in 1950. Even though he was decisively reelected to a third term that year, Republican Governor Dewey did not carry Bronx County. At the time, the trend of Republican decline in New York City was offset by Republican's winning in fifty-six of the fifty-seven counties outside the City.[124] Going forward Democrat inroads into the suburbs and smaller cities Upstate would erode Republican majorities there.

Limits for the Pioneer Generation Women

Women hoped the length and breadth of their work in the legislature would yield new opportunities. Sometimes as with Graves the opportunity sought was a higher legislative office. Others like Byrne or Ryan left the legislature voluntarily for other appointments or electoral contests outside the legislature. Toward the end of the pioneer era, we find more women securing their initial nomination to run for a legislative seat because of lengthy party service, jobs, or both. But party leaders generally continued to control access to electoral and appointive opportunities in ways that could stymie a woman's ambition. Graves's challenge for the Senate seat remained the exception.

Jane Todd of Westchester is a more typical illustration regarding limits on women's legislative career advancement in this period.[125] Party service yielded some electoral opportunities, but party leaders decided when such electoral options would be available. Still, because these women had been party stalwarts, leaders recognized they would have to take care of women members through appointment or patronage.

Since the 1920s, Todd had served the Republican Party consistently at both the state and county levels. She was elected president of the Westchester County Women's Republican Club in 1929, which, at that time, had a membership of 5,000. That same year Todd was appointed vice chair of the Republican County Committee, the highest position for a Republican woman in Westchester. By the early 1930s, she was included in meetings to choose candidates for the fall election and helped develop the state party platform. Yet, after longtime Westchester County chair and statewide political leader William Ward died in 1933, Todd had to fight to be part of a group of three that ran the county's affairs until a successor was finally chosen in May 1934. Todd was not considered for the chair's post but she was offered the nomination for the 4th State Assembly District. While her party service suggested she had earned the nomination, Todd got it only after several politicians pressed the leadership on her behalf. On paper, the 4th District was a relatively safe seat with a Republican majority. But this was during the Depression and New York, like the rest of the nation, had turned to the Democrats for answers. Republicans further weakened their 1934 electoral prospects when they nominated Robert Moses for governor. He was a poor candidate who failed to connect with the public, losing by some 808,000 votes. Todd won her race by only 417 votes out of over 31,000 cast. She was the only Republican woman in the Assembly for the 1935 session and one of only three women in the entire legislature. Todd stayed in the legislature for ten years (1935–1945) where she introduced over 165 bills, some 60 of which became law, with the permissive jury service bill discussed above as her most notable achievement. In 1937 she was also named vice chair of the Republican State Committee, which made her the leader of the state's women Republicans. According to the *New York Times*, Todd "enjoys a popularity transcending party lines, although she is a regular Republican."[126] During World War II Todd fought to expand employment opportunities for women along with pay equal to men in those same jobs.

Given her success in the legislature and as a political leader of women, Todd felt justified in seeking additional political opportunities. However, in 1944 party leaders denied her the nomination for a newly drawn congressional seat. The new 27th Congressional District was carved out of Westchester and Putnam Counties, both traditional Republican strongholds. Westchester political leaders had free reign to shape the new district and select a nominee. Whoever won the Republican nomination was virtually assured of victory in the fall. Todd believed current Westchester County leader Livingston Platt had promised her the nomination and was stunned when he told her to stay out of the race. In the end, though, Todd acted "as a member of the Republican organization who accepted the principle of cooperation with the duly elected leader of the party" and withdrew her name as Platt demanded.[127] Stung at the rejection by the party leader, Todd announced that she would also not run for reelection to the Assembly. Still, as Republican State Vice-Chair Todd could not be completely ignored. When she left the Assembly in 1945 Governor Dewey arranged a patronage appointment as Deputy Commissioner in the Department of Commerce. Todd remained Deputy Commissioner for fifteen years where she served as the primary spokesperson on women's business issues.

Manhattan Republican Maude Ten Eyck came into the Assembly in 1946, just after Todd left. Like Todd, Ten Eyck had built an impressive résumé of party service before seeking office. She began as a precinct captain in Manhattan, became leader of a Young Women's Republican Club, and avidly supported the failed presidential bids of Wendell Wilkie in 1940 and Thomas E. Dewey in 1944 and 1948. Ten Eyck was a Dewey delegate to the Republican National Convention in 1944.[128] She came into office as one of four new Republican women elected to the Assembly in 1946. She lost the seat in 1954 when Democrats gained eight Assembly seats, all from New York City. That year fourteen of the sixteen Manhattan districts moved into Democrat hands.[129] Her loss was really part of a larger shift in power to Democrats in the Assembly that began taking shape in the 1950s and would be completed in the 1970s. Yet as a loyal soldier Ten Eyck, like Todd, was taken care of by the party. In January 1955 she was appointed deputy journal clerk of the Assembly.[130] When Democrats first gained the majority for three years from 1965 to 1968 and with it control of that office, Ten Eyck found a new position in the office of Republican State Senator Whitney North Seymour of Manhattan.[131]

Republicans did not always resist women seeking national office. Senator Janet Gordon had full Republican backing as she sought the nomination for the newly drawn 35th Congressional District in 1962. The legislature had redistricted incumbent Democrat Samuel Stratton out of his former district, which centered on his home base of Schenectady. He now had to compete in the newly drawn 35th District. It covered 180 miles, beginning in the

Figure 3.2. Janet Gordon Congressional Campaign Card, 1962.

suburbs west of Schenectady and encompassing rural areas across Central New York. Even with party backing, Gordon had a primary challenger and a bruising fight for the nomination. It seemed Republicans believed the seat would be theirs.[132] But despite a statewide campaign blitz by Governor Rockefeller, Gordon lost the fall election to Stratton.[133] Gordon returned to the private practice of law following her defeat. Her failure to advance had more to do with Democratic encroachment in the Capital Region and surrounding suburbs than anything else. By the time Gordon looked to advance, Republican dominance of rural areas Upstate had trouble withstanding shifting demographics.

Conclusion

The "political woman" that Kirkpatrick spoke of clearly existed in New York by the mid-1960s, which closes out the pioneer era. These women had grown their political skills over time. But in most cases, their exercise of political power was limited. At any given time, women legislators were a small fraction of the whole. Any power in numbers was reduced further by party and geographic divisions. Women did not think or act in a block, so leaders concluded there was no incentive to make special accommodations for women or radically increase their numbers. Still, there was deference to women who worked hard within the party to organize women. They may not get a nomination but they would somehow be taken care of by the party in other ways.

Over time, women adapted to a legislative environment controlled by male party leaders because they had no other alternative. Women compromised on first principles more than the legislature changed how it conducted its business or how the parties chose candidates for office. Even with efforts to adapt to the legislature culture, these pioneers saw their progress constrained by the persistence of cultural stereotypes. To run successfully for office in the first place, women had to show that they were not abandoning traditional roles as wives and mothers. Too often that meant a shortened career window for interested women. Once in office, the legislature was not a place where women could just choose the moral high ground in opposition to party demands and survive. Yet, a woman who seemed to surrender the moral high ground found herself equally vulnerable to criticism for being too political.

Despite these challenges, women persisted in running for legislative office. They "threaded the needle" between issues and party by promoting the idea of constituent service. Here women did effect change in the overall legislative environment. Savvy women legislators also successfully championed issues that had broad, if not total, support from women. Women's political knowledge of how the system worked led to several legislative achievements. The persistent embrace of an issues-oriented philosophy would become an asset going forward. For in the 1960s, the legislative culture would undergo significant changes. Among other shifts, the old party- and leader-driven loyalty system in the legislature would give way to a framework that placed much greater value on issues expertise. Legislative women would be well-positioned to leverage their strengths as issues advocates in this changed environment.

Finally, while pioneer women may not have been elected in large numbers, they did become part of the mosaic that made up New York politics. Their actions contribute to a better understanding of how politics played out between 1919 and 1964. Just like with men, women's ability to make their mark politically was determined by what party and part of the state they represented. Championing the dairy farmer did not depend on Rhoda Graves being a woman as much as it did on her own business experience and being in the majority party. The story of rural challenges in twentieth-century New York is not complete without her in it.

Chapter 4

Activism and the Woman Legislator, 1965–1980

Activist-Era Legislators

	Party	Body/Year Elected	through Year	Body/Year Elected	through Year	Region Represented
Constance Cook	R	A/1962	1974			Southern Tier
Shirley Chisholm	D	A/1964	1968			New York City
Constance Motley	D	S/1964	1965*			New York City
Dorothy Rose	D	A/1964	1968			Western NY
Gail Hellenbrand	R	A/1966	1970			New York City
Rosemary Gunning	R	A/1968	1976			New York City
Mary Anne Krupsak	D	A/1968	1972	S/1972	1974	Mohawk Valley
Carol Bellamy	D	S/1972	1977			New York City
Karen Burstein	D	S/1972	1978			New York City
Elizabeth Connelly	D	A/1973	2000			New York City
Estella Diggs	D	A/1972	1980			New York City
Jean Amatucci Fox	R	A/1974	1978			Mid-Hudson
Mary Goodhue	R	A/1974	1978	S/1978	1992	Mid-Hudson
Marie Runyon	D	A/1974	1976			New York City
Linda Winikow	D	S/1974	1984			Mid-Hudson
Jeanette Gadson	D	A/1974	1976			New York City
Gerdi Lipschutz	D	A/1976	1986			New York City
Mary Rose McGee	D	A/1976	1978			Long Island
Carol Berman	D	S/1978	1984			Long Island
Audre Cooke	R	A/1978	1990			Finger Lakes
Rhoda Jacobs	D	A/1978	2014			New York City
Olga Mendez	D	S/1978	2002	S/2002	2004**	New York City
May Newburger	D	A/1978	1986			Long Island
Antonia Rettaliata	R	A/1978	1987			Long Island
Joan Smith	R	A/1978	1982			Capital District
Florence Sullivan	R	A/1978	1982			New York City

Assembly = A, Senate = S.
* Special election spring 1964, and then again in the regular fall cycle.
** Switched Party registration from D to R after the 2002 election.

Activist-Era Legislators

 Carol Bellamy
 Carol Berman
 Karen Burstein
 Shirley Chisholm

 Elizabeth Connelly
 Constance Cook
 Audre Cooke
 Estella Diggs

 Jean Amatucci Fox
 Jeanette Gadson
 Mary Goodhue
 Rosemary Gunning

 Gail Hellenbrand
 Rhoda Jacobs
 Mary Anne Krupsak
 Gerdi Lipschutz

 Mary Rose McGee
 Olga Mendez
 Constance Baker Motley
 May Newburger

Antonia Rettaliata   Dorothy Rose   Marie Runyon   Joan Smith

Florence Sullivan   Linda Winikow

Overview

The 1960s and 1970s were a tumultuous time in American life. Twenty-six women served in the legislature as the country and New York State dealt with issues of discrimination and urban unrest, along with changing cultural attitudes about gender, sex, and crime. The number of women in the legislature modestly increased, but it was the impact of larger societal shifts, coupled with structural changes in the legislative system, that reshaped how women legislators saw themselves and their political roles. Much of the presuffrage legacy of women's separate political culture that had been present in the pioneer period was displaced by other considerations. Many women became politically active through their participation in rights movements. But, perhaps surprisingly, the New York legislature did not attract large numbers of self-identified feminists. For what such members found was that the legislative apparatus itself worked against any sort of revolution. The legislature developed a professionalized structure with greater centralization of power in the chambers' leadership. The changes were meant to counter executive assertions of authority. The new system was not designed to bring about big changes overnight. Faced with that restructuring, some women legislators shortened their time there and sought other political opportunities both at the state and national levels. Such women hoped to find a better venue for more immediate change and wide-ranging influence. At the same time, other women in this period stayed in the legislature and built political careers there. They became mentors for the women who would later follow.

The shifts are significant enough that, in order to give this cohort of women justice, we need both to take a broad view of the changing characteristics of the woman politician generally and assess the impact of changed external circumstances on several specific legislators' experiences. This chapter focuses on that broad analysis, while the following chapter takes an in-depth look at examples of how an activist mind-set could lead either to impatience with the legislature or an embrace of the possibilities there.

Transition to the New Era

In 1965 Aileen Ryan of the Bronx (D) (A1958–1966) was the lone holdover in the legislature from the pioneer era and one of only two women legislators overall. She would leave in 1966 to run for and win a seat on the New York City Council. Ryan had come to the legislature as a former teacher and widow, a common profile for her generation. She delivered her maiden speech in the 1959 session in support of the "spanking bill," legislation allowing teachers to administer punishment to what Ryan termed "recalcitrant" students.[1] Often her advocacy on issues was framed as speaking for the housewife's interest, whether it was about more safety on the subways or calling for a repeal of the 10 percent tax on pocketbooks.[2] Constance Cook (R) (A1962–1974) of Tompkins County Upstate had joined Ryan in the Assembly in 1963.[3] Cook was a lawyer who practiced for five years before marrying and starting a family. She was a working mother who ran for the open seat being vacated by her boss, Assemblyman Ray Ashberry.[4]

Together, the two women are emblematic of the transition to a new generation of women legislators. Overall, the twenty-six women legislators elected over this fifteen-year period confirm a sea change in several key areas: the sheer number elected to office, their growing professionalization as political actors, and their heightened activism on behalf of issues related to women's disadvantaged position in society. The women's progress on these fronts was not linear in all cases. Individually, they were aided or frustrated in their goals by considerations of party, geography, the structure and culture of the legislature itself, and other issues dominating the state and the nation at the time. The women who served in the legislature did so in a highly charged atmosphere rife with the hope of rapid political and social change.

More than their predecessors this cohort of legislators embraced their identity as women in politics. The nineteen women of the forty-five year pioneer generation had spent their time in office as somewhat isolated islands, which had made them reticent to connect themselves too much to their gender. They concentrated on winning acceptance from fellow legislators and in normalizing the idea of the woman legislator. Pioneer-era women's concern for issues was more outwardly driven, focused on those they believed called on to help. Activist-era legislators did not abandon the role of woman as caretaker of the community. But they recognized that women were a part of that community and women's concerns needed to be addressed.[5] Again, the effect was mixed, much like the public's mixed reaction to the organized women's movement's agenda at the time. The goal of equality was lauded by all these legislators, though they did not agree on the specifics of every issue. Where it got complicated was when heightened expectations for change met the realities of lawmaking in New York. Regardless of whether they stayed or moved on, this generation of women legislators were not shy about challenging their colleagues to address inequality and discrimination.

In 1964 three more women, two of whom were minorities, won seats: New York City Democrats Shirley Chisholm (D) (A1964–1968) in the Assembly and Constance Baker Motley (D) (S1964–1965) in the Senate. The third new woman legislator was Dorothy Rose (D) (A1964–1968) from Buffalo. Between 1966 and 1972, five more new women joined the legislature and one went from the Assembly to the Senate. If one judged progress solely by the aggregate number of successful women candidates, women appeared to being making progress in changing the composition of the legislature. Especially significant was the fact that eight women in the activist era would serve in the Senate.[6] There were only two women senators between 1919 and 1964.

The majority of these women came from the metropolitan New York City area: one of the five City boroughs or Nassau, Suffolk, Westchester, and Rockland Counties. Seventeen activist legislators were Democrats though party affiliation was not the sole determinant of where a woman stood on a given issue. The rise in the number of Downstate Democrats was more about population shifts, court-mandated increases in minority districts, and a greater concentration of liberal political voices there. At the same time, Republicans were mirroring national shifts away from moderate positions on issues to more conservative ones.[7] The growing influence of the Democratic Party in New York especially benefited New York City metropolitan area male leadership in the Assembly. When Democrats took control of the chamber, temporarily from 1965 to 1968 and permanently from 1974 on, the speakership went to a New York City–area legislator. That unwritten rule has remained going forward. While women in the Assembly did not have a chance at a leadership position, there was a base of support from Downstate representatives for much of the legislation women would introduce in that chamber. Male colleagues even cosponsored several key pieces of legislation.

A Different Kind of Preparation for Office

Female and male legislators overall appeared increasingly alike in their education and political background, which were two indicators traditionally seen as signs of readiness for office. Nationally, the overall trend for legislators in the twentieth century has been for more to hold college and advanced degrees. A 2015 study by the Pew Trusts found that especially true in the more populous states like New York where 86 percent of the legislature held a Bachelor of Arts or other advanced degree.[8] The women legislators of the activist era actually outpaced the broader statistic, achieving an 88 percent score by 1980. In New York the largest single credential held has become and remains the law degree. In a 2015 survey, 48 percent of Assembly members and 49 percent of senators were lawyers. In this era nine women legislators had law degrees, the largest single group within the cohort.[9] An additional seven women, while not lawyers themselves, could still claim a connection to the legal profession. Two women had family members who were or had been judges, and five had worked in some capacity for the court system.[10] New York's women thus reflect what political science researchers observed nationally, by the 1980s women's and men's career paths and socioeconomic characteristics were converging and resulting in more women elected to office.[11]

Unlike the five women lawyers of the pioneer era, female lawyers now did not seem as pressured to build up a strong résumé of community service before running for office.[12] The pioneer-generation women had come out of and reflected a cultural dynamic that emphasized the differences between men and women. As noted earlier, the women who ran for the legislature then stressed their lengthy experience out in the community over their professional credentials. Their decision to run more often grew out of community activities geared toward social uplift and family concerns than it did from a lifelong preoccupation with politics.[13] Now, younger women like Karen Burstein (D) (S1972–1978) of Nassau County accepted the challenge of running for a congressional seat in 1970, albeit unsuccessfully, while she was still in law school.[14] In 1972, at age thirty, she won election to the New York State Senate. Two other female lawyers were elected with her; Carol Bellamy of Brooklyn (D) (S1972–1977) was also thirty while Mary Anne Krupsak was forty. Krupsak (D) (A1968–1972 and S1972–1974) had never been shy about having political ambition. Her first job out of college was in a civil service position in Governor Averill Harriman's office. The advice she received from the male officials there was to go to law school. In a 1993 oral interview she recalled, "It was almost like a credential that you had to have in those days."[15] After graduating, Krupsak went to work as an assistant counsel in the Senate. From there, in 1968 she beat the sixteen-year incumbent from Montgomery County for a seat in the Assembly. A 1972 *New York Times* profile of the three candidates commented on their youth, noting an average age of thirty-three and labeling them "full time activists."[16] Going forward, the younger representatives would admit to a degree of impatience in wanting to tackle big issues.

One social science researcher in the 1970s observed that New York's female legislators' backgrounds appeared somewhat unique in comparison to legislative women in surrounding states. In 1971, political Scientist Irene Diamond surveyed women legislators in New England. She supplemented that data with in-depth interviews of a subset of female and male legislators in Connecticut and New Hampshire. None of these women were lawyers. She also included in her analysis written interviews with four unnamed New York legislators from the 1973 session, all of whom were lawyers. Five of the seven women in New York's legislature that year had law degrees—the three new Democratic senators plus incumbent Republicans Assemblywomen Cook and Rosemary Gunning (Conservative/R) (A1968–1976) of Queens. Cook received her law degree from Cornell University in 1943 at the age of twenty-four. She spent two years as a confidential law assistant on Governor Dewey's staff before moving to Ithaca and marrying in 1954.[17] Cook was the only female legislator who had school-age children in 1973. Based on quotes from Diamond's studies dealing with family-work tensions, Cook can be identified with certainty as one of the four. Gunning's route to law school and career path to the legislature was the most unusual of the five. She was part of the last class admitted to law school that allowed one to apply without a college degree. Though she obtained her law degree at twenty-two and was admitted to the bar at twenty-five in 1930, Gunning did not run for the legislature until 1968 at the age of sixty.[18] Again, the quotes attributed to New York's female lawyer legislators suggest Gunning was also one of the four. A lawyer quoted in the study was self-deprecating about being so much older than most of her male colleagues.[19] Krupsak is likely the third interviewee based on a comment about beginning her elective career by winning a district her party had written off.[20] That leaves either Burstein or Bellamy as the fourth woman interviewed by Diamond.

The pattern set here of younger lawyers seeking office at an early stage will continue going forward as would the view that a law degree was a strong indicator of readiness for office. Helene Weinstein (D) (A1980–present), another lawyer and a legislator whose career will be emblematic of the professional era after 1980, was only twenty-six in 1978 when she challenged Assembly Majority Leader Stanley Steingut in Brooklyn. In turn, her opponent challenged her residency and got Weinstein removed from the ballot only eleven days before the September 1978 primary. Murray Weinstein, her father, stepped in as substitute and beat Steingut. In another departure from the pioneer era pattern, here the male served as stand-in for a female family member; he held the seat for his daughter until the 1980 election.[21] His role as placeholder is part of the shift to what I will call a professional era around 1980. Helene Weinstein would win the seat outright in 1980, and has become the longest-serving female in the New York State Assembly.[22]

Association with the legal profession aside, the next most common type of preparation for these women was party service.[23] Even more that in the pioneer era, these women grew up with the option of party membership as a form of community activism. Still, the long-standing locations of power—county leaders with their machines and political clubs—were weakening in influence, which afforded these women more options inside and outside the parties. Several women were part of attempts to create rival local political clubs bent on wresting power from the established leadership. That is what Weinstein did. New York City Councilman Theodore Silverman's 25th District overlapped Majority Leader Steingut's 41st Assembly District. Steingut controlled the area as district leader. Silverman had begun his political life in 1969 as an opponent of Steingut. After a failed effort to coexist with the fellow Brooklynite, Silverman left the Steingut-controlled Madison Democratic Club to form the New Way Democratic Club. Weinstein lived across the street from Silverman's club and was drawn into political discussions there, which explains how she became Steingut's challenger in 1978.[24]

Women also gained a political education through nonparty organizations seeking change. Carol Berman (D) (S 1978–1984) combined the roles of party worker and community activist. Her successful quest for a Senate seat in 1978 was spurred by her leadership of an ultimately unsuccessful movement to prevent the Concorde jet from landing at JFK Airport. The district, which included parts Nassau County and Queens, would be directly in the flight path of the newly developed plane and locals feared a massive increase to existing noise pollution.[25] She had been in and around politics for decades as both an elected representative to her local school board and a paid local aide to legislators in home district offices. But it was her activism on behalf of residents concerned about the planes that secured her the Senate nomination and the victory in a district divided almost equally between Queens Democrats and Nassau Republicans.[26]

It was clear that law and political experience best reflected the women legislators' résumés in this period. Fewer women's backgrounds resembled pioneer-era legislators. Excluding Gunning who earned a law degree directly after high school, only four did not go on to some post–high school education and, instead, emphasized volunteer work in the community. Only two listed teaching experience as part of their professional background and another was a school nurse. Finally, one legislator was a trained social worker.[27]

Challenging the Legislative Culture

Another way in which these women departed from their pioneer predecessors was in how many saw themselves as movement leaders, warriors for causes that would intentionally upend old norms and power structures. For some, simply running and winning office challenged the entrenched legislative culture. When Bellamy, Burstein, and Krupsak won seats in the Senate in 1972, they formally requested to be listed as "Ms." on the Senate voting sheets.[28] This was a rebuke to having endured being called "little lady" and having a cheek pinched by Assembly Minority Leader Steingut "every time he saw me," said one. While another reported having been told they would be welcomed as "ornaments to this chamber."[29] In describing the newly elected Burstein, the *New York Times* led off with calling her an "attractively packaged bundle of energy," followed by listing the color of her eyes, brown, and her hairstyle, tightly curled and brown.[30] During their first year in office, Burstein and Bellamy gained a reputation for being more vocal than other freshmen. A *New York Times* piece singled the two out for their active involvement in floor debate, questioning and "needling more than any other two members of the Senate."[31] The same article noted each member was also "fighting the male establishment" outside the legislature. Bellamy had her application for membership in the all-male Brooklyn (political) Club denied. Burstein tried but failed to find a sponsor for membership in the all-male Fort Orange Club in Albany.

In considering her fellow legislators' reputation, Assemblywoman Gunning observed that historically there had been fewer women in the Senate than Assembly, which perhaps made the women's behavior seem so challenging to that membership. She believed that Bellamy and Burstein were disadvantaged both by being in the minority party and by being "aggressive gals," though Bellamy and Burstein would have disagreed about the characterization. Gunning believed the women in the Assembly were less confrontational.[32] Her comment implies that not all women legislators endorsed their female colleague's approach to dealing with demeaning reactions from male members. But these assemblywomen clearly knew and experienced gender bias. Gunning herself admitted that there was a culture of socialization among the male members that was not welcoming to women. "At first I went out to dinner (with them) . . ." she remembered. "I was really spoiling it . . . I soon dropped the idea."[33] Shirley Chisholm remembered what she called "an active, shall we say, night life" among the male legislators.[34] Linda Winikow (D) (S 1974–1984) who joined the three women senators in 1974 agreed that there was an ever-present "drinking culture," but she never tried to break into it. She drove back home to Rockland County each night to see her elementary-school-age children.[35] Apart from the socializing limits, women legislators were frequently "overlooked" in the sense that many in and around government just assumed they worked for someone else rather than being the legislator themselves. Assemblywoman Elizabeth Connelly (D) (A1972–2000) recalled how, while waiting in Speaker Steingut's office to see him, a lobbyist remarked that she looked familiar and asked who she worked for. Connelly replied she was in the Assembly, to which the lobbyist responded, "I know but who do you work for?" He left in embarrassment when the secretary set him straight on Connelly's position.[36] In sum, the women did encounter a culture where gender bias was commonly accepted. While the women confronted it on the individual level, they failed to alter the broader environment that still relied on male camaraderie to get things done.[37] A more significant blow to that culture would come from the professionalization of the legislature.

Still, the women were astute enough about gender dynamics in the legislature to occasionally make them work on their behalf. Assemblywoman Diggs put herself up as a contrast to the challenging demeanor of her younger, female colleagues. Diggs, fifty-six when first elected in 1972, was affectionately known as "the lady" due to her dignified demeanor.[38] She was described by her daughter as a "very traditional lady" who got more done with diplomacy than by being aggressive.[39] Gunning said she "played the vulnerable" card in order to get a bill passed that would require men leaving their wives to disclose three years assets in a divorce proceeding. By appealing to her colleagues' chivalry Gunning's bill prevented husbands from shielding their assets in court.[40] On the lighter side, being a woman could get you freed from the lengthy legislative sessions of the 1970s. Assemblywoman Jean Amatucci (D) (A1974–1978) left an extended 1975 session that had deadlocked over a tax package to relieve New York City's fiscal distress so she could attend her own wedding.[41] Assemblywomen Krupsak and Cook left a locked 1971 session by saying they had to go to the bathroom. At the time, the women's lavatory was on another floor in the building. Reporters caught up with them later at a local restaurant where they were having dinner.[42]

Women's restrooms loomed large as a cultural symbol of discrimination in America broadly and in the New York State Legislature specifically. Assemblywoman Connelly remembered how demeaning it was to have to ask the Majority Leader for a pass to go to the "ladies' " room because there was not one connected to the chamber. Several legislators from that era and beyond recalled aspects of the quest for bathroom access equivalent to the men. The women did not consider it sufficient to just put a sound system into their distant bathroom. While some of the specific details remain hazy, there is a general sense that the defining moment of the struggle can be traced to a reception for women organized at the Capitol. There the female membership presented Speaker Stanley Fink with a pink toilet seat cover as a visual symbol of disadvantage. The women's point was not lost on him. By the following session in 1985, the men's room had been remodeled into a separate male and female facility.[43]

On a broader scale, Senator Burstein sponsored a successful bill in 1975 to ban pay toilets in public facilities. At the time, such facilities typically included some free toilets but also some that required the user to deposit a dime or quarter to open the stall door. Private establishments serving the public, like a restaurant, might opt to have only pay toilets. Some thought the pay toilet a more sanitary option. Regardless, there was no equivalent in the male restrooms. Burstein claimed pay toilets humiliated women. Male legislators admitted they were unaware of the importance of the issue before the women brought it up. But as one male observed, "This is a national movement." That was a reference to some twenty pay toilet bans being considered by state legislatures at the time.[44]

Part of the difficulty in changing the legislative culture was twofold. For all that women's numbers increased, they were still a small percentage of the whole. For the 1968 session, the four women in the Assembly were only 2½ percent of the chamber. There were no women in the fifty-seven-seat Senate that year. The women's small numbers, their party affiliations, and the area of the state the women represented were other considerations that limited unity of purpose and action.

Rights Activism versus Professionalization

The other factor that divided women and limited their ability to reform the legislative culture is what I see as an expectation gap driven either by impatience with the speed of change or lack of experience with political organizations and the legislative process. Sometimes it was both. There were some women who reflected the attitude of many in the 1960s, that demanded speedy change, speedy reform. They were impatient with the traditions of the legislature, with limits on how quickly they could turn their issues into laws. They openly balked at what they deemed restrictions and often left to pursue their agendas in other venues. They stirred things up in the legislature while they were there, sometimes generating criticism from male colleagues. Upon election to her first term in office, Assemblywoman Rhoda Jacobs (D) (A1978–2014) observed that while the voting public had generally accepted the woman politician, "I am not so sure that the politicians (in the legislature) have reached that same level of acceptance."[45] Some of the women's combative behavior may have played a role in that body's reluctance to embrace them.

What had changed is that women were increasingly challenging incumbents in elections and winning. Jacobs herself was no shrinking violet. She took on incumbent Brooklyn Assemblyman George Cincotta in 1976 and lost. Jacobs then beat him in a second match-up in 1978. She was well aware of persistent gender stereotyping where women politicians were continually asked about family obligations, for she had three children in high school in 1978.[46] But she had done a stint as a local district leader, thereby building up a network of grassroots support and infrastructure for her campaigns.[47] She believed women had to embrace the political basics since even the men had to work their way up the ladder to a degree. But she also appreciated that there was a place for women to assert themselves.[48] Her career in the Assembly ended only in 2014. However, Krupsak, Bellamy,

Burstein, and Marie Runyon (D) (A1974–1976) all expressed frustration or came to believe other vehicles would better suit their agendas. These women's legislative careers are a focus of attention in chapter 5.

In general, women like Bellamy, Krupsak, and Burstein may have placed too much faith in the women's movement to foster change in the legislative environment for women. These legislators also encountered the limits of what a modest increase of in the number of women legislators, particularly in the Senate, could accomplish. Women legislators who presented themselves as primarily women's rights activists still had to demonstrate interest and expertise in other areas. Women who put together large, broad legislative portfolios that included women's issues tended to have more success with a feminist agenda. As one New York legislator in the Diamond study referenced earlier made clear, "You have to convince people that our legitimacy is more than just legitimacy as a woman . . . that you have the capacity to handle any issue."[49] Because of their small numbers the pioneer generation had mostly tried to avoid being typed and thus marginalized as women. Now, these activist legislators found that not all women approached issues the same way, even issues about women themselves. The 1975 ballot proposition to amend the state constitution to include an equal rights amendment failed by over 400,000 votes, or 57 percent opposed to 47 percent in favor. Some New York women were even beginning to organize in opposition to parts of the women's movement agenda. In the case of the ERA, on the national level it was Phyllis Schlafly's STOP ERA organization. New York had its own iteration in Operation Wake-Up, which had about 100,000 members and was led by a Long Island mother, Annette Stern.[50] The diversity among women and how that affected their leverage on women's issues is the subject of chapter 7. But in the 1970s legislature, it is fair to say on the ERA issue that New York's women legislators, who were all supportive, were surprised by the ERA's failure in New York. This surprise even included Rosemary Gunning, who as a member of the Conservative Party was considered the most traditional of the women legislators.

The ERA highlighted a tension specific to New York. Increased power for leadership clashed with some women legislators' active commitment to a movement agenda regardless of other considerations. In the New York Senate specifically, the majority leader has certain tools that allow tight control of which bills can come to the floor. The majority leader has the power to "star" a bill, which effectively freezes it until the star is lifted. As chair of the Rules Committee, the majority leader also holds absolute power over end of session bills; nothing comes to the floor without Rules approval.

Increased power for the majority leader was tied to the expansion of staff and professionalization of the legislature in the 1960s and 1970s.[51] Members of both parties who bucked leadership ran the risk of losing important committee assignments and having their bills fail to move forward. The women's movement expectation of continuous, rapid change came directly up against a system that was slower and where party control trumped other considerations. A 1981 *New York Times* headline "Voting in Albany: A Test of Loyalty and Endurance," aptly summarized the legislative environment. That year's session was among the longest at the time, lasting until July 10th. In the article, Senator Olga Mendez (D) (S1978–2004) claimed, "My friends have sequestered me and they are brainwashing me, brainwashing me, trying to break my will."[52] The question at hand was a tax plan to rescue the metropolitan transit system. Fellow Senator Linda Winikow avoided the browbeating by hiding in another room with a colleague until the vote.[53]

The pressure on state legislators to follow party cues existed even in the ERA battle. Political scientist David Hill studied roll-call votes on the national ERA from every state that held them, which included most states in the country. He thus had "a rare situation in which legislators in an extensive variety of political contexts voted on precisely the same piece of legislation."[54] He found what he termed "party cues" trumped other factors even on this issue. In terms of the New York Senate's vote on the state ERA, all three members as Democrats had no conflict with a party that endorsed the measure. But on other women's issues going forward there would be divisions that can partly be traced to party pressures. Michelle Barnello studied all the roll-call votes in the 1993 New York State Assembly during the legislative session. She found that women and men mainly cast votes as a response to party cues and their electoral constituency, even when the issue focused on women, children, or the family. The 19 percent of the Assembly who were women adhered to party discipline, in part because it was such a strong component of the New York State legislative culture.[55]

Some women were frustrated by this new legislative organization. This new environment valued loyalty and expertise built up over time. To a degree, these attributes replaced personal connections as the path to influence in the legislature. Stanley Fink was Assembly Speaker from 1979 to 1986. He remarked on the presence of new, younger voices like these women arriving in the legislature. But in a 1991 interview he affirmed the dominance of that more structured environment. "My contention, then and now, is that people gain power, particularly in the legislature, by the accumulation of knowledge."[56] The changing landscape included development of separate budget and research staffs, expansion and professionalization of the legislative staff, computerization of laws, building of a separate Legislative Office Building, creation of legislative campaign resources managed by the leaders of the parties in each house, and the expansion of the legislative session such that the job now operated more as full time.[57] Political Scientist David Hill found in a 1981 study that women's representation in a legislature was inversely proportional to how professionalized it was.[58] In part, that may be because representatives in more professionalized legislatures approach those offices as steps in a political career and competition can be steep.[59] Still, during this period New York women showed they could be successful in a professionalized legislature. Women who set their mind to mastering the system, to doing the job as it was structured, did well. Their success also provided opportunities to promote women's issues. This was not unique to New York. Suzanne Schenken has studied Iowa's women lawmakers. Iowa's legislature underwent a similar professionalization at about the same time as New York. The emphasis on women there who won office was not their feminist agenda but their capability for the job.[60] The New York Legislature had women like that, too. Two of those women, Constance Cook and Elizabeth Connelly, are profiled in chapter 5.

Aspects of Mary Goodhue's career (R) (A1974–1978) (S1978–1992) resembled fellow female legislators who forged longer careers. Goodhue understood that being in the majority party gave you gave you an advantage in getting things done. Goodhue acted on that knowledge after only a short time in the legislature. She came to the Assembly in 1974 as a Republican. This was the year that Democrats took control of that body for good, which left her in the minority with zero seniority. In the Assembly, Goodhue could not get any of her bills out of the Democratically controlled committees.[61] Not surprisingly, she put herself into competition for a special election in 1978 to replace recently deceased State Senator Bernard Gordon as a way to "get something done." Most of her Assembly District lay within the lines of the Senate District, which made her a formidable candidate who bested several primary challengers.

Once in the Senate, Goodhue chaired the Child Care Committee where she initiated significant legislation regarding day-care centers as well as focusing on tightening laws related to punishing child abusers and on child custody in divorces. Childcare issues received significant attention due to publicity surrounding the McMartin Preschool child-abuse scandal and trials in California that lasted from 1983 to 1990. The multiyear investigation and two trials ended in the acquittal of the owner, Barbara McMartin, and two deadlocked juries on her son, Ray Buckley. The long-term consensus has been to dub the scandal a "hysteria" without evidentiary foundation. The trials have become a cautionary tale about unreliable expert testimony. But in the short-term, prosecutors across the country fielded allegations of abuse and politicians considered numerous regulatory and policy changes. In 1985, New York considered forty-three bills related to child abuse. Goodhue defended her actions when she said, "I don't think we're overreacting. . . . Potential victims are young children, inarticulate, easily scared and ignorant about sexual abuse. I don't see how anybody could take the position that the state shouldn't try to protect them."[62]

During the 1990 session, Goodhue was prime sponsor on some ninety bills that passed in both houses.[62] She brought to bear her legal training and her facility with how the legislature operated. For example, Goodhue was widely credited with having salvaged a bill during the 1981 session mandating that judges consider joint custody in divorces if either party requested it. After she negotiated a compromise that both houses accepted, the *New York Times* ran a piece, "Mrs. Goodhue's Role in Joint-Custody Bill," that alluded to "the power she has obtained in her seven years in Albany." Goodhue astutely pointed out that one needed to combine being in the majority and having seniority before one had any real power in the legislature. What kept women legislators back was the lack of that seniority. "I lost four years by being in the Assembly," Goodhue reflected.[63]

Goodhue's Westchester was an affluent county with growing suburban areas close enough for commuting into New York City. It had been a Republican stronghold since before women won the right to vote in 1917. In 1934, Republican Jane Todd had been first female elected from Westchester to the legislature. But now the political composition of the county was shifting toward the Democrats. When Goodhue first ran for Senate, area Republicans in had a three-to-two advantage in registered voters. But by 1984 Westchester Democrats held a slight majority. Still, Goodhue's seat seemed safe. She was a moderate in her Republicanism, which meant she was fiscally conservative and socially moderate. Democrats struggled to draw big distinctions based on party. She and her Democrat opponent in 1982 differed only on the death penalty. Since Republicans controlled redistricting in the Senate, over time leadership compensated for increasing Democratic numbers in Westchester by shifting Goodhue's district lines to include more and more of Putnam County to the north. Putnam was a heavily Republican county. Party control of a house at redistricting time was a powerful tool to keep the party in power. Throughout the 1980s, Goodhue benefited from that process. Things changed in the 1990s. Goodhue's unsuccessful struggle against the Republican leadership to retain her Senate seat in 1992 is covered in chapter 8.

There might have been a few more women with expansive legislative careers had they not entered elective politics at an older age. It had been characteristic of women in the pioneer era to be unmarried or to wait until they were older to run, most often because of family considerations. More of the women in the activist period ran with children still at home, though the second birth to a woman serving in office would not come until 1987, when Senator Velmanette Montgomery gave birth to a son.[64] Jean Amatucci Fox chose to leave the Assembly in 1978, after two terms, because she was just starting her family. In contrast, Rosemary Gunning, Estella Diggs (D) (A1972–1980), May Newburger (D), (A1978–1986), Florence Sullivan (R) (A1978–1982), and Audrey Cooke (R) (A1978–1990) were all in their fifties when they first won seats in the Assembly.

Minority Women's Experiences

While some stereotypes about women continued to impede their entry into politics, circumstances in the 1960s and 1970s gave minority women a better chance of winning office than ever before. Civil rights struggles gave these women important public exposure and advocacy experience that they combined with an understanding of how the political system worked. As with their white counterparts, some had career goals that took them quickly beyond the legislature while others focused on working there.

As discussed in chapter 1, court decision in the 1960s and 1970s profoundly affected representation and district configuration in the state. The Democratic Party and the influence of New York City increased dramatically. District boundaries were drawn to enhance the ability of more minorities to win elections. In some cases, the opportunity to run for office came from these changes. Shirley Chisholm certainly believed so.

> 1964 was the first big year for black candidates in New York State. Redistricting . . . had wiped out some of the cleverly drawn district lines that had split the black vote and kept white women in office. When I went to Albany I went as one of eight, six black assemblymen and two state senators. I was the only woman but not the first.[65]

Shirley Chisholm (D) (A1964–1968), wanted to be a change agent. Throughout the 1950s, Chisholm's Brooklyn political club, which covered the 17th Assembly District, was tightly controlled by an all-white leadership despite there being a black majority population. After a frustrating period of trying to work within the existing structure, she became part of a group of six insurgents who formed the Unity Democratic Club (UDC) in 1960. As she remembered it, at the time there were efforts all around the City challenging established clubs.[66] Her club secured control of the 17th Assembly District by 1962. Chisholm declared herself a candidate for the Assembly in 1964, when the current incumbent left for a civil court judgeship. Even though registered black women outnumbered men by 17,000 in the district, the UDC balked at a woman candidate. The party backed her only after her primary victory and never offered much monetary support during the general election.[67] Her November victory ended the reluctance about her electability.

By 1966, Shirley Chisholm was part of a group that organized as the New York State Black and Puerto Rican Legislative Caucus.[68] These legislators then began to negotiate as a unit for more power in the legislature. Over time, the caucus has expanded its reach and changed its name to reflect a broader constituency. The last change came in 2005, when the group became the Black, Puerto Rican, Hispanic and Asian Legislative Caucus.

1964 was also the year Constance Motley was approached to run for the State Senate. Motley (D) (S1964–1965) was the most well-known of the women lawyers to serve in the legislature during this era. She graduated from Columbia Law School in 1946, and went to work for the National Association for the Advancement of Colored People's (NAACP's) Legal Defense Fund where she had already been volunteering. Motley saw the law as a way to aggressively press for change, in her case change focused on civil rights issues.[69] Motley worked on a number of segregation challenges and directed the legal campaign that resulted in the admission of James Meredith to the University of Mississippi in 1962.[70] Her reputation was a significant factor in outgoing State Senator James Watson's effort to recruit her to run for his seat in a special election in 1964. In a 1994 interview Motley admitted, "I have a name as they say in politics—that's ninety percent of it."[71]

Neither Motley nor Chisholm stayed long in the legislature. They were energized by the activism of the decade as were many others. The two also benefited from a unique moment in time that allowed them to move successfully to positions of greater scope. They both were experienced professionals. The late 1960s was that moment when the women's movement's energy fed off the civil rights movement's recent success in getting federal legislation banning discrimination in employment. The result was that these two legislators were desired commodities because they were ready right then to walk through the figurative open doors in front of them.

In 1968, Chisholm's Assembly district made up a good portion of the newly redrawn 12th Congressional District. Its lines had been drawn with electing Brooklyn's first Black representative in mind. She declared early, in January, and outlasted minority rivals in both the primary and general elections. She devised her own campaign slogan, "Unbought and unbossed."[72] The slogan paid homage to both her gender and her race. Neither women nor minorities had had influence in the Brooklyn Democratic machine until now. Chisholm read the moment correctly when she said in her memoir, "They would still be exploiting my abilities if I had not rebelled. Increasingly, other women are reaching the same conclusion."[73]

Figure 4.1. Constance Baker Motley with Majority Leader Joseph Zaretsky, 1965

Black Democratic leadership approached Motley to run for the State Senate in a special election in February 1964. J. Raymond Jones, currently a member of the New York City Council and soon to be elected the first Black Tammany leader in Manhattan in 1965, fought to name her the candidate rather than have a minority chosen through white influence. Her reputation was intended to overwhelm a faction supporting a different and controversial candidate, Noel Ellison, a man with three criminal convictions for policy gambling.[74] At first it appeared that the meeting to choose a senate candidate had settled on Ellison. But it turned out that Ellison's razor thin plurality of three votes was achieved by manipulating the process, which then led to his removal. Motley's supporters insisted on and got the nomination for her.[75] Considered a hot commodity as a candidate, as the challenge played out Motley turned down both the Republican and Liberal Party nominations offered her. The eventual Liberal Party nominee, Mrs. Cora Alexander, then called on all her supporters to vote for Motley who won the February 4th special election.[76] Even then, Jones expressed hope that the Senate would be only the beginning of Motley's political rise.[77] In February 1965, Jones had the chance to promote Motley to the Manhattan Borough presidency because of a vacancy. He successfully fought to secure for her the interim appointment and then supported her as she won a full term in the fall election. While Jones readily admitted that Motley's success would reflect well on his leadership, he also was aware of its importance for the Harlem community and for Black women. "I wanted to see a woman representing the Harlem community," he remembered. "Mrs. Motley's candidacy would have great significance for Black women in New York City and State, and this added to the value of her candidacy."[78] Motley's unique résumé also brought her to the attention of President Lyndon Johnson, who nominated her for a federal judgeship in 1966. Her departure from New York City government was bittersweet for Jones, who had hoped to make her the first Black and first female Mayor of New York City in 1969.[79]

Estella Diggs (D) (A1972–1980) was the first Black woman elected to the legislature from the Bronx. She also worked her way up through the party ranks, beginning as a poll watcher and ending as district leader. But Diggs equally valued her community and race activism which she saw as inextricably tied together. Diggs organized the Bronx Citizens Committee in 1964 to address issues of homelessness, hunger, underfunded schools, and instances of discrimination.[80] She raised money for civil rights groups and organized 300 community residents to participate in the 1963 March on Washington. Diggs was a member of the NAACP, Congress on Racial

Equality (CORE), and the Urban League. Upon her death in 2013, a legislative resolution recognizing her service noted "Estella B. Diggs fought for the Bronx when it was burning."[81] This is a reference to the deterioration of Bronx properties throughout the late 1960s and 1970s, and the numerous fires there, many set by landlords who either could not or no longer wanted to keep the buildings up. The devastation had brought President Carter to her district in 1977.[82] At the time he toured what the *New York Times* described as a "rubble strewn Charlotte St. Block" that symbolized the Bronx's distress.[83]

Olga Mendez was the first woman of Puerto Rican heritage to be elected to any legislature in the United States.[84] Her lengthy New York State Senate career is particularly remarkable, given that for all but the last two years in office she was in the minority party.[85] Her district of East Harlem, Upper Manhattan, and the South Bronx was among the poorest in the City and a mixture of Hispanic and Black residents. As a senator, Mendez advocated for the concerns of all her constituents, at the same time being mindful of how underrepresented the Hispanic community was in politics. One columnist titled a profile of Mendez, "She Speaks; Hispanics Listen."[86] The profile described Mendez as a grassroots politician, "one of them" rather than presenting herself through her doctorate in educational psychology. It talked about her efforts to get more Hispanics registered to vote and how her offices overflowed with constituents needing help.

Mendez was elected to the Senate in a special election in April 1978. Over the years her opponents tried to paint her as either unresponsive or as someone enriching herself and her family through office holding.[87] None of the charges took hold. Nor were efforts to redistrict away her Puerto Rican voter base sufficient to unseat her. Mendez did believe she had a responsibility to be the voice of Puerto Rican New Yorkers, regardless of the consequences. In 1985 she resigned membership in the Black and Puerto Rican Caucus when it failed to endorse Herman Badillo for New York City mayor.[88] Her concern was that the Black members exerted disproportionate influence over caucus decisions. At the time she tried and failed to get the other five Latino members to follow her exit.[89] Still, she worked with those Latino members to create a Puerto Rican/Hispanic Task Force in 1987. In 1989 Mendez was named its chair.[90]

Yet during her time in office Mendez was not immune from criticism. She crossed party lines to endorse Mayors Giuliani and Bloomberg and Governor Pataki. Even when she supported Democratic New York City Mayor Ed Koch there were rumblings that she was too passive in her dealings with the City and political leaders in authority.[91] In late 2002, Mendez finally changed her own party registration from Democrat to Republican. She justified the shift as a pragmatic effort to get more resources for her poverty-stricken district.[92] If that were so, it remains unclear why she waited so long in her Senate tenure to take that step. When she switched, Mendez expressed confidence that her constituents would back her. It did not hurt that she had just won reelection in 2002 with 95 percent of the vote, a figure which at least one press report suggested would embolden her.[93] But her optimism about ethnic solidarity was misplaced. In 2004, Mendez lost to her Democratic challenger in a district that had been restructured to rob her of a portion of that traditional base.[94]

The minority women of the activist era signified the beginning of a sustained and growing number of minority women legislators. By 1980, there were signs that a new group of female political leaders at the district level were coming into their own as power brokers who could successfully leverage these changing demographics into legislative office. This included Black women in districts that had been represented previously by a white legislator. A 1977 profile in the *Amsterdam News* called Geraldine Daniels, coleader of her Assembly District in Manhattan, "symbolic of a new type of female leader" who vowed she would not play second fiddle to her male counterpart.[95] Daniels had some twenty years political experience in the trenches and was the vice chair of the New York County Democratic Committee when she successfully challenged Assemblyman George Miller in 1980. Miller was a ten-year incumbent who held the position of majority whip. By 1983, Daniels was the chair of the New York County Democratic Committee in her own right, the first woman to hold that position, and was appointed assistant majority whip in the Assembly.[96]

Not All Change Was Positive

But opportunity for some meant loss for others, including some women legislators. Gail Hellenbrand (D) (A1966–1970) came from Brooklyn. When she ran the first time, though her district was only about one-third white, middle- and upper-class residents dominated the politics of the district. Hellenbrand was described as "a typical, busy, league of women voters type, sponsor of many cultural activities . . . (who) sends her son to a private school ten miles outside the neighborhood."[97] But in 1970 she declined to seek a third term, noting that "the winds of change have come to the 54th."[98]

Others who saw their districts redrawn to improve election prospects of minorities included Bellamy and Burstein in the Senate in 1974, and Jacobs and Weinstein in the Assembly multiple times. In their cases the women withstood efforts to shift the racial composition of the legislator. By 1996, Jacobs's district was 70 percent Black and 14 percent Hispanic, yet she still won reelection. Her challenger asserted that the demographics showed the district should be represented by a minority but the Black political leaders stayed on the sidelines because they liked Jacobs.

Not so in the case of Assemblywoman Marie Runyon (D) (A1974–1976) from Harlem. She remembers having multiple challengers when she ran for reelection in 1976, as many as six of whom were minorities. David Dinkins, then chair of the Council of Elected Democrats (and later Mayor of the New York City) considered this a "traditionally Black seat."[99] Runyon said she understood and appreciated that the district wanted Black representation, but questioned whether any of her opponents had as deep a commitment to their community.[100] The sheer number of minority challengers ultimately enabled the only other white candidate on the primary ballot to defeat Runyon and the rest of the field.[101] It appears that women's reputation as warrior for the communities remained a powerful weapon they could use in their fights to retain office.

The argument that the representative had to reflect the majority race in a district could prove to be a double-edged sword. Minority members worked hard to distinguish themselves as individual legislators rather than just members of a group. Upon first winning her seat in 1972, Assemblywoman Diggs addressed the problem head on when she said, "I am not going to be 'another Shirley Chisholm' . . . I'm going to be Estella Diggs."[102] Minorities could also find themselves pitted against one another in these specially designated areas, with the result being the substitution of one minority for another rather than the development of expanded opportunities for all. Diggs first won her seat in the Bronx over a minority opponent. Bernard Jackson was a Black lawyer and former policeman.[103] She lost her primary in 1980 to another minority woman, Gloria Davis, the former district leader. This was Davis's second challenge to Diggs; she had failed to unseat her in 1978.[104]

Davis would stay in office until January of 2003, when she pled guilty to a bribery charge for taking kickbacks.[105] She had been able to stay in office for twenty-three years largely because of support from the dominant political boss in the Bronx, Roberto Ramirez. In a 1998 *New York Times* article, Ramirez, the first Hispanic county chair, was described as an autocrat who was not averse to using the machine to crush an insurgent if it kept the political peace.¹⁰⁶ In reporting on Davis's conviction, the *Amsterdam News* lamented that she had failed to deliver on the promise of the majority-minority districts. "When she was first elected, there was much hope for the Bronx and its new minority politicians, who were expected to change the face of the poverty program in the Bronx and get rid of the cult of criminality that had been the hallmark of Bronx political leadership." The piece called hers a "wasted life."¹⁰⁷

Davis is a cautionary tale about women navigating a legislative environment that existed before their arrival. New York politics has always had unfortunate associations with corruption and illegality. Historically, the Tammany Hall machine in Manhattan was the most well-known political entity in that regard. But there were political scandals at the state level as well. Rather than uplifting the legislative culture by their presence, some women became embroiled in its worse aspects. From the beginning of women's election to office in New York, the public has shown little tolerance for women politicians thought to be using their position for personal gain. In 1925, Republican Florence E. Knapp was elected secretary of State in New York, which made her the first woman to hold a statewide office after suffrage.¹⁰⁸ During her two-year term, from 1926 to 1927, she oversaw the last separately taken New York State census where she managed a significant allocation for the hiring of census takers and enumerators. However, after leaving office accusations of malfeasance forced Governor Al Smith to order an investigation into the census process, which led to her indictment and subsequent conviction on charges of forgery and grand larceny. Though several Republican political figures were also implicated in the scandal, only Knapp was indicted. At the start of the investigation a *New York Times* editorial had opined, "[if the] charges are sustained, the situation will carry a peculiar irony for those who had looked to her to demonstrate what could be accomplished in public life by the woman with the broom!"¹⁰⁹ The traditional association of women with morality, which dates back to the suffrage fight itself, lingers on in the public's perception of its female politicians. Even the perception of impropriety can disproportionately and negatively affect the woman candidate or officeholder. The misdeed is magnified for the woman.

Assemblywoman Gerdi Lipschutz was essentially driven out of office in 1987 for having acquiesced to behavior that, though technically illegal, had been practiced by multiple members in the past. In 1987 she admitted to a felony in exchange for immunity so she could testify against Richard Rubin, a powerful Queens politician, legislative lobbyist, and the current legislative aide to the Assembly speaker. Rubin had his personal secretary on Lipschutz's office payroll between 1983 and 1986. Here Lipschutz was abetting a "no-show" job for a person she had inherited from a colleague, David Cohen, also of Queens. Cohen lost his Assembly seat in the 1982 election and one of the two individuals he had on his payroll moved over to Lipschutz. Both Lipschutz and Cohen testified that they did not intentionally violate the law. Rather, Cohen said it was common for someone to be on one legislator's payroll while working in another legislative office. He did not realize that these people worked as Rubin's private law secretaries. Lipschutz also alluded to the practice as relatively common; in her case she was repaying a favor of support from the Queens Democratic organization. Though not charged herself, press coverage openly suggested that she needed to resign.[110] The Assembly Ethics Committee was harsh in its recommendation that she be publicly reprimanded on the Assembly floor and formally censured. Lipschutz resigned instead on March 9, which may have been the goal of the leadership all along. An op-ed on the scandal by political scientist, journalist, and radio commentator, Alan Chartock, asked the question "Did Gerdi Take a Fall for Everyone Else?"[111] Chartock quoted Speaker Mel Miller as definitively denying that no-show jobs still existed. Miller called Lipschutz "a throwback" who did not realize times had changed. In all other respects, however, the speaker praised her. Yet the Ethics Committee had been brutal in its treatment of her, which Chartock interpreted as a way of preserving the legislature's image rather than doing something substantive. And the reform legislation passed by both chambers two weeks later was viewed by Governor Mario Cuomo as "unacceptably weak."[112] All this took place as state and federal prosecutors were investigating "possible payroll irregularities and other corrupt practices in several legislative offices."[113]

Linda Winikow's career in the Senate did not founder on a specific allegation of impropriety but more on a sense that she exhibited characteristics atypical for a woman. Her career did not start out that way. The Democrat won the seat in Republican-dominated Rockland County in 1974; she held it by effectively associating herself with aspects of being a woman in politics that her constituents liked. Winikow focused on service to district residents and eschewed association with the social habits of male politicians. Instead, she emphasized her commitment to home and family life. Her earliest political experience at the town level had been to create a consumer advisory board, which gave her visibility as a watchdog for that community. Despite being in the minority, Winikow got legislation passed by cooperating with Republicans on issues of interest to her district.[114] She advocated for women's issues but was not considered to be as extreme as her contemporaries (Bellamy, Burstein, and Krupsak) in that regard. She appears to have avoided being narrowly defined and thus marginalized as a feminist activist.

Winikow's "downfall," if you can call it that, revolved around what some referred to as her naked political ambition. Historically, women had been more about issues and people than their own careers. Her colleagues who did build legislative careers in this era were careful to craft an image that did not suggest ambition as a primary motive. For such an image bore too much association to an older, masculine political world and by extension its history of political corruption. Press reports on her career conveyed a mixed message. A newspaper profile pointed this out when it said that to some Winikow was "hardworking, energetic, sensitive, an achiever," while to others she was "egotistical, . . . dangerously ambitious, vindictive, a hype." That same piece noted she was similar to male colleagues in her ambition.[115] When Winikow dropped her long-standing opposition against the death penalty and voted for a bill to restore it in 1982, the press speculated that it was because her redrawn district in the next election included a substantial portion of conservative Orange County. The shift did not cost her much, for she knew the legislature would not have the two-thirds needed to override a promised veto from Governor Carey.[116] Thus, the move was considered significant only for its openly political motivation.

Winikow left the legislature in 1984 to accept the senior vice presidency at Orange and Rockland Utilities. The local press speculated that she was frustrated. Winikow was known to have wanted to run for higher office, ideally that of county executive. But her home county of Rockland had repeatedly voted against creating such a position. She left office with a 70,000-dollar campaign fund surplus. Its disposal came under scrutiny and resulted in a new law the following year that required such funds be used only for governmental or campaign purposes. The new law, colloquially referred to as the "Winikow Memorial Law" would not let elected officials invest the money in government bonds as Winikow had done. She had justified the action as acceptable because the investment and its yield might be used in some future campaign.[117] Her new career fell apart in 1993, when she was accused of receiving commercial bribes and making illegal campaign contributions. Winikow had funneled utility monies to candidates using other companies and individuals to shield the utility's identity. She had also illegally funneled funds to two local newspapers in exchange for a pledge that the papers would no longer run articles criticizing the utility and its executives. Her professional demise was called "a remarkable fall from grace for a woman who had been cheered by voters for railing against Orange and Rockland's rates while she was a senator."[118]

Women continued to face the challenge that carried over from the pioneer era of having to assert their independence. Immediately after suffrage, women's individual political identity was sometimes seen as a reflection of male political figures. Challenges to Doris Byrne in the Assembly in the 1930s were partially about her being seen as the protégé of the Bronx County Democratic leader, Edward Flynn. More benign, but still an example of the tendency to treat women as reflections of men, were the widows selected to run for their recently deceased husband's seats. But at this point, women considered it important to push back on older assumptions and define themselves separately from the prior occupant of the seat. Shirley Chisholm recounted how, at the start of her first term in the Assembly in 1965, her male colleagues assumed she would vote for Stanley Steingut as Assembly speaker. Why? Because her male predecessor had been close to him. Chisholm bucked that assessment and instead supported his opponent, Anthony Travia.[119]

The associational conundrum got more complicated if the woman was perceived to work too closely with or have a personal relationship to someone involved in a conflict, scandal, or criminal investigation. She might be suspected of participating in the contested activity or be open to criticism because she, as a woman, should have acted to stop it. Some women succeeded in distancing themselves from tainted associations; others could not shake their prior connections. New York City Councilman Samuel Wright was a Democratic power broker in Brooklyn's Ocean Hill–Brownsville district in the 1970s. He was opposed by another Brooklyn Democratic faction led by Congresswoman Shirley Chisholm and Major Owens. In 1973, Wright relinquished the local school board post he also held because he was under criminal investigation for possible misuse of funds; Wright would be convicted in 1977.[120] In a move decried by opponents, Wright supposedly engineered the appointment of Jeanette Gadson, a longtime associate, to replace him on that board. Gadson is almost always referred to as a Wright loyalist, suggesting he would continue to control the board through her.[121] Before his election to the City Council, Wright had been in the State Assembly. Gadson followed in his footsteps there as well, serving one term in 1974–1976. She left the legislature to unsuccessfully challenge Owens for the area's State Senate seat. In all of this, Gadson never shook off the assumption that she was following Wright's instructions.[122] The association seems somewhat unfair, given that Gadson had a long and varied political career of her own. Gadson had Chisholm's endorsement for her challenge to Owen. Chisholm in all likelihood would not have supported Gadson had she believed her to be Wright's puppet; Chisholm had beaten Wright's challenge to her congressional seat the year before and there was no goodwill there.[123] In addition to long-term service on the 23rd District school board, Gadson was both administrator and head of Community Board 16, a member of the New York Board of Elections, and deputy borough president of Brooklyn through 2001. The last three positions were all undertaken separately from any connection to Wright.

Moving forward, women legislators have been more successful in rebranding the label of protégé as something positive. Mentorship and experience on someone's staff, would be seen more as preparation for becoming part of the professionalized legislature. Working for someone now became an apprenticeship in the details of the bureaucracy and familiarity with the players and process. That shift can be seen to begin in earnest with May Newburger's election to the Assembly in 1976, to replace Albert Blumenthal. He had been a leader in the chamber who retired after winning dismissal of twelve counts of perjury and bribery against him. Newburger beat out several others for the nomination partly because she had experience in the legislature, most recently as legislative director of the Assembly's Higher Education Committee.[124] By the mid-1990s, female senior staff like Cecille Singer (R) (A1988–1994), Naomi Matusow (D) (A1992–2000), Joni Yoswein (D) (A1992), Francine Delmonte (D) (A1998–2010), and others could assert their readiness to succeed their legislative bosses and were taken seriously on their own merits.

Transition to a New Era

The difference between the activist era ending and the professional era beginning around 1980 is illustrated by the careers of two women, Audre Cooke (R) (A1978–1990) and Antonia Rettaliata (R) (A1978–1987). Both entered the legislature in the same year, Cooke representing Rochester and by extension Upstate interests, while Rettaliata was from Suffolk County on Long Island. Each had a preferred nickname as well; Antonia became "Toni" and Audre was known as "Pinny" by colleagues. Both had lengthy careers in politics. But how they framed those careers was quite different.

Cooke's career looked backward for inspiration. She centered on children and their issues, specifically disabled children.[125] Her other great asset was her focus on constituents.[126] One newspaper endorsing Cooke for reelection in 1980 noted "her strength is her sense of people and her accessibility." In 1979, the Republican Party made efforts to promote its support of women running for office by citing the example of "Pinny" Cooke, who championed what she termed "the human service issues."[127] Like Assemblywoman Connelly, Cooke fought to have adequate environments for disabled living and learning, as well as for teenage safety on the roads. But because Cooke was in the minority in the Assembly, her record of achievements was more limited. Unlike Connelly, who benefited from the Democratic takeover of the Assembly, Cooke could only be the "ranking member" of the Alcoholism and Drug Abuse Committee. Cooke's twelve years in the Assembly was lengthy, but arguably it was more in the tradition of community uplift so characteristic of the pioneer generation. Her political career began at fifty-four, after she had raised three children, and it ended when she left the legislature.

Toni Rettaliata, also in the minority, made the most of what her time in the legislature could do for her. She was twenty years younger than Cooke when elected in 1978, and represented an area of growing Republican strength on Long Island. Her career star rose in the 1980s in parallel to the strength of Reagan Republicanism. In New York that influence was personified by the election of another Long Islander, Alphonse D'Amato, to the US Senate in 1980. Rettaliata chose tax relief as her signature issue, for it was the number one concern of Long Islanders, regardless of whether they were represented by a Democrat or Republican.[128] It positioned her both to avoid being constrained by association only with women's traditional issues and to transcend party difference by aligning with her Democratic colleagues from the Island. Her connection to the other members of the Long Island delegation helped her avoid seeing her district carved up as part of the 1984 reapportionment process.[129] In 1983, Rettaliata was named chair of the Minority Steering Committee in the Assembly. While not particularly powerful at the moment, the *New York Times* observed that "the minority positions have proved to be launching pads for statewide office, as well as for majority positions if the political tables turn."[130] Her visibility due to that position catapulted her into being one of two finalists for the lieutenant governor position on the Republican ticket in 1986.[131] That year, Rettaliata did not run with Andrew O'Rourke against incumbent Governor Mario

Cuomo, who was reelected, but instead was reelected to the Assembly. The following year, 1987, she left to run for and win the position of Huntington Town Supervisor on Long Island. She lost her reelection bid as supervisor in 1989. Rettaliata's choice here presages the career trajectory of a number of women legislators going forward. Some women legislators will have more success and lengthy careers that move around from the legislature to higher positions or to ones closer to home. The key takeaway is that, more and more, the sum total of those careers will be definitively political.

Chapter 5

Activist-Era Profiles

Contrasting Career Paths

Overview

The women legislators of the activist era tended to fall into one of two categories: those who were intent on shaking up the status quo and those who had mastered it. The former moved through the legislature, turning their attention to the next challenge. The latter invested in the view that professionalization and expertise were useful tools for getting things done in the legislature. Encouraged by the rights movements of the 1960s and 1970s, women in the early stages of their careers like Carol Bellamy, Karen Burstein, and Mary Anne Krupsak came into the legislature determined to make change happen. And one need not be young to be an activist, as the brief career of Marie Runyon demonstrates. The legislature frustrated these women. In contrast, by choosing to stay in the legislature Assemblywomen Constance Cook and Elizabeth Connelly showed that one could exert influence by mastering its policies and procedures.

Constance Cook and Elizabeth Connelly had productive careers within this system. Common attributes that speak to their success include developing expertise on areas or issues separate from feminist ones, understanding and effectively maneuvering within the system, and a willingness to stay there to gain influence through seniority.[1] Success there required a willingness to compromise on issues. Ironically, as Cook noted, that was one of the hardest aspects for women. Diamond found that the women legislators she studied in 1971 seemed negatively disposed to the idea of bargaining on legislation.[2] Kirkpatrick saw women's motivation to run coming from a desire to be problem solvers for their communities and not professional politicians.³ These gendered predispositions can be traced back to the unique path many women took to become public activists and politicians early in the twentieth century. Thus, both the rights-based activism embraced by some, coupled with the legacy of women's separate path to politicization, constituted complicating factors for women's career aspirations in the New York State legislature in this period. Still, there were women who made women's tradition of fighting for the health and well-being of their communities a part of their successful legislative careers. Each individual emphasized different elements within that broad designation but the idea that women were the voice of those that needed a voice most represents the connective tissue across their varying definitions of service. Women in service to community hearkened back to women's early public activism. What was new was how these women married that concern to electoral politics.

Mary Anne Krupsak (D) (A1968–1972), (S) (1972–1974)

In particular, Mary Anne Krupsak appeared to relish challenging the male hierarchy on a nearly constant basis. Her determination to get something done quickly left her little time to build bridges to others within the Democratic Party and the legislature. She credited this drive to both the women's movement of the 1960s and the political upheavals related to the anti–Vietnam War movement.⁴ Krupsak was convinced that women would have to "win elections, be there ourselves, and make it happen. . . . I don't want to spend my life waiting."⁵ In 1968, she unseated incumbent Republican Assemblyman Donald Campbell who represented the Upstate counties of Albany, Schenectady, and Montgomery. Even though it was supposedly a Republican-leaning area, Krupsak's family was well-known politically. Her father was a Montgomery County supervisor. She framed her campaign as an attack on entrenched power, in particular criticizing the pension plan that the lawmakers had approved for themselves in the prior session. During her first session as legislator, some incumbent members who were still smarting from her criticisms refused to support her benign piece of legislation on deer hunting.⁶ Going forward, even minor bills if introduced by her went nowhere.

Krupsak labeled her legislative career "tough." She ran for the Senate in 1972 because she was redistricted intentionally out of her Assembly seat. Leadership created a new district where "troublemakers," be they Democrat or Republican, had to run against each other.[7] So she ran for the Senate seat from her area. The press gave Krupsak and the other two women running for Senate that year, Bellamy and Burstein, significant press. Krupsak felt she had a good relationship with the press; they played her up as a fighter, which she liked.[8] She won a seat that had been expected to go Republican. The press also connected the three directly to the feminist movement, though each cited a variety of factors influencing their political activism.

Yet Krupsak was stymied in her efforts to make change happen. She was in the minority in both houses which marginalized her efforts to get legislation passed. That led her to refer to Republican Senate leaders as "arm twisting dictators."[9] Her two female Democratic colleagues expressed the same frustration along with chafing at what Krupsak described as a slower pace overall in that chamber.[10] The three women also believed their association with the women's rights movement further strained relationships with male colleagues.[11]

Krupsak was the first of the three to seek a different office. In 1974 she entered the Democratic primary for lieutenant governor and stayed in the primary race even after the Democratic State Convention officially supported Mario Cuomo for the position. Candidates who received 25 percent of the votes at the convention could do so. That was also how Hugh Carey managed to appear on the primary ballot since the convention had endorsed Howard Samuels for governor. Confident that she knew the state and could do the job, Krupsak resisted pressure to withdraw. Political observers credited her victory to good ballot placement, (one of the top five positions, all drawn by lottery), a year of general political apathy when it came to state races, and the fact that she was the only woman in the race.[12] Krupsak contended that she would not have had to fight for the nomination had she been a man, that the nomination "would have been hers for the asking." Still, she chose as her campaign slogan, "She's not just one of the boys."[13]

Both Carey and Krupsak succeeded in their challenges and the two became united in a single ticket, though neither had sought the other out previously or knew if they were compatible. Krupsak proved a campaign asset as her political skills were considerable. She secured some high-profile endorsements for herself and in the general campaigned hard Upstate for the ticket.[14] The mid-1970s was also a period when women's heightened political awareness yielded some party crossover support by women for women candidates like Krupsak.[15]

After the election, Krupsak intended to be an active lieutenant governor. Unfortunately, the position itself did not fit well with her expectations.

Figure 5.1. Mary Anne Krupsak campaigning in Albany, 1974.

There were few constitutionally mandated duties other than presiding over the Senate and serving as the chief executive should the governor be out of state. Neither activity had any real power. In his analysis of the Carey administration, political scientist Daniel Kramer concludes, "It was almost inevitable that Carey would not pay much attention to her and that the press would soon be speaking about the 'strain' between the two."[16] It was partly a function of the office. Still, Carey did not dismiss out of hand Krupsak's desire to make more of it. He doubled the lieutenant governor's budget, which allowed her to set up two regional offices, one in Rochester and one in Harlem.[17] This fit with how Krupsak had defined the woman politician's role back when she first ran for the Senate. The three women running then would be full-time politicians who were "community expeditors and ombudsmen" in recognition of women politicians' special and close relationship with their constituents.[18] But Krupsak felt excluded from Carey's inner circle of advisers and frustrated at the Republican Senate leadership that frequently challenged her on parliamentary procedure. Early in his administration Carey had to hold a press conference where he vowed to be less chauvinistic toward women in government, generally, and Krupsak, specifically. This followed on veiled threats from Krupsak about resigning from the office because of her treatment.[19]

By year two of Carey's first term, the early bumps in their relationship seemed to have smoothed out. At the end of year three, Carey openly expressed his preference for Krupsak to be his running mate in next year's election.[20] And Krupsak felt she had the upper hand against Republican leaders in the Senate who tried to undermine her authority. The New York State Court of Appeals, the state's highest court, had ruled in Krupsak's favor in her claim that she had handled the 1975 election of new State Regents properly. Krupsak argued that she had been right to declare the Senate in recess and send the membership over to a joint session with the Assembly to select the regents. Republican Senate leaders challenged that interpretation, arguing there had been no adjournment and the membership she sent did not constitute a quorum. Republicans claimed the Regents' appointments were illegal. The Court of Appeals reversed two lower courts that had sided with Republicans and against Krupsak.[21]

Regardless of efforts to present a united front, the two had not grown closer. Carey aides kept Krupsak at a distance. They thought her too ambitious for herself and they questioned whether her feminism clashed too much with the Carey agenda.[22] For example, the two had supported different candidates in the 1977 New York City mayoral election. Carey had been instrumental in getting his Secretary of State Mario Cuomo to run and stood behind him while Krupsak vocally supported former Congresswoman Bella Abzug.[23] During her time as lieutenant governor, Krupsak had emerged as a national figure in the feminist movement. She was a featured speaker at the 1975 march and rally for International Women's Day and lauded again in 1976 as one of only three female lieutenant governors nationwide. Legislatively, she came out early in her term for the New York Women's Lobby fifteen-point agenda of proposed legislation. Her very victory in 1974 was seen as part of a broader breakthrough for women nationally and justified women building their own network outside the regular party structures that they claimed sidelined them. A separate network might then afford women independence from party control.[24]

All these different factors influenced Krupsak first to withdraw from the ticket in the spring of 1978, and then challenge Carey for the gubernatorial nomination itself. The specifics around her withdrawal are not entirely clear. Each side has its story. What is undisputed is that Krupsak was committed to being on Carey's team up until less than a week before the state convention was scheduled to start on June 14. But on June 11, during a phone call with the governor, she declined the nomination. Her decision became public on June 12. Broadly speaking, Krupsak claimed the governor was inaccessible to her, which convinced her that the governor would never use her and her skills properly.[25] The move surprised Democratic leaders and even her friends. Some privately admitted she had a point about Carey's dismissive and distant attitude.[26] Still, on June 15, she seemed to soften toward the governor, implying she might endorse the Carey-Cuomo (Mario) ticket.[27]

Yet, on June 26, Krupsak officially announced her own primary challenge to Carey. Political observers wondered why, given the disadvantages her campaign faced. Establishment Democrats would rally behind Carey making it very hard to raise money. She had no infrastructure in place to run a campaign. Finding a campaign message would be hard given that she was still part of the administration.[28] When asked about why she chose to run, Krupsak played down the idea that she did so out of bitterness or anger. Rather, she referenced being inspired by a conversation she had with a group of Black maids while staying at a New York City hotel. Equally significant, she believed this moment demanded activist women push to advance politically. "It won't happen unless we make it happen," Krupsak recalled later.[29]

All the predicted liabilities came to pass plus an unexpected newspaper strike in New York City that took away valuable publicity for her. The campaign suffered from its own Upstate-Downstate divide. Krupsak's Upstate organization did not work well with a New York City–based group that included Bella Abzug, a divisive figure within the Democratic Party. Krupsak tried to tamp down disagreements by naming two campaign chairs, but that just left the impression no one was in charge. Ultimately, Krupsak distanced her campaign from Abzug but some damage was done.[30] It was one thing for traditional Democratic leaders, mostly male, to support Carey's reelection. It was somewhat more disappointing to Krupsak that women officials, including those with whom she had served in the Senate and who had criticized Carey's lack of commitment to women's issues, also went over to Carey.[31] One particularly devastating headline said it all: "Women Reject Krupsak, Race Back to Carey."[32] Gender as a unifying force paled in comparison to the twin traditions of the power of incumbency and control of the political apparatus of the Democratic Party in the state.[33] Finally, what Krupsak characterized as independence and a grassroots rebellion against the power structure others called a lack of trustworthiness and loyalty to party.[34] Women, like men, had to think about their standing in the party.

Carey moved quickly to defuse Krupsak's charge that he was antiwomen by meeting with scores of them and holding photo ops.[35] Carey beat Krupsak in the primary by 52 to 34 percent.[36]

Still, the goal of a supportive network among women was not completely misguided. Two years later Krupsak unsuccessfully ran for Congress. This time, she received help from women officeholders around the state and in Congress. The now supportive Burstein and Bellamy were two names Krupsak had not seen in her column for the gubernatorial run. Nationally, she benefited from the Congresswoman's Caucus. Started in 1978 by New York Congresswoman Elizabeth Holtzman and Massachusetts Congresswoman Margaret Heckler, the organization was dedicated to increasing women's representation in Congress. Assembly Speaker Fink and Lieutenant Governor Cuomo also made campaign appearances with Krupsak, which suggests she realized the importance of mending fences with the party leadership. Unfortunately, it was an uphill battle, where Krupsak was vulnerable to charges of carpetbagging. She moved to the 30th Congressional District in the North Country shortly before declaring for the open seat.[37] She lost to Republican David Martin in the general election but landed on her feet with an appointment as special counsel to Speaker Fink. The political fence-mending may have come too late; she never won elective office again.

Carol Bellamy (D) (S1972–1977)

Carol Bellamy of Manhattan also found her minority status and the pace of the Senate frustrating. Like Krupsak, Bellamy was not shy about making her concerns known, which left her vulnerable to charges that she lacked loyalty. She experienced both challenges to getting her name on the ballot and then being redistricted at reelection time. The latter tactic was a typical way for the majority to silence problematic voices. During her initial run for Senate in 1972, Bellamy had to rally her supporters to review voter registration cards. This was to ensure that she had a margin of victory about four times more than needed to withstand charges of voter fraud leveled at her petitions as a way to keep her off the ballot.[38]

Right from the start of her first term, Bellamy stood out for her willingness to raise her voice on issues she deemed important. Some actions were inspired by her feminism but not all. The 1973 session had barely begun when she objected to what she called the small number of women, just 3 out of 100, being appointed to administration jobs that required

Senate approval.[39] In 1974, she was the lone dissenting voice on a package of reforms in Senate rules and procedures because they failed to require that Democrat-sponsored bills at least receive a hearing in committee.[40] Bellamy did develop more traditional and successful legislative skills as well. Also in 1974, Governor Malcolm Wilson signed a bill eliminating corroboration requirements in rape cases. Previously, allegations of rape had to be corroborated by medical or eyewitness testimony independent of the victim's testimony before they could be prosecuted. Bellamy had been a leader in the fight to remove those requirements and was supported by the Manhattan Women's Political Caucus and the National Organization for Women.[41] Two years earlier, the Manhattan group had tried to increase pressure on legislators regarding women's issues. There had been talk of a "one to one" project where a woman caucus member would be assigned to each legislator to "drive him crazy" in their advocacy for women's bills.[42] Now the caucus's lobbying efforts were credited with securing the 130-to-0 vote in the Assembly for the rape reform bill.[43] Here Bellamy made use of her more traditional role as legislator as well as judiciously securing outside pressure from women's groups.

In her second term, Bellamy's legislative experience was crucial for shepherding the proposed Equal Rights Amendment to the New York State Constitution through the Senate for a second year so it could appear on the 1975 November ballot as a referendum. Changes to the state constitution must be passed by two consecutive legislative sessions and a voter referendum. There was an effort on this second go-around to amend the language of the ERA bill to exclude "any laws of New York State which extend protections or exemptions to women." She characterized it as an attempt to actually kill the bill by forcing the effort to begin the full approval process anew.[44] Senators Bellamy, Burstein, and Winikow remained the first line of defense on the floor while lieutenant governor Krupsak adjudicated floor objections.[45] In the end, though, the ERA failed to win a majority of New Yorkers' votes. In a postdefeat assessment of voting patterns, ERA supporters concluded sadly that it was women who provided the margin of defeat. Why? The most common explanation was fear that the amendment would usher in too many changes and that frightened women. Equally depressing was the possibility that the 1974 election of Mary Anne Krupsak as New York's lieutenant governor and Ella Grasso as governor of Connecticut the previous year might have represented the high point of momentum for women's issues and politicians.[46]

Bellamy asserted her district was dismembered in 1974 because she was too outspoken a feminist in the legislature. Some politicians were said to have seen her district as the most expendable "from the organization's point of view."[47] Bellamy believed the Democratic minority leader, Joseph Zaretsky, was complicit in drawing up the redistricting plan to oust her.[48] When the legislature voted on the new district lines, several Democrats voted with the Republican majority to reapportion her district into fragments. Undeterred, Bellamy used intensive, grassroots campaigning to win the nomination for the new 25th District seat that included one-third of what had been her old district and was earmarked by organizational Democrats for Paul Bookson.

Even though she won a third term in 1976, Bellamy was described as "noticeably restless recently in the Senate " 'and looking for a new challenge.' "[49] She had headed a task force charged with overseeing the financial rescue package for a near-bankrupt New York City, and wanted greater input directly on the City's issues. The thirty-five-year-old senator announced her candidacy for City Council president in the spring of 1977. The press characterized Bellamy as an "active feminist," though not as flamboyant a one as former Congresswoman Abzug, whom Bellamy had aided in an unsuccessful run for the US Senate the previous year.[50] Bellamy, though described as a reformer and advocate for women's rights, won praise for her hard work in a legislature described as a "rigidly disciplined body."[51] During her last session in the Senate before going on to win the borough Council presidency, Bellamy finally secured a law to award disability benefits to pregnant workers. Though she railed at how Albany operated in slow motion, she had persisted with this issue for five years.[52] Ironically, the next chapter of Bellamy's political career placed her in a situation that would have the same kinds of frustrations she was leaving behind in the Senate. While she would represent the entire City, the position was clearly a number two behind the mayor and without significant powers of its own. Still, Bellamy expressed optimism that she could push for reform in the position.[53]

Karen Burstein (D) (S1972–1978) and Marie Runyon (D) (A1974–1976)

Karen Burstein entered the State Senate in 1972, with two labels: antiwar activist and feminist.[54] Like Bellamy, Burstein chafed at not being able to get things done. She disliked both being in the Senate minority and the only Democrat in the Nassau County legislative delegation. A 1975 piece on Nassau County women politicians noted heightened expectations for office and power. Among those interviewed, however, Burstein cautioned that women still had to be twice as good as their male counterparts to get any recognition.[55] Governor Carey's offer of a position on the Public Service Commission late in 1977 came at an opportune time; at the age of thirty-five, Burstein had already decided not to seek another Senate term in 1978.[56]

Though impatience, youth, and minority status in the chamber described Krupsak, Bellamy, and Burstein's situations, there was at least one member of the Assembly who shared only the first attribute, impatience, with the others. Marie Runyon won her Assembly seat in 1974 at fifty-eight, just as the majority shifted to Democrat in reaction to the Watergate investigations on the national level and the Attica prison uprising in New York a few years earlier at the state level. Her 30th Assembly District covered Morningside Heights and part of Harlem in Manhattan. The area was experiencing tension between the Black population of Harlem and the expansionist interests of Columbia University. Runyon had no history of working within the Democratic Party or of having any connections there at all. But she did have a history of being an activist dating back to the mid-1950s. She was especially passionate about housing and tenant's rights, though she more broadly described herself to the media as "very active at the street level in the politics of confrontation."[57] Runyon's efforts to keep affordable housing in the area gave her name recognition and incentivized a group of local Black leaders to approach her about running.[58] Runyon tried to defer, indicating that since the district population was majority Black their support should go to a minority. She was overruled and successfully primaried the sitting Assemblyman, Jesse Gray, who was Black, and then beat her Hispanic female opponent in the general. Runyon had an interesting backstory. Born in North Carolina, she migrated north to the University of Wisconsin for graduate work in psychology. After some time working in mental hospitals, Runyon moved to New York City and changed her career focus. There was a stint as a copy editor at the *Daily News* and a several-years period fundraising for the ACLU, which included raising money for the Black Panthers. While housing issues were her passion, Runyon was proud that she had a long arrest record for her activism.

Runyon was similar to the other activists in that she challenged party discipline and leaders, refusing to bow to the way things had always been done. She remembered one time when she had backed a Republican-sponsored bill in committee, with the result that it went to the floor for full debate.

Leadership lectured her that as a Democrat she was supposed to vote only for bills supported by Democrats. "So what," Runyon remembers retorting. "I liked it and I voted for it. Tell him [the governor] I'm sorry."[59] Runyon differed from the activist senators in her lack of interest in the women's movement; it did not motivate her in the way other issues did. After the Democrat establishment knocked her off in the 1976 primary, Runyon went back to housing advocacy. She spent twenty years fighting Columbia University to be able to stay in the apartment she had lived in since 1950. Her building was among a group of seven purchased by Columbia with the intent to knock them down as part of an expansion initiative.[60] Runyon won her case, or it may have been that Columbia finally threw in the towel. The entrance to her building on Morningside Drive now has a plaque that reads "Marie Runyon Court."

These activist female legislators were responding to cues from the broader society where demands for action were part of the rights movements of the era. It seemed as though some then blamed the position or the system or both for their inability to make big changes happen in office rather than consider other possibilities. Governor Carey was not coming through with promises to appoint more women to office, so lieutenant Governor Krupsak challenged him for the job. Even when women understood that a particular office might not have enough authority to push an agenda, the women believed/hoped they could change the office, make it more powerful. Both Bellamy and Krupsak tried and failed with that, Bellamy as New York City Council president and Krupsak as lieutenant governor.

Constance Cook (D) (A1962–1974)

Constance Cook was regarded as a legislative expert long before she was elected to office. Following graduation from law school in 1943, she served on Governor Dewey's legislative staff where she was counsel to the public health, fire laws, and unemployment insurance committees.[61] Cook was also the legal assistant to Assemblyman Ray Ashberry, whose seat she won upon his retirement. She cited that legal work when she gave testimony in 1966 before the Temporary State Commission on the Constitution. There she offered a series of suggestions on how to improve the functioning of the legislature. Those suggestions were intended to ensure accountability and transparency as well as check the growing power of leadership. Cook's ideas included more accountability for each legislator by publishing all votes, even in committee; mandating that the paid legislative staff be appointed strictly on merit; and a petition procedure that would increase the ability to move a bill out committee.[62] Petitioning would enable legislators to overcome leadership resistance to bringing a bill to the floor for a full debate and vote. Sadly, the few ideas that were embodied in proposed changes to the state constitution that went to the voters were not approved in the 1967 referendum.[63]

Assembly colleagues respected Cook for her expertise on education issues, which she used as chair of the Education Committee. In the early 1970s, the committee fought with the executive on school funding levels. Even though it was her own Republican Party in the majority, she successfully led the fight against Governor Rockefeller's proposed education cuts in 1970. In this case, Cook did so by compromising on language and accepting the governor's commitment to add additional funding in a supplemental allocation. Rockefeller was able to save face by not having his budget directly repudiated, while Cook and her committee gained the funding they wanted.[64] The year before, Rockefeller had appointed Cook to a blue ribbon commission on reforming the state's elementary and secondary education system. The "Fleischman Commission," as it was known, issued a three-volume, fifteen-chapter report in 1972, which recommended the state take over the collection and distribution of funds for education via a statewide property tax.[65] The controversial idea was dead on arrival. Before leaving the legislature, Cook fended off a Rockefeller effort to appoint an inspector general of elementary and secondary education. She attacked the idea as a foolish expansion of the bureaucracy and a ploy by the governor's office to secure direct oversight of education. Cook got the proposal "tabled" in the Assembly.[66]

At the opening of the 1971 legislative session, Assembly Speaker Perry Duryea singled Cook out "as an outstanding lady legislator." This fit right in with Cook's belief that progress on a set of feminist issues could be made because of the men "realizing women have a lot to contribute."[67] Cook stood her ground on a number of those issues, most important of which was the fight to reform New York's abortion law. That fight is covered as a separate topic in chapter 7. During the 1967 constitutional convention, Cook advocated for the addition of a state ERA, albeit unsuccessfully. She was more successful in having the ban on sex discrimination that applied to employers also extended to the employment agencies that screened job applicants for those employers.[68] And she led the fight to allow the broad availability and sale of contraceptives to the public.

Elizabeth Connelly

Elizabeth Connelly's arrival in the Assembly only briefly overlapped with Cook; the two served together for just the 1974 session. Their résumés could not have looked more different. Cook was a lawyer from Upstate Tompkins County, while Connelly was the first woman elected to the legislature from Staten Island. Cook's legislative record showed more support for what were termed feminist issues than Connelly's. Connelly had no college or career but was very active in her local community. She was honored for her volunteer work at the Staten Island Hospital where she was on the advisory board. Heightened concern about health issues, particularly mental health, inspired her to run for an open Assembly seat in a special election in 1973. Her lengthy work with the Democratic Party on Staten Island got her the unanimous endorsement of the Democrats and a cross endorsement from the Conservative Party.[69]

Figure 5.2. Elizabeth Connelly at the Capitol, 1978.

Connelly's victory was a bit of a surprise, even to her, since the seat had been held by a Republican and most of Staten Island's elected officials were Republican. Both she and her area stood out from the rest of the City as being more conservative and rural.[70] "I always felt geographically it was separate and again philosophically very different," Connelly later remembered.[71] Her voting record did not resemble that of other women legislators from the City. The borough's sense of otherness and disadvantage ultimately generated an unsuccessful effort to secede from New York City. Connelly was at its forefront, sponsoring a bill in 1989 to put the question on the ballot as a referendum that the voters approved in 1990. Connelly then sponsored legislation, which Governor Mario Cuomo signed, that put into motion Staten Island's formal pursuit of independence. Voters again approved a final plan for secession developed by a Charter Commission set up through Connelly's legislation. But in 1997 Speaker Sheldon Silver killed the movement when the Court of Appeals upheld his contention that the New York City Council had to issue a "home rule" message affirming he could act on final legislation. Since the other boroughs opposed the separation, it died.[72]

Connelly, like Cook, saw value in the systems being put into place to make the legislature more efficient and effective. In particular, she supported the requirement to use plain language in memoranda explaining bills. She thought that after the Assembly majority went over to the Democrats in 1975, Speakers Stanley Fink and Mel Miller opened up deliberations more and shared information with committee chairs more widely. Democrats were in the minority when Connelly first arrived. She remembered it was frustrating that "(minority) bills didn't get considered; they'd get lost. If you had a good idea, they (Republicans) took it."[73] Unlike some others, both the professionalization and the shift in power to her party incentivized her to stay in the legislature for twenty-seven years. Connelly achieved a number of legislative goals because of the benefits attached to being in the majority. In 1977, Connelly became the first Democrat woman to chair a standing Assembly committee, the Committee on Mental Health, Mental Retardation, Developmental Disabilities, Alcohol and Substance Abuse. She continued as chair until 1992. (The last two elements became their own committee in 1986.) Committee chairs benefited from expanded staff who could research and draft bills. After 1981, Connelly also served on the powerful Rules Committee, the gatekeeper for legislation onto the floor. Finally, in 1995, Speaker Silver appointed Connelly Speaker Pro Tempore. At the time it was the highest-ranking leadership position ever held by a woman in that body.[74] Somewhat ironically Connelly's seniority actually gave her more flexibility to disagree with majority leadership. She called it a sign of independence that she voted "no" more often that 84 percent of her fellow Democrats on Democrat sponsored legislation.[75]

Connelly believed she could make a difference when it came to mental health issues. She remembered a number of women's groups expressed disappointment with this focus. They thought Connelly was being marginalized in an area tangential to the women's movement. "It took a number of years for a lot of the women's groups to realize and to think that I had really taken on a major responsibility. For many years I tried to get women's groups to take this issue (mental health) as a women's issue."[76] As her career progressed, she could point to many legislative achievements aimed at supporting the disabled. In 1985, Connelly had the most bills signed into law of any member of the Assembly. By then she was widely acknowledged as a power in the state's social service establishment.[77]

When Connelly first entered the legislature, the state was reeling from the scandal at the Willowbrook State School on Staten Island. From 1951 on, it had operated as a facility for children with intellectual disabilities. But it was always overcrowded and the care more "warehousing" than treatment. By 1975 there were 6,000 children in a facility designed for 4,500. A series of television news reports in 1972 brought the abuses there into America's living rooms. Upon entering office in 1973, Connelly jumped squarely into the problem when she set up her local office on the Willowbrook campus itself. She believed her presence would focus attention on disability issues.[78] The state signed a consent decree in 1975 that committed it to community placement for what was called the "Willowbrook class."[79] In 1977, she was main sponsor on a series of bills that overhauled the state's Department of Mental Hygiene. It was split into three separate agencies and more treatment authority was given to local governments. Those changes meant more patients were housed in local communities. According to the consent decree, Willowbrook, renamed the Staten Island Development Center (SIDC), had to be down to just 251 residents by 1981.[80] Connelly took a good deal of public criticism for questioning the speed and rationale for handling the needs of the most severely disabled, those who could not be transitioned to smaller community facilities. It was her reputation as a mental health advocate that allowed her to ask those questions.[81] Connelly was honored for her advocacy in 1981, when a remodeled dorm to house 130 of the severely disabled still on the grounds was named for her.[82] Later, in 1987 as the SIDC finally closed, Connelly was honored again with the dedication of the Elizabeth A. Connelly Community Resource Center on the northern portion of the old Willowbrook grounds.[83]

Willowbrook was just one part of Connelly's broader advocacy on mental health issues. She included drug and alcohol abuse in her portfolio, securing funding for special alcohol treatment centers for women in 1979 and legislation to raise the drinking age from eighteen to nineteen in 1982. With respect to DWI legislation, she remembers taking it on because "nobody wanted to touch that issue and I did. . . . it was a woman that had to do it."[84] The increase in age was part of a larger set of bills she sponsored in the early 1980s that increased alcohol education for teens, gave the police more tools to apprehend drunk drivers, and specified escalating penalties for convictions.[85]

Connelly was aware that her lengthy career as a woman legislator was not the norm. When first elected, she joined only three other women in the Assembly: Cook, Gunning, and Diggs. She remembers the next woman to come and stay as she did was Rhoda Jacobs in 1978: "I think there were one or two women who came and went (in that period)."[86] She was not far off. Runyon was there for her one term, as were Jeanette Gadson and Mary Rose McGee (D) (A1976–1978). All three were from New York City.

Conclusion

Regardless of these women's assessment of their legislative possibilities, they all realized that women's influence remained bound up with their gender identity. Such recognition incentivized women to act on that identity as individual legislators. But they also understood that more might be done by harnessing the power of their collective voice to effect change on issues important to women. We turn next to how these efforts played out for New York's women legislators.

Chapter 6

Women Organize as Women
Maximizing Leverage in the Office

Overview

From the time that the first woman took her seat in the legislature in 1919, these female legislators realized they needed a way to strengthen the power of their representation if they were going influence the legislative agenda and environment. This chapter looks at one path women took to address that need, which is the creation of organized caucuses at both the state and national levels. Caucuses are organizations whose members share a common interest or have constituencies with a common interest. In her recent study of state-centered women's caucuses, Anna Mahoney defines these entities as "bipartisan, institutionalized associations of legislators that seeks to improve women's lives."[1] She argues caucuses matter because they express an identity, convey symbolic power for the group, and pressure policy makers to include women's voices and perspective.[2] In the end, however, she concludes that women's success at organizing owes more to the local conditions and legislative environment than anything else. The level of party control over members and whether the legislature is split between the parties weigh heavily on efforts to create a functioning group.[3] But it is not just structural considerations that matter; the investment of the women themselves is almost as important. Mahoney points to the presence of a "savvy champion" and a cohort of women legislators invested in the concept as key indicators of whether a women's caucus can be created and sustained.[4]

In Mahoney's view, the varied nature of local dynamics and women's investment in organizing yield two types of state caucuses: social and policy focused.[5] The former concentrates on using socializing to build relationships. The latter either constructs a women's agenda of legislation or supports individual legislative initiatives. Scholars mostly agree that the presence of a critical mass of women in the legislature is an important component for accomplishing legislative goals important to women.[6] But the pioneer women were too few in number. Only Graves might be said to have broken the mold and carved out a preeminent place as an individual woman politician, though others asserted themselves at times on specific issues. New York did not have a critical mass of women to warrant a caucus within the legislature itself. Connecticut spearheaded the first caucus initiative, though when approached, New York's women legislators were open to joining the initiative.

Connecticut's women legislators were also aware of the numbers problem. They responded by mounting an effort to create a national organization. That first effort was the National Order of Women Legislators (NOWL). As we will see, NOWL struggled, never achieving the kind of solidarity or influence hoped for by its members. But the idea that a women's bloc could be important remained alive because women continued to see it as a way to give greater voice to a minority constituency. With the establishment of the Black and Puerto Rican Caucus in the New York State Legislature in 1966 as an example, New York's women created their own counterpart with the Legislative Women's Caucus (LWC) in 1983. At about the same time, the women in the Assembly succeeded in getting legislative approval for a special task force on women's issues. Those developments show that women believed it was important to highlight a distinctive women's presence in government. As of 2016, Mahoney counted twenty-two active state-centered caucuses, with New York's as one of only five with a policy-oriented focus.

National Organizing Efforts

In the 1920s and 1930s, the few women in legislatures around the country were dominated by political parties that simply expected women to follow party dictates. As early as 1919, Walter Lloyd George, an English novelist writing on women in politics for *Harper's Magazine*, predicted that "[party] loyalty will certainly be a feature of the woman legislator."[7] Suffragists' efforts to counter that influence with their own organizations never became a threat to party dominance. One reason is because the women went a nonpartisan route, a path likely chosen to maximize numbers. Nonpartisanship was in keeping with women's activism before the vote and thus familiar to women generally. The League of Women Voters, formed out of NAWSA after the Nineteenth Amendment was ratified, adopted nonpartisanship as its framework. Yet the League did not generate high membership or have any real influence on the existing political power structure. This should have been a cautionary example, as women politicians operating in partisan environments contemplated how best to work with one another.

In 1927, Julia Emery, a member of the Connecticut Legislature, invited the women legislators in her state to join a Connecticut Order of Women Legislators (OWL). A 1984 profile on the organization says it was created partly in response to women's exclusion from the male-only dining room frequented by legislators. In one of its first actions, the new group opened their own, female-only dining room, which outlived the male counterpart and was still operating in 1984. Emery's original goal for the group was modest—to help show new female members around the capital and educate them on how the legislature operated. The current president at the time of the profile described OWL as "a combination of a social group and a support group, as well as a group to push some legislation."[8] The 1984 Connecticut OWL emphasized that advocacy was mainly in the form of educating fellow members on issues from a woman's perspective.

In 1938, on behalf of the pioneer group Emery sent out a call for a national gathering of women legislators to take place on April 20th in Washington, DC.[9] Representatives from a dozen states attended a social tea. There was no New York representation, though the women in the legislature (Todd, Byrne, and Graves) sent a letter of interest regarding the initiative. Nor was New York there at the 1st Annual Meeting in 1939 that was attended by thirty-six women from twelve states. Emery's summary of that first organizational meeting stated clearly that the national order would be nonpartisan.[10] The new NOWL Constitution had as its objective "to promote a spirit of helpfulness among past, present and future women legislators . . . [and] to encourage greater participation of trained and competent women in public affairs."[11]

NOWL suspended its conventions during World War II. In her letter announcing the suspension, then President Mildred Rich of Utah implored the membership not to let NOWL disintegrate.[12] She called on members to seek out new recruits and create new state chapters, implying that parts of the country were not affiliated. NOWL seemed to be struggling. When Rich canvassed the current governing board of eighteen members on the plan for suspension, while four board members did not reply at all. New York State Senator Rhoda Graves was serving as parliamentarian at the time though there is no information on her personal response.

Over the years, NOWL held annual meetings in Washington, DC, and conventions in locations around the country. Those meetings and NOWL's publication, the *OWLetter*, emphasized information-sharing more than advocacy on a specific agenda. Women held panels and spoke about how their states were addressing specific issues. In 1947, then Assemblywoman Janet Gordon delivered an address on state aid to schools in New York at the annual convention in New Jersey.[13] Also that year, the convention held a symposium on conflicts among the states' marriage and divorce laws. In 1949, attendees heard a roundtable on election laws and a talk on fifty-fifty representation on party committees. The convention then approved a resolution calling for "more recognition for all women on party committees."[14]

There appears to have been more effort to get NOWL to address issues of discrimination against women specifically during the 1970s and 1980s. This coincides with the years that New York's women legislators pressed for a similar agenda at home. It was also the time when some of those women were active in NOWL.[15] New York's yearly membership averaged 4.3 in the 1970s; it nearly doubled between 1980 and 1987, with an average of eight New York women.[16] The numbers are somewhat misleading in that women members could be current or retired legislators. Several New Yorkers remained active after retirement, with a few even holding an officer position. Jane Todd was elected first vice president in 1948, three years after leaving the legislature; Doris Byrne, who left the legislature in 1937, chaired the law committee from 1952 to 1954; and Elizabeth Gillette, who served a single term in the Assembly in 1920, was second vice president from 1950 to 1952.[17] It appears some women legislators found value in interacting with women with whom they could share similar experiences. Retired legislators' participation suggests that these women found being in the legislature an important part of their lives, however brief the service. Still, even with an active New York presence, efforts to move NOWL toward substantive action on women's issues was not particularly successful. The organization created a legislative committee in 1973, which included New York State Senator Mary Ann Krupsak. But the annual convention in 1975 defeated a resolution twenty-six yes to forty-six no that would have had the committee survey state legislatures on actions taken specifically affecting women.[18] Members defeated a resolution supporting the ERA in a close vote at the 1978 convention. Former Assemblywoman Rosemary Gunning tried and failed the next day to get the group to reconsider. In 1982, Gunning was the only New Yorker at the yearly convention.[19]

Available NOWL records include organization scrapbooks by year, which are unfortunately incomplete.[20] Those scrapbooks include issues of the *OWLetter*. The publication gave attention to news from the states where activities by women legislators appeared. Activities were not restricted to what the women were currently doing in their state legislatures, though that type of entry appeared most frequently. Though not stated anywhere in the publication, we can infer that the information was submitted either by the women themselves or by a NOWL member from that state. However the material reached the editor, the NOWL updates reflect what women saw as significant about their political lives at the time. Krupsak was often featured in this section between 1973 and 1975, when she went from senator to lieutenant governor.[21] Still, a 1971 *OWLetter* reported that Dorothy Rose, current head librarian at Erie Community College, was running for a seat on the Evans Town Council. Rose had served in the New York State Legislature from 1964 to 1968.[22] One New Yorker was in the throes of an active political career, while another was interested in restarting one.

The NOWL scrapbook for 1950–1960 contained clippings about past and present New York legislators Doris Byrne, Janet Gordon, Rhoda Graves, Frances Marlatt, and Genesta Strong. Neither Byrne nor Graves was a current legislator. In June of 1950, Byrne was appointed the first woman justice of a New York City Court. Janet Gordon, still in the Assembly, gave birth to a daughter in January of that year. That same month, Rhoda Graves died and her obituary was included in the scrapbook. There was a page of articles on Genesta Strong's successful fight in 1952 to legalize the sale of colored oleo in New York. Finally, Frances Marlatt was profiled as she began her first term in the Assembly in 1954. Each of these entries spoke to a unique aspect of the New York woman legislator. Byrne's public career began in the Assembly at the young age of twenty-eight. It continued with a number of high-profile positions and several firsts well beyond her time in the Assembly. Byrne was executive deputy Secretary of State and a New York City magistrate before being appointed Justice of the City Court. Over time, more and more of New York's legislators followed the type of career path women like Byrne pioneered. Women would move among public sector jobs, some elective and some appointive. Gordon's motherhood was another notable first for a New York Woman legislator. The event was the first step in breaking the perceptual barrier against women serving if they had small children. Graves's obituary summarized a remarkable career in both houses, eight in the Assembly and fourteen in the Senate. Graves was the preeminent woman legislator of her era. The items on Strong lauded her policy victory with oleo margarine. Strong was reported as having "received a standing ovation, was embraced and kissed and presented with bouquets of yellow roses and yellow snapdragons by colleagues in the Assembly." Frances Marlatt indicated that she planned to take up anew the fight for divorce reform, signaling that women would not abandon that contentious issue.[23] New York's women not only got individual attention in the 1950s, but Albany hosted the September 1953 convention. Some fifty women from fourteen states attended.[24] Former Assemblywoman Jane Todd and current Assemblywoman Maude Ten Eyck had prominent roles as both hostesses and presenters.

Assemblywoman Mildred Frick Taylor was the most prominent of the New York NOWL members in the 1950s. She was NOWL's first vice president in 1953 and its second vice president the year before.[25] Taylor missed the 1954 annual May meeting due to illness and, perhaps, later wished she had not. Shortly after it ended, the NOWL recording secretary informed Taylor that she had been elected president for next year "in absentia."[26] Taylor then dashed off a letter to the outgoing president expressing her "surprise" at the honor she had not sought.[27] She was more forthright about feeling boxed in when she wrote to Mayme Collins, a legislative colleague from Maryland and fellow NOWL member. Taylor lamented, "As the newly elected President I had no opportunity to accept or reject, so here I am as president."[28] Her assembly office issued a press release announcing her election. Taylor's surprise, frustration, and resignation at the honor came through when she was quoted as saying, "It is a surprise and a tremendous honor and certainly I shall do my best to fulfill the confidence shown in me," at the same time citing her lack of knowledge about the actions of the nominating committee, given that she had "shown reluctance to continue as an officer due to her many duties in the state [of New York]."[29]

Taylor inherited an organization in some disarray. She could find neither a full nor accurate list of women legislators in the country or of the women members of NOWL. In November, after having requested the information from the states, Taylor wrote to another friend and member asking if she had a list of members from her state. "I have had so many lists sent to me from various sources," Taylor wrote, "I do not know now which is membership and which is potential."[30] During her presidency Taylor notified the membership (or what she thought was the membership) that she wanted to resurrect a newsletter focused on legislative progress in the states. NOWL had produced one in the past. She repeated an earlier request for this type of information, saying she did not yet have sufficient material. Taylor fell ill in the spring of 1955, which resulted in the annual meeting being canceled. By the next convention Taylor was replaced as president by Isabelle Rylander of Connecticut. That event drew representatives from only twelve states.[31] Taylor's difficulties and frustrations are emblematic of an organization struggling for relevance and never quite achieving it.

NOWL was the only national group specifically focused on women legislators in the states. There are snippets of information about other efforts involving New York women legislators that either did not last long or that concentrated more on women elected to office at the national level. The most famous national initiative was the National Women's Political Caucus (NWPC). In July 1971, Shirley Chisholm, as well as activists Betty Friedan, Gloria Steinem, and others responded to New York Congresswoman Bella Abzug's prodding about the need for a women's group focused on politics by creating the NWPC.[32] Approximately 320 women from twenty-six states met in Washington, DC that month to formalize the organization's structure. The goal was to see more women secure positions at every level of political and public life in the country. Realizing the value of having an activist inside government, Abzug, at age fifty, had been inspired in 1970 to run for and win a congressional seat representing the eastern side of Manhattan.[33] Her congressional campaign slogan had been "This woman's place is in the house, the House of Representatives." The slogan for the NWPC, "Make policy, not coffee," encapsulated women's intention to lead rather than support those in power.[34]

The NWPC began as a nonpartisan effort, though participants early on realized that the emerging issues agenda would make that commitment hard to maintain. Margot Polivy, Abzug's congressional administrative assistant and a lawyer, reflected on the NWPC and its partisanship conundrum. "With the founding of the caucus, there was a new avenue for everybody to express themselves," She remembered. "And, of course there was the question of bipartisanship—how to find acceptable Republicans, or willing ones . . . at least for a couple of years it worked well."[35] In 1981 during the Reagan administration there were open calls at the NWPC convention for it to stop supporting Republican women candidates who voted in favor of the administration's budget cuts. The majority of members appeared willing to end bipartisan support for feminist Republican members, which was an admission that the caucus as originally conceived no long worked.[36] The NWPC ultimately shifted to a mission position described on its website today as "pro-choice [and] multi-partisan."[37] The statement serves as an admission that women politicians come at issues from multiple perspectives, not all of which can be successfully grouped together.

The story of women in national office organizing at the congressional level proceeded somewhat differently. In 1977, fifteen of the eighteen women representatives in Washington created a bipartisan organization within the US House of Representatives. Originally called the Congresswoman's Caucus, the women members changed its name in 1981 to the Congressional Caucus for Women's Issues to allow men to join and to enable the group to receive operational funding. When Congress eliminated such support in 1995, the group reorganized again into a members group open only to women representatives. From the start, the Congressional Caucus has credited its success to its bipartisanship, believing that women legislators can come together to improve the lives of women and families, and are willing to put their partisan differences aside to do it.[38] Still, Democrat and Republican members have admitted some difficulty in identifying nondivisive issues. Some Republican women have left because the balance felt too one-sided.[39]

New York's Women Organize

New York State's women tried to create their own women's political caucus. The February 1974 organizing convention for a New York State Women's Political Caucus (NYSWPC) brought together some 400 female political activists. But there were reports of difficulty satisfying women of different backgrounds and parties at the event. In the end, the convention was characterized as "an overwhelmingly Democratic gathering."[40] State Senator Mary Anne Krupsak had addressed the group on its opening day; she focused on increasing the number of women candidates rather than talking about any policy positions.[41] That fall, A *New York Times* postelection analysis speculated that her successful primary campaign for the lieutenant governor's nomination succeeded in part because of just such a women's political network.[42] Studies confirm that on the whole women legislators tend to be more liberal than their male counterparts, and that this holds true for both parties.[43] Given that predisposition and Krupsak's close association with the women's movement, some female New Yorkers in a state known for the idea of liberal Republicanism may have been willing to cross party lines for her. But that would have been in the general and not the primary, since New York does not permit same-day registration or open primaries where registered voters are not bound to vote only for candidates in their declared party. Still, the enthusiasm of that first convention and its endorsement of Krupsak's then unofficial candidacy likely helped her decide to formally run for the office. Unfortunately, the NYSWPC failed to do the paperwork that would have allowed the national caucus to endorse her at its 1974 convention that July.[44] The NYSWPC may also have been a factor in Krupsak's decision to challenge Carey for the governorship in 1978. As early as the 1975 convention, attendees at the closing ceremony were treated to chants of "Bella [Abzug] 2016 for Senator and Krupsak for Governor."[45] Abzug would run unsuccessfully for the US Senate nomination in 1976 and Krupsak for governor in 1978. Today, the national organization lists fifteen state chapters, including one in New York—though newspaper database searches show the New York Chapter to have no public footprint going forward from the 1980s.

There was also a brief, targeted effort to build a women's caucus in Brooklyn. Carol Bellamy was one of the organizers of a Brooklyn Women's Club in 1972, during her initial run for the State Senate. The organization provided volunteers for women's campaigns. But it collapsed almost immediately afterward, largely due to infighting among Brooklyn politicians.[46] The Brooklyn Women's Club shaped up as a Democratic group supporting candidates challenging more entrenched Democratic interests, particularly the power of City Councilman Samuel Wright. Congresswoman Shirley Chisholm, another club founder, by 1974 became a polarizing figure in some mainstream Democratic clubs because of her opposition to Wright.

There are several lessons from all these efforts that New York's women legislators appear to have learned. The first is that there is a distinct divide between organizations that seek to get women into political positions and organizations of women already in those positions. Second, a focus on electing women to office generally founders on the issue of partisanship. Third, women in office do find some kind of organized support system worthwhile, though to be most helpful the organization needs to be concentrated. The organization works best when female members are in close proximity because that leads to shared experiences. A shared environment is important for group cohesion. Hence, NOWL failed, but the Congressional Caucus for Women's Issues remains vital.

New York's Legislative Women's Caucus

Eighteen women members of the New York State Legislature created the Legislative Women's Caucus (LWC) in 1983. From its inception, the LWC has been and remains bipartisan. Composed of women elected to either house of the state legislature, the LWC works to "improve the participation of women in all areas of government, support issues that affect and benefit women and families in New York State, and provide a network of support for women in the State Legislature."[47] The self-funded group remains an active caucus today, with rotating officers and a small staff. It has become important as an informational resource center on budget issues and current legislation. Each session, LWC members coalesce around one or two issues to maximize their influence on the governor and the budget.[48]

Particularly in its early years, the LWC was an important tool for ensuring that women legislators received equal treatment and women's voices would be heard. Two early LWC members of different parties, Florence Sullivan (R/Conservative) (A1978–1982) of Brooklyn and Aurelia Greene (D) (A1982–2009) of the Bronx both credit the LWC with doing just that. Sullivan saw the LWC as an important element in women legislators' quest to bring about public awareness on breast cancer. While today the month of October is dedicated to that issue, such awareness was not a feature of life in the early 1980s.[49] Greene remembered how she was mentored by these women, most especially by Assemblywoman Connelly, one of the LWC founders, whom Greene called "absolutely fantastic."[50]

Going forward, the commitment to bipartisanship has limited the caucus's choice of which issues to highlight. Francine Delmonte (D) (A1998–2010) was an LWC member throughout her legislative service. She recalls members shared certain general concerns and saw them through the lens of women's experience. For example, Barbara Clark (D) (A1986–2016) chaired the LWC in 2000, and used the group's influence to educate officials considering reform of the so-called Rockefeller Drug Laws about how those laws had specifically impacted women.[51] At the same time, Delmonte also came away from the legislature convinced that using gender as the sole organizing principle had its limits. She cited geography as one differentiating factor. Plain old personal likes could be another. While the LWC is a formally recognized caucus in the legislature, which gives it more visibility and gets it more attention from the leadership, Delmonte also found common ground in an informal sportsmen's caucus, which brought together members of both sexes interested in the outdoor sports practiced in Upstate areas such as her own.[52]

While the LWC pursues issues advocacy delicately, the caucus has made and continues to make important contributions to documenting the history and activities women legislators in New York. This is done through a series of publications, some focused directly on the legislators and others connecting New York's political women to other female figures and to women's history more broadly. The LWC has produced two compilations of brief biographical sketches on each woman in the legislature. The first, published in 1988, covers women elected between the years 1918 and 1988. The second edition came out in 1998, with additional biographies; it also includes a single page on a significant trend/event in each decade between the 1920s and 1990s. These publications make some basic information on legislative women available in a single location rather than scattered in various editions of the *New York Red Book*, which contains short bios of every legislator, and in other secondary sources. These works reinforce the importance of the shared experience of being a woman legislator in New York. They also show that women have legislative histories of their own. In the end, women organized successfully with the Legislative Women's Caucus in New York because the single state environment allowed them to build a sense of camaraderie and shared experiences. Women supported each other's careers, even as they struggled to find consensus on issues. In many ways the common identity of woman politician serves as a kind of glue, giving women of all backgrounds and positions in the legislature a forum where colleagues can honestly say to each other, "I get what you mean" about their time in the legislature. As we will see next, issues can divide as well as unite, regardless of whether they fall within women's traditional sphere of social influence, as with education, or whether women have been inspired to secure increased control over their own individual lives, as with abortion reform.

Chapter 7

Advocates for Women's Issues

Overview

Figure 7.1. Group photo: Constance Cook, (June Martin), Rosemary Gunning, and Mary Anne Krupsak, 1973.

Activist-era women manifested important differences from the pioneer generation when it came to their understanding of women's voice. Their sense of responsibility for leading on women's issues was heightened by the influence of the various rights movements at the time, most particularly the woman's movement, coupled with their own modestly increased numbers. They were more aggressive about focusing on women's own disadvantages. Political scientist Drude Dahlerup believes that it is important to evaluate the progress elected women legislators made at balancing their independence of action with their effectiveness at advancing policies.[1] There remained a generalized belief among the public that women had greater authority on certain issues because they were women. Focus on an issue might also transcend other forms of division, like party affiliation. We will see that women's voices grew stronger but remained varied when it came to leadership on issues.

The women who first entered legislative politics in 1919 faced a dizzying and somewhat contradictory set of expectations. Some of the most effective arguments for suffrage had emphasized how women would improve politics and governance because they were elected to office as true outsiders. So, in one sense there was an expectation that the legislative environment would change because women would improve it. This was a generic expectation without accompanying details. Acting on their difference could mean that women would fundamentally change the structure and process of politics or it could mean women would champion a set of "women's issues." Or it could mean both.

Historically, women have been associated with issues that touch on home and family and even community. Women had entered the public square on such issues with some success. Over time, some of the issues became about the women themselves, as in the case of suffrage and securing a legal identity. But an argument could be made even there that, though women were the immediate beneficiaries, they were now better positioned to champion other groups whom they were "by nature" drawn to protect. By the mid-1920s, political parties realized that women did not vote in a bloc even on these "women's issues." Women, like men, filtered issues through their own personal lens, which included where they lived, their family backgrounds, and their economic needs.[2] Even as an organized women's movement emerged in the 1960s, women also organized in opposition to portions of the movement's agenda. Full agreement among all the women in the legislature on a big movement issue was achieved only on the Equal Rights Amendment proposed to the New York State Constitution in the mid-1970s. There an argument can be made that women's united front was important to getting it through the legislature for a second time in 1975, and out to the voters in a referendum. It was the voting public that failed to support it at the polls.

Women Organize for Issues: Education

Since the very founding of the Republic, the state has acknowledged women's responsibility for raising the next generation to be responsible American citizens. At the time, the designation "Republican Mother" connected women to the Republic and articulated an educational role for them that was to be their contribution to the new country.[3] The connection of women to education remained strong as a public education system developed in the nineteenth century. One element of that emerging system was the degree to which local oversight remained important, even as state influence increased. Teaching was among the first professions open to women, albeit with the requirement that they remain single or relinquish their positions. Women's organizations of the late nineteenth and early twentieth centuries often promoted some type of education reform as with the WCTU's push for "scientific" temperance instructional mandates. The women who entered the legislature affirmed that, as mothers, they would carry on this legacy. Their interest in education was not just about their own children but was part of the broader commitment to community uplift. The synergy between womanhood, education, and community gave all women an opening to get involved in education policy in the legislature, even those who were unmarried or had no children of their own or any prior experience with education.

A majority of pioneer-era legislators had teaching experience. But by the 1960s, state education policy reflected a growing complexity that went beyond the teacher-student relationship. Questions of financing were key, as was the growing tension over how centralized education oversight should be. Older controversies whose origins can be traced to the mid-nineteenth century also persisted, particularly concerning the relation between the public and private educational sectors. Shirley Chisholm and Constance Cook's actions illustrate how more traditional education concerns intermingled with new worries about increasingly limited funding and how to deal with racial and sexual discrimination in education. Rosemary Gunning's story illustrates how education activism served as the specific springboard for a legislative career.

Shirley Chisholm grew up in a family that stressed education; she trained to be an early childhood educator and married with some expectation of having a family of her own, though she never had children.[4] As a child in the 1930s, her mother insisted her girls do well in school. Chisholm remembered, "We had to read, too, even if we did not want to. We all had library cards and every other Saturday Mother took us to the library to check out the limit, three books each."[5] She attended schools where 80 percent of the student body was white and schools where minorities were at least 50 percent. As a student she experienced the effect of changing racial demographics in New York City. Areas were transitioning from white to minority as a consequence of the reshuffling of the minority population to what would later be tagged the "inner city" of the post–World War II era.[6] Elements of her background informed her work on education issues in the Assembly. Chisholm sponsored the Search for Education, Elevation and Knowledge (SEEK) bill, which when passed allocated funds to support disadvantaged high school students attending college, and she won a victory for teachers when her bill protecting the tenure rights of teachers who went out on maternity leave became law.[7]

Chisholm's concern about funding for education in her heavily minority district was behind her disapproval of two bills, an original and supplemental passed in 1965 and 1966, that together authorized public schools to provide private (mainly parochial) schools with textbooks. She objected to the bills on two grounds.[8] First, she and others decried what they saw as the erosion of the separation between church and state. Second, she saw the legislation as ultimately taking away financial resources from struggling New York City public schools. Chisholm accused the bill's supporters of "hiding behind the emotional argument that they are helping 'the poor little children.'"[9] Separation of parochial and state schools in New York City dates back to passage of the Maclay Bill by the state legislature in 1842. At the time, Catholic Bishop John Hughes of New York City actively challenged the Protestant Public School Society that then administered public education in the city. The Bishop created a rival network of Catholic schools and pushed for some public funding for those schools. Widespread nativist sentiment made that impossible. The legislature instead extended the state public education system to the City, taking control away from Public School Society and giving it to a newly established taxpayer funded public system. The City was divided into wards to be run by elected commissioners. Lip service was paid to the idea that parents and taxpayers ought to have input into the running of their local schools. The reality was that local politicians took control of the positions and resources in the short term. More importantly from the Bishop's perspective, the law barred state funds from any school teaching religious doctrine.[10] Given that history, Chisholm saw these two new laws as both unconstitutional and expensive. By the 1960s, New York City public schools were severely underfunded. Statewide school debt increased from 100 million dollars in 1950 to 330 million dollars in 1959. As the per-pupil cost of education increased, state aid as a percentage of that cost decreased from 40 to 30 percent.[11] In areas like Brooklyn, the local taxpayer base could not keep up.

Assemblywoman Cook's defense of education funding covered in chapter 3 was part of her work as chair of the Assembly's Education Committee, as was her service on the blue-ribbon commission set up by Governor Rockefeller to examine problems in public education. That commission concluded that inadequate resources were a fundamental problem everywhere in the state, but its recommendation to overhaul the existing, decentralized funding system was thought too radical and not seriously considered.

While Cook was credited with expertise on issues at the macrolevel, she began her time in the Assembly championing a local education issue she came to see as having statewide implications. In 1966, an area near one local school in Ithaca objected to the school board's decision to end busing for children living too close to the school to qualify. The parents argued it was unsafe to walk. The dispute revolved around what constituted a "child safety zone" under New York State Education law. Cook supported the parents' efforts to broaden that definition legally.[12] Otherwise, eligibility for busing could only be determined along mileage lines.[13] In 1967, she sponsored legislation to amend state education law on transportation in her area of Tompkins County, which then got paired with another bill to give school boards around the state the ability to designate a "hazardous zone." The statewide bill was sponsored by another Upstate legislator, John Terry of Onondaga County.[14] Governor Rockefeller vetoed these 1967 bills, but state education law was successfully amended in 1992 to allow school districts to designate a child safety zone and authorize transportation based on hazardous conditions.[15] Cook stayed true to her belief that busing was important for children's safety. She was the only Republican in the 1972 session to vote against a one-year moratorium on all busing to schools. She refused to be part of this symbolic gesture in support of then President Nixon's call for a national moratorium.[16] In 1972, Nixon's antibusing stance was part of a broader overture to Southern Democrats who opposed mandatory busing laws for racial balancing purposes.

Cook was regarded as someone with expertise in both education and women's issues, which thrust her into the limelight over controversies in higher education. In late 1971, Chancellor Robert Kibbee invited her to join an Advisory Committee on the Status of Women in the City University of New York system (CUNY). Kibbee was responding to complaints about unaddressed sexual discrimination within CUNY. Kibbee had been approached and asked to work directly with a liaison group of women from each college to deal with the allegations. Instead, he assembled the advisory group from among prominent CUNY women graduates and other women like Cook "active in the field of sex discrimination."[17]

The endeavor was problematic from the start. Prominent women inside and outside of CUNY feared the committee would be a sham controlled by the administration. Carol Greitzer was a CUNY grad and current member of the New York City Council. She refused to serve on the committee and tried unsuccessfully to get Cook to decline.[18] Shortly after Cook agreed to participate, a newly formed CUNY women's organization appealed to her to resign, citing their belief that the "Chancellor's appointed committee is an attempt to keep women divided from each other."[19] It was clear from the minutes of the committee's first meeting that its members were aware of those concerns and took pains to rebuff the chancellor's moves to control the group's actions.[20] It insisted on communicating directly with the chancellor rather than his designee. The committee also determined to hold two days of public hearings for women at CUNY, during which it heard testimony from fifty-seven different witnesses.[21] The group issued a final 272-page report in December. The opening line of its summary declared that "women employees of the City University of New York are the victims of sex discrimination in hiring, promotion and salary determination."[22] While Cook was active on the committee at the early stages of its investigation, at least through the first round of public hearings, her name was not part of the committee roster that submitted the final report. But as late as March, Cook was still identifying cases the committee should look into.[23] Cook's records say nothing about why she left the group, but there are other women whose service on the committee also did not last for the full year.[24] The bulk of the work took place in New York City, which made it hard for Cook to attend. There was also the pressure from CUNY women themselves that may have influenced her to bow out.

One year later, Cook again became embroiled in controversy over sex discrimination, this time at her alma mater Cornell University. In early 1973, Cornell's Board of Directors commissioned a study on the school's practices for hiring administrators. Cook headed the committee charged with the analysis.[25] Not surprisingly, the study was critical of Cornell's efforts to diversify, especially at the senior level. Her interest in the Cornell situation may have been piqued by having recently herself been passed over for nomination to the State Court of Appeals. In March 1972, Governor Rockefeller made a public show of asking both Democrats and Republicans to put forward women candidates. At one point, Cook appeared to be the strongest candidate in the field and the only woman recommended by either Republicans or Democrats. Normally, judicial candidates remain behind the scenes but Cook told the *New York Times* she was "fighting like mad" for the nomination. She was not chosen then and blamed the State Bar Association's negative comments about her not having judicial experience. Cook tried and failed again for a judicial nomination in late 1973, when another vacancy arose. She was more successful at Cornell. Two years after her retirement from the legislature in 1974, Cornell appointed Cook its first woman vice president in charge of land grant affairs. Her committee's final report had strongly advised the institution to diversify its administration.

More so than any other legislator in the 1960s and 1970s, it would be Assemblywoman Rosemary Gunning of Queens who wrapped herself in education concerns, primarily the issue of busing. Her approach to education was very traditional; she was determined to preserve the neighborhood character of schools. To Gunning, individual schools were community sites. She feared that they were being made pawns in a larger fight to address racial discrimination in education, which she believed was behind decisions about busing.[26] Gunning first got involved in debates about school integration in 1963, as political leaders were redrawing school district maps and reconfiguring grade assignments in individual schools in an effort to racially balance the student population. Ultimately, Gunning determined that grassroots action to stop such changes was insufficient and fixed on changing the law and even the state constitution. To do that required her to be a part of that process. In January of 1969, this married, but childless, sixty-year-old woman went to Albany as a newly elected legislator.

Gunning admits her name recognition and path to the legislature came from her education activism.[27] The Parents and Taxpayers Citywide Coordinating Council (PAT) initially formed in October 1963 to resist proposed mass pupil transfers between PS 149 and PS 980 in Queens. PAT contended that the transfers would destroy the neighborhood school framework.[28] PAT was the umbrella organization that brought together numerous ad hoc groups throughout the five boroughs that opposed the City Board of

Education's plans for integration. At various times the organization claimed between 300,000 and 500,000 members, though there were no means of verifying the statistic.[29] Gunning, referred to most frequently as the executive secretary, soon emerged as the chief spokesperson for PAT.[30]

Two sides squared off in 1964 over the issue of student transfers. Gunning's group defended neighborhood school assignments while civil rights groups, most specifically the Citywide Committee for Integrated Schooling, demanded better racial balance in schools across the City. Pro-transfer groups led a school boycott on February 3. The participants demanded immediate action. At the request of the City Board of Education, State Education Commissioner Dr. James Allen proposed a plan to pair thirty schools having majority white enrollment with thirty schools of mainly minority students as a way to equalize the racial composition of every paired school. The number was later reduced to eight and then four, with large student transfers not to begin until junior high school grades five through seven.[31] The City's schools were not a state problem to solve per se and Gunning got Allen to admit he could not mandate specific changes.[32] However, the controversy had been stirred up initially by Commissioner Allen's official finding that any New York State schools with more than 50 percent minority enrollment were de facto failing to provide equal education opportunities. For New York City schools it meant that only the racial composition of a school mattered, not the teachers, staff, or educational programs in that school.[33]

The state had stoked a divide without any good plan to overcome it. The press tended to play up the difficulties as a black versus white issue, though Gunning disputed that. She believed minority mothers objected to busing just as white mothers did, not because of race but because it would take children out of their neighborhoods.[34] Yet the *Wall Street Journal* did a story on what it called the "integration furor," which portrayed the conflict as largely racial. The headline read in part "White Parents in New York Protest Plan to 'Pair' Schools." Still, the story admitted that the benefits would be felt mainly through the "upgrading of inferior Negro schools" and that minority parents were more willing to overlook concerns about the distance their children would have to travel if it meant enrollment in a better-equipped school. The report also called it "interesting" that "not all Negro parents favored the school board's integration plan." The piece ended with an ominous prediction "that a long and heated controversy lies ahead before integration of the sort the school board has in mind can be achieved."[35]

A substantive cross-racial organization emerged to challenge the impression that PAT and the white perspective were synonymous. The grassroots organization EQUAL was created in the spring of 1964. It was made up of committed activists, most of whom were white, and dedicated to total mandatory integration.[36] Irene Lurie, a white parent, became the heart, soul, and voice of EQUAL between 1964 and 1966. She had become a supporter of integration in the 1950s, while honing her skills as a community organizer in East Harlem.[37] As a mother, Lurie directly experienced the integration debate while serving on her local school board for Consolidated Districts 12, 13, and 14 in 1962 and 1963, in the Washington Heights and Inwood sections of northern Manhattan. Lurie tried to be the example that advanced the integrationist cause. She withdrew her two oldest children from their local elementary school PS 187 and enrolled them in the heavily minority PS 161 for two years. Both returned to the neighborhood for junior high school grades.[38] Though Lurie and EQUAL viewed the education issue very differently than PAT, both groups appreciated the power and history of the neighborhood school, of how such schools were stand-ins for the very idea of neighborhood itself.[39] Lurie saw many of the mothers in her own neighborhood become active as parents concerned about their neighborhood and against busing. It was dismaying to her that the letters the school board received suggested the start of what would become the PAT position.[40]

Gunning and PAT and Irene Lurie and EQUAL illustrated the power women could wield on education issues. Lurie's voice had the added authority of a mother with "skin in the game," so to speak. For her part, Gunning responded to questions about her childlessness by connecting education to civic affairs more broadly, articulating a modern version of the Progressive Era mantra of mothering the community. That generation's middle-class woman had the free time and interest to dedicate herself to issues like education. Gunning presented her childlessness as a positive when she observed, "If I had children, I wouldn't have time to do this."[41] For its part, a *New York Times* profile on Gunning in the summer of 1964 supported the idea that being a woman was integral to her leadership of the group. Though the article's headline listed her as "Gunning" (she went by her maiden name professionally), the piece mainly referred to her as "Mrs. Moffat." She was described as "motherly" and someone who acted out of principle rather than political interest, a nod to the moral authority traditionally associated with women.[42] At other times, the press referred to Gunning as a "Ridgewood (Queens) housewife" who heads PAT "from her living room."[43]

Yet Gunning was a trained lawyer who did not rely on grassroots rallies and boycotts alone. In the spring of 1964, PAT simultaneously pursued a demonstration at City Hall that drew 15,000, set up candidate nights to vet those seeking election to the City Council, lobbied for a Neighborhood School Concept Bill in the state legislature, and aided a court challenge by three Queens families seeking to block the transfer of their children.[44] The legislation was sponsored by George Van Cott of Westchester, who served in the Assembly from 1962 to 1972. Cott represented a portion of suburban Westchester that increasingly became associated with opposition to school integration and busing.[45] As summer arrived, PAT also canvassed and secured what it believed were more than enough signatures to place a referendum on the fall ballot to change the New York City Charter to prohibit busing. But on the last day in August, the State Supreme Court upheld the City's challenge to the referendum.[46] Also, earlier in the summer, the Courts had determined that the parent suit against the Board of Education had no merit.[47]

Frustrated, in September PAT acted on its threat to boycott schools "if all else fails."[48] Over the course of the summer the cumulative effect of PATs pressure and involvement by Mayor Robert Wagner's office had negotiated down the number of paired schools to four. Gunning still considered that unacceptable since some 25,000 students could potentially be forced out of their neighborhoods. After a last-ditch negotiation meeting with City school officials on September 5 failed, both sides indicated that further meetings would not be productive. On September 15, the opening day of school, there were 237,638 students absent for 27 percent of the total enrollment. A normal absenteeism rate was 10 percent. In comparison, the pro-integrationist forces boycott back in February of that year had numbered 464,362 or 44 percent of the student body. Though PAT threatened an open ended, citywide boycott, the effort was over after the second day when participation dropped to 22 percent.[49] Instead, PAT announced it would focus intensively on state legislation to define and protect the neighborhood school. The organization would also pursue changing how the City Board of Education was selected, hoping to shift from an appointive procedure to direct election, believing "it would be more responsive to the public's will than appointed ones."[50] PAT presumed its view represented that will.

From this point on, Gunning's career took an overtly political turn. In July 1965, she accepted the Conservative Party nomination for president of the New York City Council. The full ticket was composed of William F. Buckley for mayor, Hugh Markey for comptroller, and Gunning.[51] This was a moment where the newly formed Conservative Party was flexing its youthful muscles. Created in 1962 to push New York's liberal Republican Party to the right, the Conservative Party wanted to show that its power to cross endorse could help Republicans regain losses suffered statewide in the 1964 elections. For Conservatives, the 1965 campaign in New York City pitted them against John Lindsay, nominated by the Republicans and cross-endorsed by the Liberal Party, and Abraham Beame, Democratic nominee. Historian of the Conservative Party, Timothy Sullivan, called the Conservative enmity toward Lindsay "almost visceral."[52] Lindsay, however, won the election with 43 percent of the vote. The City's Conservative ticket had run strongest in Queens and Staten Island, with Queens as Gunning's home turf. It took heart from increased name recognition and publicity from the campaign. Gunning continued to be connected to the Conservatives over the next few years. In early 1968, Republican State Senate majority leader Earl Brydges appointed Gunning to his legislative staff where she served as Conservative Party liaison with sympathetic Republican legislators.[53] That summer she was persuaded to accept the nomination for the Assembly seat in her district of Queens.[54] Gunning's election coincided with the Conservative Party, becoming the top vote-getting minor party in state history. Gunning and Charles Jerabek in Suffolk County, the two candidates who ran as Conservatives with Republican endorsement, beat incumbent Democrats.[55] In 1970, the number of Republican candidates accepting cross endorsement increased from 50 to 65. The *New York Times* estimated that the outcome of thirty-six of those elections would hinge on votes received on the Conservative line.[56] The article also noted that one thing limiting the Conservative Party's ability to negotiate for power, particularly patronage, was the party's ideological purity; leaders and members kept their focus on issues. Gunning seemed to prove that point as she entered the legislature insisting, "I'm here to pass my anti-busing bill and I think I can do it."[57]

But by then the education battle had shifted appreciably. The goal of integration through pupil transfer was replaced by the concept of decentralization or local community control. Given the demographics, shifting students for racial balance was unreachable. Instead, Mayor Lindsay supported the minority community's new vision to have authority to run their schools, to reimagine who should teach and what they should teach. The Ford Foundation offered funding for a trial run. In April of 1967 the City Board of Education approved three experimental districts for the next year. The experiment failed miserably, with plenty of blame to spread around. Locally elected community school boards thought they had full power to run their schools, but the Board of Education never clearly defined the powers and authority of those boards. The central board's vision of decentralization was more in line with giving greater control to existing administrators.[58] Activists were unbending in their vision of affirming Black culture through processes they controlled and personnel they hired.[59] The United Federation of Teachers (UFT), the union representing instructors and administrators throughout the City, had fought hard over the years for guarantees of impartial hiring practices, due process on complaints, and a system of advancement that rested on civil service examinations. It would not allow community boards to undermine that system. Between May and October 1968, the Bedford-Stuyvesant district become the main area of controversy. It was the focus of countless administrative actions and counteractions, court suits, and three citywide strikes by UFT teachers. The settlement reached appeared to leave out the voice of the local community school board in the interests of reopening the schools and keeping them open. Still unsettled, as the strikes ended, was consideration of legislation to revamp the City's system of education administration. It stalled in Albany as officials waited to see how the situation in Brooklyn played out.

Now it was up to the legislature in the 1969 session to resolve that issue. Gunning was right in the middle of negotiations as it appeared that Conservative legislators, those elected on the Conservative line or with Conservative cross endorsement, held the deciding votes in a conflict pitting supporters of expansive, decentralized authority against advocates for holding onto union-negotiated protections. Gunning herself seemed unwilling at first to shift her focus away from busing. In this Gunning was unlike the leadership of EQUAL, which historian Diane Ravitch says "followed the lead of militant blacks in switching from a strident advocacy of integration to a strident advocacy of community control."[60] Negotiations on an education bill in the spring dragged on for weeks. One hold-up was Gunning's dogged insistence that the bill include a provision banning busing to achieve racial balance, a position that had no chance of passing.[61] Gunning and her group of conservatives did win on the demand for a stronger central board of elected members, one from each borough, which ran counter to what the decentralization forces had wanted.

The final bill divided the City into thirty-two districts with at least 20,000 students, each with locally elected school boards. These decentralized districts oversaw only the elementary and middle schools. Each board hired district superintendents to manage the schools. But the local boards' areas of authority were limited; they had to clear budgets with the chancellor, the head of the City's schools, who was hired by the central Board of Education.⁶² Many of the financial decisions remained completely out of local board control. The chancellor and board fully controlled the administration of the City's high schools. The legislation authorized each borough to elect one member to the central board and the mayor to appoint two other members. That aspect was immediately challenged in court as violating the one-person-one-vote principle. In 1973 Gunning sponsored the compromise that brought the Board of Education method of selection into final legal compliance. Each borough president would now choose one member and the mayor two to serve concurrent, renewable four-year terms.⁶³

How did this arrangement square with Gunning's commitment to the idea of neighborhood schools as the foundation of community? Ravitch believes that Conservative Party support generally, and Gunning's in particular, was an effort to co-opt decentralization for conservative purposes.⁶⁴ If that were totally true, then it does not fit well with the conservative insistence that the power of those boards be reigned in and that the central board be made relatively strong.⁶⁵ Rather, Gunning may have accepted a compromise that at least kept the integrity of the neighborhood framework through the creation of so many districts within New York City. Gunning herself insisted her goal was to give Queens some sort of representation. "If they (the people) don't use it properly," she added, "well at least you've done your duty as a legislator."⁶⁶ Gunning's one blind spot remained her belief that busing was the chief threat to neighborhood integrity in education, long after that issue had become irrelevant.⁶⁷ Gunning was more prescient about the possibility of community school boards not using their power wisely and instead becoming pawns of interest groups, political clubs, and power brokers. Political scientist Wilbur Rich looked at these boards some thirty years later and found mixed results. He noted that the *New York Times* called community boards a "nest of corruption." But he also saw the boards as a valuable path into New York politics, especially for minorities. The boards have developed an identity as an interest group and successfully lobbied against changes that would diminish their power at the expense of the central board.⁶⁸

Fighting for neighborhood integrity and local control of education were brought to the forefront again when New York City faced draconian budget cuts to stave off financial collapse. In the spring of 1976, the same year Gunning retired from the Assembly, Harlem residents repeatedly demonstrated against the closing of several neighborhood schools as part of a fiscal consolidation effort. Demonstrators countered that the Board of Education was using a flawed definition of an underutilized school, one based strictly on student enrollment numbers in relation to the capacity of a building. In their study of the Harlem demonstrations, Kim Phillips-Fein and Esther Cyna show that the residents believed the schools essential to neighborhood identity and symbolic of the City's broader commitment to their neighborhood. In many instances, the schools were often the only viable public institutions in areas devoid of parks, gyms, and other recreation areas.[69] City-imposed cuts on public education would be seen as a full repudiation of the City's support for community control of that education.[70] Harlem education activist Babette Edwards came to that conclusion. In the late 1960s she had been a huge advocate of full community control of local schools. But she grew frustrated at the way the centralized City Board of Education emasculated the power of community-run school boards. This was based on firsthand experience as a school board member of the board of IS 201 in Harlem; she resigned in protest in 1971. Her resignation letter accused the principals and teachers of sacrificing the interests of the students in favor of safeguarding their own careers.[71] Edwards's commitment to local control ultimately moved her to support a voucher system whereby the state would allow the per-pupil dollars to follow those students to the school of their choice. She and her nonprofit organization, Harlem Parents Union, drafted a voucher bill that was introduced in the State Senate by Joseph Galiber of the Bronx in 1977. The Galiber Bill wanted to set up four voucher demonstration districts in Harlem. But Edwards was not alone in seeing vouchers as the logical next step in the fight for local autonomy in education. During that session, the legislature also considered a bill drafted and supported by the newly retired Gunning. Her version would offer vouchers in all the City's districts to any pupil. Edwards's effort was clearly connected to the importance of local control in minority districts with a history of failing educational outcomes. Gunning's vision appeared more aimed at middle-class parents who would be able to supplement the voucher amounts and thereby widen their school-choice options.[72] Neither bill succeeded.

Education remained a close-to-home issue, especially for women legislators like Chisholm, Cook, and Gunning. The views of each legislator were formed out of the experiences they had with how education was delivered in their particular communities. Such formative experiences made the women confident advocates for what they believed would best serve students and their families in the communities they represented. It did not necessarily prepare them for the ways that educational concerns were subsumed within other struggles, be they over finances, racial or gender equity, or bureaucratic turf wars.

Reproductive Policy: The Fight for Abortion Reform[73]

More than any other issue, the fight to liberalize New York State's abortion law called on women legislators to make hard, personal decisions about the line between bodily autonomy and the sanctity of life. While a male member of the Assembly first introduced the legislation, it would be Assemblywoman Constance Cook who became the acknowledged leader in that fight.

In 1967, Albert Blumenthal canvassed fellow Assembly members looking for cosponsors on his bill to allow therapeutic abortions at less than twenty-four weeks gestation, in the case of rape, following the identification of significant fetal abnormalities, if the person was less than sixteen years in age, or if the person was deemed incompetent.[74] This was Blumenthal's second push for abortion reform. Like its predecessor, this bill never made it out of committee onto the floor. New York's abortion law, first passed in 1829, had last been amended in 1883 to permit abortion only when the life of the mother was at stake. With regard to the Blumenthal bill, Cook said she would support it if it were released but that she was not overly involved with it.[75] That was partly because, as a Republican, she was in the minority. Still, as the only female Republican in the Assembly that term, she was seen to represent that party's voice on this woman's issue. Cook was also gaining a reputation as a reformer—someone willing to support changes to the status quo. On the floor she had argued for the 1965 bill that ended the state's ban on the distribution of birth control devices and information.[76]

Stacie Taranto, historian of New York's Right to Life movement in this period, sees the demand for access to abortion emerging as the core tenet of the modern women's liberation movement.[77] This position, in turn, inspired a countermovement by opposition women in New York in the 1970s. Hints of that divide were already evident in 1967, in the positions taken on abortion by the four women in the Assembly that year.[78] The *Ithaca Sentinel* interviewed Assemblywomen Cook, Chisholm, Hellenbrand, and Rose. Chisholm and Hellenbrand, both Democrats from Brooklyn, fully embraced women's right to abortion. Democrat Dorothy Rose from Angola, a small village south of Buffalo in Western New York, was staunchly against it. Rose's reason, her recent conversion to Roman Catholicism, matched the core element that would drive the suburban women who created the New York State Right to Life Party. Cook's comments in the 1967 piece were the most nuanced of the four. She rested her potential support for changing the law on the reality that illegal abortions were currently being performed under dangerous conditions. In another interview, Cook indicated that she was reserving final judgment while she gauged public opinion in her own Upstate district.[79] Cook's caution mirrored that of the legislative leadership that year. There was concern that passage of reform would generate a backlash outside of the urban areas in the state and from the influential Catholic Church. Blumenthal, sponsor of the reform bill, lost chairmanship of the Democratic Advisory Committee, which supported candidates at election time, because his fellow members "consider[ed] his reform views too far out."[80]

Over the next three years, Cook took on a much greater activist role on abortion. She met with Betty Friedan and NOW and gave them a crash course on political lobbying tactics. The pro-abortion forces created the National Association for the Repeal of All Abortion Laws (NARAL), which brought more attention to the feminist arguments for change. Closer to home, in 1968 Rockefeller convened a New York State Governor's Committee to Review New York State Abortion Law. The Committee heard from fifty-three witnesses, including some prominent feminists like Freidan. Its final majority report recommended legislation similar to the 1967 Blumenthal bill in that it identified specific grounds where abortion would be legal.[81] The committee stopped short of recommending full repeal. Still, the governor's committee and the public relations campaign of feminists were shifting public opinion and the political will toward changing the state's abortion law. Other states began considering changes to their abortion laws and several state courts heard challenges to existing statutes.[82] By 1969 Cook was solidly in the full repeal camp and ready to introduce legislation to that effect. Repeal differed from reform in that the former would fully decriminalize abortion and remove all restrictions. Reform would mean expanded but not full access to abortion. Republicans retook control of the Assembly after the November 1968 election, so Cook was now part of the majority party. Even so, the repeal bill she and Democrat Senator Franz Leichter of the Upper West Side of Manhattan introduced was shunted aside and only another Blumenthal reform effort got attention, though it was defeated in a somewhat close vote on the Assembly floor.[83] The tough going for changing abortion law stemmed from Assembly Speaker Perry Duryea's lukewarm support of the legislation and Senate Majority Leader Earl Brydges's outright opposition.

Apparently Cook and the reform camp in the legislature decided to join forces in 1970 rather than having their bills cancel each other out. Supporters would coalesce around Cook's repeal bill, which would be introduced first in the Senate by Leichter, and only move to the Blumenthal reform bill if repeal seemed unlikely to pass.[84] Blumenthal was a cosponsor on the

Cook repeal bill and was reported to prefer it above his own legislation.[85] Blumenthal's willingness to take a backseat to the process in 1970 focused all attention on the Cook-Leichter initiative. All subsequent negotiating and compromising would be on the language of that bill.

Cook was an extraordinarily effective advocate for her bill. As Assembly Speaker Perry Duryea put it, she deemphasized the emotions surrounding the issue and in his words she did not "overplay her femininity on this."[86] Her main argument in favor of the 1970 bill and those that had failed in the preceding sessions was always the logic behind decriminalizing abortion. The reality, she repeatedly declared, was that abortions already take place. Under the current system, poor women must seek out back-alley abortions while women with means can get safer ones. "What we are here to do," Cook asserted in Assembly debate, "is put the illegal abortionist out of business."[87]

Figure 7.2. Constance Cook as Abortion Reform Bill Passes, 1970.

In the end, it was her skill as a politician that secured passage of abortion reform. On March 18 the Senate bill passed thirty-one in favor to twenty-six opposed. Majority Leader Brydges had softened his position over time as he saw public opinion shifting. To get it through the Senate, Cook had agreed to amend her bill to require that licensed physicians perform abortions. This represented a modest tampering with the focus on repealing abortion proscriptions fully, though some radical activists felt betrayed.[88] Still, Catholic officials turned their guns on the Assembly's consideration of the bill determined to defeat it. Nuns lobbied the Assembly, Bishops' letters exhorted parishioners to oppose the bill. Then Assemblywoman Mary Ann Krupsak, a Roman Catholic, bowed to the pressure and voted against the bill on March 30. Krupsak had voted for reform in 1969 and was targeted for her vote by Republicans in the next election, who charged that she had violated the tenets of her own Catholic faith.[89] At the start of the 1970 session she had been one of the cosponsors of the Cook bill in the Assembly. She claimed her "no" vote rested technical problems with the bill.[90] The other two women in the Assembly, Democrat Hellenbrand and Conservative/Republican Gunning, split their votes. Gunning, another Roman Catholic, voted no because she believed the rights of the unborn needed protection.[91] Hellenbrand remained consistent with her 1967 pro position.

Cook's frustration at the defeat was not directed at her female colleagues but at Speaker Duryea. She had gotten him to pledge to vote "yes" should the measure get seventy-five votes, one shy of the seventy-six needed for a majority. That would have been the case but for Duryea's decision not to count the votes of two supportive members who had left the chamber after debate but before the final tally. The bill failed, seventy-three in support to seventy-one against. Cook had even accepted another late change to the Senate version that would limit abortions to six months, in hopes of winning more votes.[92] Supporters of the bill felt betrayed by what they considered Duryea's promise. Duryea supporters countered that the Speaker normally only voted to break a tie.[93] Cook refused to consider the bill dead. At the last moment she used a parliamentary maneuver to table it for future consideration, essentially erasing the unfavorable vote, and vowing to bring it back to the floor. When Cook called for a motion to reconsider the bill, Speaker Duryea held up final action on the motion until twelve missing Assembly members were brought to the chamber. Every member's position was going to be on the record for this issue. It was not that Duryea opposed abortion reform as Brydges had for so long. Rather, Duryea was seen as being in bind. He was personally in favor of reform, but the majority of the opposition came from Republicans. He could not do anything that would make it look as though he was thwarting members of his own party.

Cook's last-ditch effort to win votes forced her to compromise yet again, amending the bill to allow abortions only through the first twenty-four weeks of pregnancy. In agreeing to the change, Cook knew she was giving up on repeal and accepting reform. She was willing to do that to win passage. Even with the accommodation, the Catholic Church had succeeded in getting three formerly "yes" votes to switch to "no." This time, though, Assemblywoman Krupsak resisted pressure and shifted in the other direction, from "no" to "yes." Other Catholic legislators who did not change their votes nonetheless reported experiencing intense pressure. One legislator said he was called "murderer" by his parish priest while he and his family sat in the pew for Sunday service.[94]

Cook opened the final Assembly debate by trying to keep the focus on making the abortions already taking place safer for the women involved. But the arguments offered that day were mostly a rehash of earlier debates and unlikely to be the driving factor in changing any votes. What did move Assemblyman George Michaels of Auburn to cast the pivotal vote in favor were the pleas made by his own sons who supported the legislation. They did not want his vote to be the one that resulted in the bill's defeat. Convinced that his Upstate, rural district opposed the bill, Michaels initially voted "no." But when it appeared that the bill would fall one vote short of passage he stood and requested his vote be changed. Now, the seventy-five "yes" votes allowed Speaker Duryea to cast the decisive seventy-sixth vote in favor.[95] Governor Rockefeller had already said he would sign the reform bill. It was high drama, as the *New York Times* headline said. For Assemblyman Michaels openly admitted his action would cost him his political career. That June he lost his bid for reelection in a four-way primary and he never held elective office again.[96]

Cook spent the next three years defending the access to abortion her bill allowed. Governor Rockefeller brokered a budget deal in 1971 that included to a ban on using Medicaid funds for elective abortions. Cook and Assemblyman Blumenthal championed a failed bill in 1972 that would have reversed that decision.[97] Their efforts were ultimately foreclosed by a federal ban on the use of such funds for that purpose.[98] More worrisome that year was the push to repeal abortion reform altogether. In early May just before the final vote in the legislature, a repeal bill authored by Republican-Conservative Assemblyman Edward Crawford of Oswego received an unexpected boost from President Richard Nixon, who sent a letter to New York's Cardinal Cooke expressing his support for repeal. Assemblywoman Cook was "appalled" by what she saw as a strictly political move.[99] Nixon's intervention stirred things up only briefly.

Most of the energy around the push for repeal was coming from pro-life women around the state. Following passage of the 1970 law, suburban and predominantly Catholic women organized Right to Life Committees (RTLC). This loose network of what the press dubbed "church ladies" provided workers for writing campaigns and visits to Albany to lobby legislators. They were the ones who successfully pressured legislators to let the Cook-Blumenthal public financing of abortion bill languish in committee.[100] These women's efforts included running candidates for office, more to bring attention to the issue of abortion than to win. The committees' initial forays into politics were grafted on to a sophisticated and determined effort to create a single-issue political party. Like the Conservative Party, which was enjoying some success at pushing New York's Republican Party to become more conservative, the New York State Right to Life Party (RTLP) hoped to push legislators to change their voting position on abortion.[101]

By 1972 these repeal forces had developed into what Taranto terms a "politically mature anti-abortion movement sustained by activist women."[102] She argues that these women's voices were so well organized that legislators assumed they were representative of women's voice on abortion. The appearance of gender support, combined with another full-court press by the Catholic Church, overwhelmed the feminists advocating against repeal. Repeal passed 79-68 in the Assembly and 30-27 in the Senate. All told, abortion reform support declined by five votes in the Assembly while repeal gained four votes in the Senate. But as expected, Governor Rockefeller vetoed the bill.[103] Later that summer the State Court of Appeals rejected the argument that the unborn had a constitutional right to life, concluding that the extension of legal personhood was a matter for the legislature to take up.[104] In January of 1973, the issue in New York became moot as the US Supreme Court legalized abortion at the federal level in *Doe v. Bolton* and *Roe v. Wade*.

Cook and her colleagues did not know what the ultimate outcome would be back in the spring of 1972. In that moment, she employed her considerable political skills toward defeating the repeal bill in front of her. Her goal was to preserve the principle of abortion access, even if it meant compromising on the details. This approach mirrored her actions over the 1970 bill. Cook introduced a Rockefeller-supported alternative bill to reduce the gestational age limit on legal abortions from twenty-four to eighteen weeks.[105] Cook was realistic about the long odds against the alternate bill's passage. "It will be difficult to bring about a compromise," she said. "But I am willing to try."[106] As in 1970, Cook's most repeated argument, originally for reform and now to defeat repeal, was pragmatic rather than ideological. "The issue is not whether we have abortion in this state but where we will have it, in a hospital or in a motel room" had become so much a part of the debate that it was repeated an editorial supporting abortion in the *Atlanta Journal Constitution*.[107]

To some degree Cook became a symbol of the women's movement at the time. It is worth examining how closely her personal views represented a movement that rested its support for abortion on a woman's absolute right to control her own body and choose what she will do with it. There are some indications that Cook and the feminist movement's support for abortion reform rested on different premises and had somewhat different goals. Cook's oft-repeated arguments centered on the realism of abortion and the need for safety, which is what Cook believed would be the role hospitals would play. That position was at odds with the feminists' successful suit in New York courts to remove the restriction that all abortions had to be in hospitals.[108] Cook was also willing to compromise, first on reform and then on repeal if it made abortion more safely available. Most revealing was an interview she gave to the *Syracuse Post Standard* just after repeal passed the Assembly. There she cited what she saw as errors of political strategy. Cook also admitted that she was not "personally pro-abortion."[109] She hoped the combination of education, social, and scientific advances would render abortion obsolete.[110] In 1972, Cook cosponsored sixteen bills, four as lead sponsor, that dealt with greater access to contraception for teenagers and more sex education.[111]

Cook did share with the movement a frustration at what she termed "women's political insignificance."[112] She saw her position in the Assembly as the only way to get women's concerns heard and not dismissed. Women's issues would only move forward when women took on the role of advocate and policy maker.[113] Cook sponsored a number of bills that reflected women's inequitable treatment, including a 1970 law to require employers to compensate women serving on juries, just as they did men, and a 1972 law prohibiting discrimination in public places based on sex.[114] As discussed above, Cook was involved in efforts to open opportunities for women in higher education. She took the legal case of the Reverend Betty Bone Scheiss to the United States Equal Opportunity Commission (EEOC) in 1976.

Scheiss had been ordained into the Episcopal priesthood by a group of reform bishops, but the diocesan bishop refused to license her. The EEOC ordered him to do so and the General Convention of the church that same year passed a resolution prohibiting discrimination by sex when it came to ordination.[115] Cook's interactions with feminists and her joining NOW may have been more about not letting, as she put it, a roomful of men dictate "what women's lives shall be" than it was a full-throated embrace of abortion itself as the preeminent symbol of women's liberation.[116]

Going forward, abortion remained what Assemblywoman Estella Diggs termed "a ticklish subject" for women politicians.[117] Diggs was elected to the Assembly just after the 1972 repeal fight and did not remember it as a particular issue in that fall's campaign. Her effort to play down the subject was a consequence of being a Roman Catholic convert. Like Krupsak, who was also Catholic, Diggs understood that her faith and her advocacy for women could be in tension with one another. Unlike Krupsak, Diggs did not get involved in the feminist issues of the period. She was older, fifty-six at the time of election, with grown children. If anything, representing her race in the Assembly with dignity dominated her thinking. Diggs opposed abortion personally but supported contraception, believing it important not to impose her beliefs on others.[118] Elizabeth Connelly arrived in the Assembly the same time as Diggs. She, too, was Roman Catholic and opposed to abortion. Unlike Diggs, Connelly advocated for bills to limit access or set up additional roadblocks to abortion.[119] In 1997, she and other pro-life legislators, frustrated at not being able to get their partial birth ban bill out of committee, tried and failed to force debate on the Assembly floor. In a letter to a constituent, Connelly justified using aggressive tactics because "the issue transcends all else."[120] But public sentiment had shifted in New York such that Connelly found herself in a shrinking minority of women legislators when it came to abortion. As Connelly was preparing to retire, she admitted that hers was clearly the minority position now among women in the legislature. She responded to a Legislative Women's Caucus (LWC) questionnaire about the usefulness of different kinds of programs with a caustic comment about being "recently disinvited to an event because of my pro-life stand."[121] To its credit, the LWC concentrated on women's health issues, where there was more consensus. In 1995, when Connelly was LWC President, the main health-related issues were expanding insurance coverage to mammograms and pap smears and categorizing obstetrics and gynecology as primary care areas of expertise for women.[122]

With regard to issues, women understood that their voices could lend more power to an issue, that in certain areas women were seen as credible because they were women. Women's voices, combined with political savvy could be powerful, as with the fight for abortion reform. But women's positions on issues informed by their gender were not monolithic. All three women serving in the Assembly in 1972, the year the NWPC was created, joined the organization. But Gunning did not support abortion reform in 1970 or lobby against repeal in 1972 as her colleagues Cook and Krupsak did. As for issues, Gunning made education her signature issue. But her views there put her at odds with many in the civil rights movement, including women. Gunning's concern about neighborhoods remaining central to children's education was somewhat overwhelmed by other concerns, such as funding limits. Still, Gunning was one of the voices that argued successfully for the long-term continuation of locally selected school boards within the larger City education bureaucracy. And even though women were not united on abortion reform, Cook's pragmatic political approach, coupled with deference to a woman's voice on the issue, secured the initial reform in 1970 and staved off repeal for the next two years.

Chapter 8

New York's "Year of the Woman"
Gender and Politics in the 1992 Legislative Elections

Women Legislators from Westchester in the Election of 1992

	Party	Body/Year Elected	through Year	Body/Year Elected	through Year
Sandra Galef	D	A/1992	present		
Mary Goodhue	R	A/1974	1978	S/1978	1992
Audrey Hochberg	D	A/1992	2000		
Naomi Matusow	D	A/1992	2000		
Suzi Oppenheimer	D	S/1984	2012		
Cecile Singer	R	A/1988	1994		

Assembly = A, Senate = S.

Overview

In 1987, the *New York Times* labeled women's aggregate representation in the state legislature anemic even as its story identified several areas of advancement.[1] The piece began with some recent, obvious firsts for the women: the recent addition of a woman's bathroom to the Assembly Chamber and the first birth to a sitting state senator, Velmanette Montgomery—only the second such birth to a sitting legislator. Equally important, the interviewees heralded a record number of women named committee chairs. Assemblywoman Catherine Nolan (D) (1984–present) said it represented women's full

Women Legislators from Westchester in the Election of 1992

Sandra Galef   Mary Goodhue   Audrey Hochberg   Naomi Matusow

Suzi Oppenheimer   Cecile Singer

integration into the seniority system, "that women have simply put in the time." Speaker Mel Miller added a woman, Joni Yoswein, to his team of top advisers as his chief of staff, which made her the first woman to formally enter into the highest-level policy deliberations. May Newburger, recently retired from the Assembly, recalled how not too long ago one newspaper had labeled her a secretary in the caption for a photo with other legislators. Assemblywoman Weinstein thought that nearly all of the predominantly male lobbying contingent had finally become comfortable interacting with women. Lobbyists had gotten over the feeling that meeting with women legislators had romantic connotations.

Yet, at the time, New York's legislature ranked in the bottom third nationwide in the number of women serving. The 150-member assembly had seventeen women while six of the sixty-one senators were women. Just the year before Karen Burstein, former state senator and current president of State Civil Service Commission, speculated that women's momentum in politics had stalled. "In New York we get a lot of firsts," she said, "but it's not clear we get seconds."[2] 1992 seemed destined to change that. That year would see an election heavily focused on women candidates, first at the national level followed by a trickling down to state races. It had taken decades for women to seemingly explode onto the scene. In reality, it was the culmination of the woman candidate's development of a political identity.

By the 1980s, women running for the New York State Legislature were increasingly comfortable labeling themselves full-time politicians. More women, though not all, had résumés equivalent to full-time politicians, even if they eschewed the label itself. Despite her twenty-eight years in the Assembly, Elizabeth Connelly refused to define herself as a politician. But reluctance to commit to a substantive career and the willingness to embrace it was changing. The "class of 1980" contained six freshmen assemblywomen. Four of them, Geraldine Daniels, Eileen Dugan, Gloria Davis, and Helene Weinstein stayed in the legislature for more than ten years: Daniels twelve, Dugan sixteen, Davis twenty-two, and a still open-ended number of years for Weinstein. Gail Shaffer, another Democrat also elected in 1980, left the legislature after the 1982 election to become Governor Mario Cuomo's Secretary of State. Her twelve years there make her the longest-serving person to date in that position. As a Republican, 1980 was the wrong time for Carol Siwek's election to the Assembly, just as the Democratic Party solidified its control there. Leadership redrew her district before the 1982 election, and she lost her seat to a Democrat. For Democratic legislators, however, longevity now opened up leadership opportunities on committees. Women in the Assembly were penetrating the inner circle of male policy makers, and they were formulating a women's agenda of legislation.[3] Ever since the legislature's passage of abortion reform in 1970, that issue increasingly dominated discussions of what such an agenda should include. Despite the *Roe v. Wade* decision legalizing abortion in 1973, a newly organized New York Right to Life Party tried to keep the issue alive. There were equally well-organized interests on the pro-choice side determined not to lose any ground. There were also peripheral issues that generated debate, such as Medicaid funding for abortions.

1992 was supposed to be different for women. By spring, the media had already dubbed the campaign season the "Year of the Woman." Election night returns appeared to validate that label as fact. More women ran for and won congressional seats than ever before. More women were elected to the legislature in New York than ever before.

Here I test the assumption that it was the "Year of the Woman" framework that accounted for women's success in New York, by taking a closer look at electoral activity during that cycle within a pivotal area in the lower Hudson Valley, primarily Westchester County, a suburban area just north of New York City. The 1992 elections put Westchester County into the record books. The county was instrumental in the Democrats' success at increasing their majority in the Assembly from 95 to 101, at the time the second-largest majority in state history.⁴ Four newly elected members of the Westchester assembly delegation were Democrats, and they accounted for 50 percent of their party's statewide gain in seats. More importantly, three of those four new Westchester members were women who, when they arrived in Albany, joined ten other female freshmen, bringing the total number of women in the 1993 legislature to thirty-six, an increase of over 50 percent in a single election cycle.⁵ The County and surrounding area also had two women senators who were up for reelection, one from each party.

But Westchester was also representative of broader changes taking place in New York State politics, namely, the erosion of Republican support in major suburban areas and smaller cities. For much of the twentieth century, Westchester had been a Republican stronghold. The county elected its first woman to the State Assembly in 1934, when Jane Todd won a close election in a dismal year for Republicans elsewhere in the state. In 1992, Westchester was poised to turn majority Democrat. The Republican Party responded by using Westchester as the test site for new candidates and strategies to fight back against further losses. Since the 1930s, New York Republicans had promoted their own version of toned-down social liberalism. Now the party reinvented itself as the voice of fiscal conservatism and social moderation. Westchester was where the party tested the new identity, and it did so against the only sitting woman Republican State senator, Mary Goodhue. Looking at the various campaigns waged by Westchester's women in 1992 will clarify what was happening politically in New York that year. We will be in a better position to gauge whether those results should be considered a breakthrough associated with the "Year of the Woman" or whether they were more a part of the political evolution of the state and its women politicians. These larger dynamics may have supported positive outcomes for some women politicians, even as others did not benefit.

Rise of the Idea of the "Year of the Woman"

In April 1992 the *New York Times* proclaimed "With Outsiders In, Female Candidates Come Forward."⁶ One month later, an op-ed by the female head of a national polling firm proclaimed cautious optimism that 1992 "is the year of the woman in American politics."⁷ The idea that 1992 was shaping up to be a banner year for women candidates permeated media coverage of the election cycle from that point on.⁸ It had gained traction following several high-profile US Senate primary victories by women, most notably Lynn Yeakel in Pennsylvania and Carol Mosley Braun in Illinois. By the fall, most stories included a nod to the concept and the fall's election results at the national level appeared to justify that optimism. There were an unusually high number of open seats at the national level. Scholars have noted women's chance of electoral success increases when they do not have to challenge an incumbent.[9] And more women took advantage of these electoral odds in 1992 than ever before—106 ran for Congress and 11 for the Senate.[10] Their success rate was remarkable. The number of women in the House rose from 23 to 47, a gain of 24 new seats. The number of women in the Senate rose from 2 to 6.[11] An important component of this success was women's wealth of political experience waiting to be tapped. Studies have shown that women have been slow to see themselves as being equally qualified to run as men.[12] They are more likely to overcompensate by delaying a candidacy in favor of building up a stellar résumé. But 1992 proved the opportune moment when a critical mass of longtime women politicians in lower-level offices with many years of experience believed their time to advance had come. As political scientist Linda Witt noted, in 1992 "opportunity met readiness."[13]

These statistics mirror what the press tended to focus on: the combined power of being a female and a Democrat. Nationally, the majority of "Year of the Woman" candidates were registered Democrats. Women Democrats were also the most likely to receive targeted fundraising and campaigning help from women's organizations. The two largest funders at the time, Emily's List (Early Money Is Like Yeast) and WISH (Women in the Senate and House), provided support only to pro-choice candidates.

On the national level, both Pennsylvania's Yeakel and Illinois's Braun had unseated incumbents in their primaries to win party nomination. To do so they bucked conventional wisdom and intentionally embraced running as women, stressing their differences on issues from men and their ability as outsiders to challenge entrenched interests.[14] These candidates said they were frustrated at how the 1991 Clarence Thomas Supreme Court confirmation hearings played out. As women, they were appalled at what they perceived to be unfair treatment of Anita Hill by the all-male Senate Judiciary Committee.[15] Hill had offered testimony of alleged sexual harassment by Thomas toward her when she had worked with him at the Equal Employment Opportunity Commission. Committeemen on the Judiciary seemed exceptionally cold and unsympathetic. The hearings convinced these candidates that women's underrepresentation in office ensured their marginalization on issues. Indeed, Yeakel ran against the chair of the Judiciary

Committee, Arlen Specter.[16] Though Yeakel failed to unseat Specter in the general election, Braun won and thereby became the first African American woman elected to the US Senate.

At first it seemed like the US Senate race in New York would become one of the marquis "Year of the Woman" matchups. It was widely expected that Democratic challenger Geraldine Ferraro would run against incumbent Republican Alphonse D'Amato. Ferraro had become the first woman nominated by a major party for a presidential ticket when Democrat Walter Mondale selected her as in vice presidential running mate in 1984. Before that Ferraro served four terms in Congress, representing Queens. But things got complicated; the primary field expanded to four, with a second female in the race. As New York City Comptroller and former Congresswoman from Brooklyn, Elizabeth Holtzman had a feminist résumé of her own. Holtzman says the Thomas hearings influenced her decision to run, as did her sense that Ferraro's weaknesses during the 1984 election would hurt her again in the Senate race.[17] In 1984, Ferraro had been repeatedly attacked for her husband's questionable business connections and allegations of corrupt business financing. Now female supporters took sides as the campaign became nasty and personal.[18] Holzman expressed surprise at the level of vitriol in this primary, given that she had run against a woman before, Bess Myerson, the first time she sought a Senate nomination in 1980. Holtzman did not remember that primary as so personal.[19] Perhaps by 1992, women better understood that deferential politics almost always lost to the bare-knuckle variety. The competition between the two women hurt front-runner Ferraro enough that State Attorney General Robert Abrams won a narrow primary victory.[20] He subsequently lost to D'Amato in the general. Intrastate contests thus played out in the shadow of these national races. In New York specifically, the contests were also influenced by ideological shifts impacting electoral prospects.

Republicans Rethink the State's History of Social Liberalism

Chapter 1 detailed the development of New York's unique brand of social liberalism in the early twentieth century. Franklin Roosevelt brought that political ideology to the national level in 1933. Back in New York, Governor Herbert Lehman continued to view governing through the same philosophic lens, as did subsequent Republican governors Dewey and Rockefeller. However, by the late 1960s, New York was becoming a cautionary tale of a state in decline, as the costs of social liberalism now exceeded the capacity to support them. In 1969, New York City Mayor John Lindsay won reelection, but it was as the Liberal Party candidate. He had been beaten by John Marchi in the Republican primary. In his biography of Nelson Rockefeller, historian Richard Norton Smith labeled the victory "the last hurrah for the New Deal Coalition" of liberal Republicans in the mold of a Fiorello La Guardia with the Democratic Party's social programs agenda. At the state level, Governor Rockefeller continued to present budgets that asked for more resources from state residents than they were willing to approve. When voters rejected a 165-million-dollar bond issue in 1964, Rockefeller asked for more in next year's budget and proposed the state's first ever sales tax.[21] But creation of the Conservative Party of New York in 1962 helped push New York's Republicans to embrace a more conservative philosophy, one that would align it more closely with where the national party was moving.[22] Going forward, New York had two different political ideologies to choose from. Democrats refused to abandon social liberalism entirely, hoping for its revival over time. Republicans shed their image as a lighter version of social liberalism and touted fiscal responsibility.

The 1992 Election in Westchester

With regards to state legislative contests, there were significant differences between the possibilities for women in the two chambers. All 61 seats in the Senate and 150 seats in the Assembly were being contested. Democrats eyeing a Senate majority tried to leverage what they thought would be the women's year by running a significant number of them statewide, twenty to the Republican's lone woman.[23] One Westchester senator, Democrat Suzi Oppenheimer, won reelection but that had no bearing on the Democrats' unrealized quest for a Senate majority. The party did not win the 5 seats needed for control. Still, by 1994, Oppenheimer was serving as Minority Whip. Oppenheimer was used to working and thriving in the minority. Her first elected office had been mayor of Mamaroneck, where she was the only woman official and a Democrat in a city dominated by Republicans.[24] It was in the Assembly where the argument could more plausibly be made that Westchester participated in the "Year of the Woman" in a meaningful way. The victories by the three Democratic women meant that for the first time a Democratic and female majority would represent Westchester: four Democrats to three Republicans and four women (three D and one R) to three men.²⁵ Going strictly by the numbers, women politicians and the media in the county claimed it was their year.

However, the individual stories of the women running paint a more complicated picture. Only one of the three nonincumbents, Naomi Matusow, declared that she entered the race because there needed to be stronger female voices on women's issues. She actively sought the help of feminist groups. The other two, Sandra Galef and Audrey Hochberg, ran as experienced local politicians with decades of elected service. The two relied on traditional party support networks. Incumbent Republican Assemblywoman Cecile Singer totally dismissed the influence of the women's movement on both her own candidacy and the issues taken up by the legislature.²⁶

Matusow was the one candidate to credit the feminist movement with inspiring her run. There was no one event she remembers that influenced her decision but rather the "seeds of the women's movement maturing."²⁷ Matusow had been a teacher in the New York City Public Schools in the 1960s and 1970s, and a lawyer since 1981. In 1989 Matusow ran for the Westchester County Board of Legislators against Republican Edward Brady, then chair and a seventeen-year incumbent, mostly because no one else stepped forward. She lost a close race by 650 votes, despite being underfunded and without much assistance from the County Democratic Committee.²⁸ So, though Matusow viewed her actions through a feminist lens, she had gravitated into politics before the "Year of the Woman."

Matusow believed national issues would play a big role in the 1992 election, so she challenged nine-term incumbent Republican Peter Sullivan in the 89th Assembly District. The 89th had a two-to-one Republican edge in registrations. However, redistricting had diminished somewhat the incumbency advantage.²⁹ If she was going to win, Matusow had to convince the Democratic Assembly Committee (DAC) to finance her run. Beginning in the 1960s leaders of both legislative houses centralized election resources under their direct control, hastening the decline of local party organizations as sources of power. The leadership reserved most funds for incumbents.³⁰ DAC asked her for a feasibility study to show how likely her victory would be. Here Matusow turned to activist Polly Rothstein, director of the Westchester Coalition for Legal Abortion. Rothstein had data showing that pro-choice voters in the district were significant enough to determine the election. Convinced by Rothstein's numbers, DAC targeted the race, which meant Matusow got money and services. Matusow's campaign contrasted her pro-choice position with Sullivan's opposition to abortion.³¹ Matusow won by 725 votes out of 49,000, though it took a recount to verify the victory.

Afterward, she was clear in her conviction that the issue of abortion rights accounted for the margin of victory.[32]

Sandra Galef and Audrey Hochberg were the other two Democratic candidates seeking Assembly seats for the first time. They had served together on the Westchester County Board of Legislators, Galef for thirteen years and Hochberg for twenty. Galef saw her bid for the Assembly strictly as a career move.[33] The newly drawn 90th District had a small Republican majority but the seat was open and winnable. Party leaders specifically encouraged her to run.[34] 1992 was an optimal time for Galef to take her political career from the county to the state level. Party leaders had asked her to run for the Assembly before but she declined because her children were still young. "I don't know how people deal with children up here [in Albany]," Galef said.[35] By 1992 her children were grown. It was time to think beyond the county level.

Galef associated herself most closely with the issue of government reform during her campaign, stressing that she would be an independent legislator and beholden to neither the leadership nor special interests.[36] To prove her point, Galef took no financial support from DAC. And once in office, Galef pledged to take no member items, which she believes freed her to speak her mind on reform.[37] None of this stopped her Republican opponent from trying to label her a professional politician.[38] Abortion was not an issue she actively talked about. If asked, Galef would answer that she was pro-choice, but "I don't signal it out to my constituency."[39]

Hochberg's résumé resembled Galef's, though she served seven more years on the county board and declared her candidacy for the 88th District before Galef announced for the 90th. The 88th included Scarsdale, Eastchester, Pelham, and most of White Plains. Democrats and Republicans each constituted about 37 to 38 percent of the district; independents held the balance of power with 25 percent enrollment. Hochberg's entry into the race forced a potential male primary challenger out.[40] Hochberg was the more senior Westchester politician at the time.

Like Galef, Hochberg emphasized her administrative achievements at the county level. She was most proud of having forced the county to provide quarterly budget reports and projections that exposed a "'phantom army' of 1,000 unfilled but financed county jobs."[41] Her campaign literature played on the theme by declaring that "government waste makes me angry."[42] But there were differences. Hochberg received DAC support for polling, though it was much less substantial than the support Matusow received. Unlike Galef, Hochberg overtly inserted gender into the campaign but not in the way Matusow did. Hochberg connected her role as wife and mother to her commitment to serve the community. She included keeping New York pro-choice as part of her formal policy agenda, albeit as the last item on the list. Her campaign sent out a targeted postcard mailer reaffirming her pro-choice position.[43] Hochberg had adjusted her campaign strategy to reflect that she faced a female Republican opponent and would have to fight for women's votes. Businesswoman Rita Blanco mounted an unexpectedly strong challenge. Local newspaper columnist David Wilson observed that Blanco "was first viewed as a sacrificial lamb offered up by the county GOP leader to ensure Hochberg's departure from the county board where the GOP has struggled to stay in power."[44] When Blanco appeared to have some success, Hochberg secured financial support from the Democratic County Committee. By reminding voters that she was a wife and mother in politics Hochberg fought back against the charge that she was an insider and not to be trusted. In the end Blanco tried but failed to undermine Hochberg's reputation for honesty.[45]

Blanco's efforts as a Republican candidate were compared to those of Cecile Singer, the lone Republican woman already in the Westchester Assembly delegation. The incumbent from the 87th Assembly District faced reelection in a redrawn district almost exclusively made up of Yonkers. But it was where Singer lived and where voters were comfortable with crossing party lines to vote for her.[46] Singer credits years of building relationships with colleagues in both parties for easing her way to reelection. When she first ran in 1988, it was the Westchester Republican leadership that courted her to succeed retiring legislator Gordon Burrows. Leaders cited Singer's twenty-seven years of experience on various legislative committees in Albany.[47] Most significantly, she was Burrow's chief of staff and he encouraged her to run. He believed her to be the best candidate and he told her directly, "Cecile, if you don't do it, you're going to regret it for the rest of your life."[48] For the first and only time, the county committee used weighted voting to choose its nominee, ensuring that Singer would triumph over an opponent from Eastchester.[49] Singer's 1988 victory made her the lone female in Westchester's Assembly delegation in 1989, although two of the four state senators at the time were women: Democrat Suzi Oppenheimer and Republican Mary Goodhue.

But in November 1992, Goodhue's name appeared only on the Independent Party line. In effect this meant she would be leaving the legislature after eighteen years: four in the Assembly and fourteen in the Senate. In 1992, the seventy-one-year-old lawyer from Mt. Kisco was the legislature's lone Republican woman senator. Beginning with her successful run for the Assembly in 1974, Goodhue had had the full support of the Republican organization. In 1978 she beat out two other candidates for the Westchester Republican endorsement for the 37th Senate District. It was an eminently winnable election since the district overlay her Assembly District and there was a three to two majority Republican enrollment.[50] In subsequent elections, Democrats acknowledged how difficult it would be to unseat her, referring to her in 1982 as "an institution" and failing to field a candidate against her in 1988. The county Democratic leader that year observed, "Right now, the only way Mary Goodhue's leaving office is through death or retirement."[51]

1992 was a different kind of year, and some party leaders were promoting Assemblyman George Pataki. Pataki had become the symbol of the growing power of a group of antitax, more conservative Republicans who organized as Change-NY in 1991. Change-NY was a 501(c)(3) that billed itself as a grassroots organization critical of Governor Cuomo and a legislature that was too compliant with his spending plans. Change-NY found a kindred spirit in the Conservative Party; together they began looking for a candidate with their fiscal values who could head a Republican-Conservative ticket for governor in 1994.[52] Pataki framed his campaign against Goodhue as one of fiscal conservativism versus liberal Republican excess in the Rockefeller mold. Goodhue had not initially been his intended political target. Pataki had raised funds in 1991 to run for Westchester County Executive, but the incumbent did not leave the position as expected. The Goodhue Senate seat became Pataki's fallback position. Earlier in his career Pataki had worked for Goodhue, who was still sometimes referred to as his mentor. But now, pressured by Change-NY, Westchester Republican leader Anthony Colavita informed Goodhue in May that he was withdrawing party support for her reelection. Surprised, angry, and hurt, Goodhue initially announced her retirement, saying, "I felt I'd been sort of kicked in the backside."[53] In less than a week she reentered the contest citing significant support from Republican leaders like Senate Majority Leader Ralph Marino and the endorsement of the Putnam County Republicans.[54] Over her tenure the district had been redrawn to include Putnam and portions of Dutchess Counties, in addition to northern Westchester. The Senate seat was pivotal for the Republicans if they hoped to hold power in the region going forward. Even now, Putnam County has remained majority Republican giving the party a chance to offset the growing Democrat enrollment in Westchester proper.[55] Conflicted, Colavita briefly shifted the Westchester endorsement back to Goodhue but then returned to Pataki.[56]

Goodhue framed her campaign around gender rather than let Pataki define the race as a choice between conservative or liberal fiscal approaches. Women and women's groups voiced outrage at the Republican machinations. Female party leaders from nearby towns labeled Colavita's actions "a kick in the pants to women."[57] " 'There are a lot of women who don't like the idea of my being pushed aside,' she (Goodhue) said. 'And there are a lot of seniors who don't like it either.' " Polly Rothstein's Westchester Coalition for Legal Abortion saw the race as critical. "In 'the year of the woman,' " she (Rothstein) said, "for somebody like that to want to knock off an experienced, viable woman is unacceptable."[58]

The bitterest fighting in the campaign centered on what it meant to say one was "pro-choice."[59] Both Democratic and Republican officials in Westchester County labeled themselves that way, recognizing the broad support that existed for that position. But there were subtle differences in how deep that support went. Goodhue criticized Pataki for voting to limit the availability of abortion despite using the rhetoric of choice. When Pataki eked out a small primary victory of several hundred votes, Rothstein distanced herself from Goodhue to avoid having the issue of abortion tied to Goodhue's defeat. Still, Rothstein understood her cause had lost its true champion. " 'Mr. Pataki distorted his position,' she said. He mischaracterized himself as pro-choice, and many voters didn't realize that.' "[60]

Overall, the dynamics of the 1992 Westchester elections offer only partial support for the "Year of the Woman" meme. More Westchester women ran than in any previous election cycle; more women won than ever before. But they did not fit neatly into the stereotypical understanding of the 1992 female candidates who "took a chance and proclaimed themselves as different."[61] Nor did they (or could they) mainly frame their campaigns as insurgencies aimed at ending women's exclusion from power. Only Matusow could legitimately claim outsider status. But she ended up receiving party funding for her campaign. Galef, Hochberg, Singer, Oppenheim, and Goodhue were all experienced politicians. Party leaders pressed Galef to run. Hochberg had enough political weight to dissuade potential primary challengers. If they benefited at all from the idea of women's exclusion from power, it was in their ability to deflect charges from opponents that they were political insiders. Here Galef and Hochberg promoted themselves as reformers, as officials who did not practice politics as usual. Their approach was consistent with the history of women in electoral politics. One of the strongest arguments the suffragists had made for the vote was to emphasize women's ability to clean up corruption in politics. The woman-with-a-broom had been a familiar image in political cartoons of the early twentieth century. But women need to be careful to balance challenging the system with achieving something within it. Subsequent analysis of the women legislators suggests they struggled with striking that balance, even as the overall delegation increased its influence in the legislature.[62] Matusow labeled herself a pragmatist but she had to fight to hold her seat each election cycle.[63] Meanwhile Galef embraced the role as the "odd duck out," distancing herself from political corruption but also from sources of power.[64] Hochberg was described as "well liked and hard-working" but "not all that adept at political maneuvering,"[65]

Another theme associated with the "Year of the Woman" was the idea that women would advance issues important to them in ways that men either would not or could not. Scholars of women in politics point to research that indicates male-dominated legislatures do not act with the interests of their female constituents in mind and thus posit that having more women legislators can make a difference.[66] With increased numbers, women would be more vocal about issues and have more voting leverage to see action taken—especially when the increased number of women came from the Democratic Party, which controlled the Assembly. Again, the history of the 1992 election and the subsequent legislative history only partially validated the theory. The Westchester women all agreed they saw themselves as issues advocates more than anything else. Political scientists Ester Fuchs has found that with women, "for the most part, those passions are directed as issues directly affecting women and their families. . . . called 'the kinder and gentler issues.'"[67] But the issues Westchester's women ran on were neither uniform nor distinctly about women. There were ways that corruption or crime could be framed as quality-of-life issues, but they were topics that all the candidates addressed. Education, long regarded as a woman's issue, was for Westchester at the time primarily about resources and property taxes.[68] Women had typically not been seen as or given the opportunity to become leaders on taxes and finance. Finally, the women themselves were divided on the idea that women saw and championed issues differently. Senator Oppenheimer thought so. She believed women had a different agenda, one that focused more on basic human needs issues like food, shelter, and even the peace movement. Singer acknowledged women's difference, or what she called "women's nurturing instinct." At the same time, Singer worried about its limits, referring to it as "a terrible trap" that can unduly influence how women shape their career lives.[69]

Abortion rights appeared to be the issue that women nationally pointed to as proof that more women needed to be elected to office. Westchester was the organization of women members formed in 1983 and dedicated to encouraging women's election to office and the promotion of issues of importance to women. By the 1990s, the caucus struggled to find issues the membership could rally around.[73] In 1992, women's rights and abortion had not yet become the source of conflict in Westchester that they were elsewhere. But the Republican Goodhue failed to generate broad outrage on her behalf among Democratic women or women's funding groups. The implication is that party affiliation would conflict with and ultimately limit women's solidarity.

The divisive trend evident in the 1992 Westchester elections rested on a different foundation. The parties were splitting apart over fiscal issues. Change-NY and the Conservative Party's support of George Pataki was part of a successful effort to reframe New York Republicans as more conservative, particularly on taxation and spending. The shift also included support for tougher criminal penalties and reforms of social programs. Goodhue's moderate Republicanism was overwhelmed by a shifting tide that ultimately carried Pataki to the governorship in 1994. The Conservative Party derisively called Goodhue a "relic of the Rockefeller era."[74] Pataki successfully tested this new message against the popular Goodhue and redeployed it two years later against Mario Cuomo, finding it especially effective with suburban voters.[75] Pataki carried every county north of New York City except Albany. The 1994 Republican nominee for attorney general, Dennis Vacco of Erie County, who was pro–death penalty and antiabortion, beat former State Senator Karen Burstein by 88,340 votes.[76]

This party reorientation left Goodhue at odds with where her party was going. Research of voting patterns at both the national and state levels indicates that Republican women have been more willing to cross party lines to vote for Democratic women than vice versa.[77] Moderate Republican women could not then expect to be "saved" in office by crossover women's votes. In the end there was really no "Year of the Woman" for Westchester's Republican woman senator.

A Final Assessment of the "Year of the Woman"

At the state level, 1992 did not make gender an ongoing salient element in campaigns beyond that single election cycle. Increases in the number of women elected to the legislature after that year have neither been steady nor related directly to women campaigning as women. Even as more women have been elected to state legislatures the result has been a lessening of areas where women find common cause on issues. Scholars are thus divided over whether or not a critical mass of women legislators, considered as 20 to 30 percent of the whole, results in significant progress on women's issues.[78] The idea that 1992 was a launching pad for women's greater political representation because of women's solidarity as women was tempered by the limited subsequent growth in the number of elected women and by the unique circumstances of individual states that may better explain women's progress or lack of it.[79] But 1992 does point to the political sophistication and readiness of New York's women politicians to run for and win office. These women's backgrounds and experience were extensive. They were able to combine that experience with nods to gender identity, as appropriate. While not "running as a woman" per se, these Westchester candidates ran as experienced politicians who, in addition, could represent a woman's perspective in the legislature.

Three final points deserve mention. The first is that women's growing political experience, while increasingly helpful, was not always a pathway to electoral victory. Joni Yoswein, who broke a kind of glass ceiling by becoming Speaker Miller's chief of staff in 1987, lost a 1992 bid for her own full term in her mentor's former seat. Miller had represented Brooklyn in the Assembly since 1971; he held the speakership from 1987 to 1991. Yoswein had begun working for Miller as an intern while still an undergraduate. She moved on to a position in his local office and to other administrative positions in the Democratic leadership before assuming the chief of staff. In all, Yoswein had fourteen years of legislative experience before running in 1992, as well as years of activity in the grassroots politics of local party clubs.[80] But Miller lost the speakership and seat following a 1991 conviction for colluding with his law partner from their private practice to cheat clients out of profits associated with real estate transactions. Yoswein never distanced herself from her boss; she and most fellow Democrats had believed he would be exonerated.[81] Yoswein said she ran—first in a January 1992 special election and then for a full term in November—"because (as she later recalled) I had earned the right to run and I did it for Mel [Miller]."[82] For good or ill, Yoswein's political fortunes were tied to Miller's. His endorsement helped her win the January special election. But her September primary opponent tarred Yoswein as the organization candidate and suggested that as Miller's aide she may have been complicit in wrongdoing. In this race her opponent, James Brennan, presented himself as the outsider and the woman as the insider. The *New York Times* called the contest the "the nastiest of the season."[83]

The second point relates to the "Year of the Woman" assumption that increasing the number of elected women was crucial to the success of a woman's agenda. While that might be a positive outcome, less attention was paid to how the mantra "running as a woman" could also stymie women legislators' efforts to avoid being pigeonholed into areas traditionally considered of interest to women. When she first arrived in the legislature in 1982, the leadership pushed Aurelia Greene to promote as her first piece of legislation, a bill requiring police to hold the undergarments of women involved in assault cases for investigation rather than discarding them after twenty-four hours. Greene was conflicted about being too much associated with women's issues and made it clear she was not there just to represent women's concerns. Even in the case of the Legislative Women's Caucus, which she helped create, Greene saw the effort as much about training members to be effective politicians as it was about identifying women's issues.[84] By 1992 Greene had already been in the Assembly for eight years. Two years later, in 1994, Greene was named chair of the Assembly Banking Committee, the first woman to hold that position. She counts her years of service there, often as the only woman among several dozen men, among her most significant accomplishments. As a minority woman and chair of the committee, Greene demonstrated her command of issues by securing what was called the nation's toughest legislation against predatory lending by financial institutions when it passed in 2001.[85] Greene remained very proud of her success at expanding her own legislative portfolio and the public's view of women's expertise into new areas.

Finally, though much of the year's politics concentrated on women's political impact as women, these electoral results were consistent with broader shifts that had begun appearing well before the 1992 electoral cycle and that affected all candidates, regardless of gender. After 1974, Democrats consistently controlled the Assembly with most of the party's electoral strength concentrated in New York City and a few Upstate cities. The party's support for more social programs and spending investments appealed to women voters. Scholarship has shown that women are typically more moderate in their views, which makes them more likely to identify as Democrats. At the same time, with the creation of the Conservative Party in 1962, Republicans began migrating away from those positions and challenging the moderation of leading New York Republicans like Governor Nelson Rockefeller and

Senator Jacob Javits. By 1992, Democrats increasingly contested Republicans for influence in suburban areas. Over time, the growing Democrat majority in the Assembly and an increased presence in the Senate would come from the suburbs. In 1992, a majority of Westchester's assembly delegation fit that profile, being Democrat and female. One could make the argument that it was the shift of the suburbs toward Democratic majorities that created the opportunities these women exploited. In that case, gender was useful but, again, not determinative of electoral success.

Circumstances on the ground in Westchester County in 1992 clearly support the importance of conducting targeted state-by-state analyses of women's electoral progress. While gender may have received the most media attention, the Westchester election was equally if not more about the efforts by Democrats and Republicans to control a county whose influence was on the rise. For Democrats, candidates who seemed like they could win got party support. For Republicans, it was a chance to test a rebranded image of themselves for future contests. In the end, the 1992 Westchester elections have proven as elusive to pin down as has been the very idea of the "Year of the Woman" itself.

Conclusion

As the twentieth century came to a close, a number of political scientists asked some variant of the question what has changed for the woman politician at the state level? What they found at the macrolevel both resembles and differs from the experiences of the women in this study. The analysts found that some characteristics of male and female legislators converged though clear differences remained. Those differences may partly explain women's lack of progress at significantly increasing their numbers in the 1990s and early 2000s.[1] Once in office, though, male and female legislators have continued to operate with noticeably different styles and emphases. Yet, the generic political skill set of women and men has converged. Neither gender holds an advantage in getting things done once elected, though they may prioritize issues differently and exhibit different leadership styles.[2]

On a national level, in the early 2000s, political scientists Kira Sanbonmatsu and Susan Carroll examined changes in the pathway to elected office for women and men.[3] Sanbonmatsu, in particular, found that women, because they traditionally came from occupational backgrounds different from men, were still excluded from what she called the "social eligibility pool" when it comes to candidate selection.[4] Nationally, she found that being a lawyer continued to be a primary background path to office for male legislators. But for women that did not hold as true. She cited women's historically different preparation for officeholding and their concentration in certain female-dominated occupations as reasons why.[5] That differing preparation was intertwined with women's traditional responsibilities for home and family. Researchers found evidence that marriage and family continued to delay women's entry into politics, that these factors were still a greater impediment for women than men.[6]

The background of New York's women legislators showed that the history of women's early political awakening did influence their careers, more so in the decades immediately after suffrage and less so as time progressed. Broadly speaking, women everywhere were affected by the professional and cultural norms that existed in American society. New York's pioneer generation crafted their résumés around their community work in private organizations, often all female. In presenting themselves that way, the women stood apart from traditional politics. They were women elected to office as opposed to women politicians. Marguerite Smith illustrates the difference between seeking to be a politician and being drawn to serve. She first refused the honor of having been nominated to run for the Assembly by the Republican Party in 1919. She initially said she had too much community work to do but later relented.[7] Going forward, New York's women legislators from the activist era on have matched their male counterparts in earning law degrees or in having direct political experience of some kind prior to running. As the twentieth century ended, women routinely applied the political label to themselves. Even in the pioneer generation, New York's women had more education overall than women in general at the time. A majority also had done some kind of work outside the home.

Still, New York women's decisions about when to run for office were affected by gendered cultural attitudes. Pioneer-era women disproportionally waited until children were grown, while others who ran often never married or ran as widows. Over time, New York's women legislators, like those nationwide, became more comfortable with combining marriage and legislative service.[8] Some activist women had small children while in office. Only Jean Amatucci, who left the legislature 1978, did so to start a family. Yet, it was a span of thirty-seven years between the first and second times a sitting legislator gave birth; Assemblywoman Gordon had a daughter in 1950 and Senator Montgomery a son in 1987. Both women stayed in the legislature, Gordon for another twelve years and Montgomery until her retirement in 2020. Overall, the trend both nationally and in New York has been for women to run for the legislature at a younger age.[9] Women still noted the extra pressure on career that came with motherhood. Nonetheless, New York women legislators grew increasingly comfortable with expressing outright political ambitions.

While the demographics surrounding who runs changed for women, women's connection to issues continued to be a more significant factor in women's decision to run than it did for men.[10] This issues focus is also something women carried over from their unique presuffrage background. The public has continued to perceive women as being both more knowledgeable and empathetic on issues that involve families, children, and the quality of community life. New York's women legislators made the most of this, increasing their connection to constituents, which prompted the legislature to adopt the concept of district offices. The limiting factor for women early on was finding themselves clustered on a narrow spectrum of committees, supposedly the closest to women's areas of interest. What time has done is allow women to expand their portfolio of issues into areas previously deemed more appropriate to male leadership, as Assemblywoman Greene did with banking and finance and Assemblywoman Weinstein with becoming chair of the Ways and Means Committee. This pattern of change has played out for both the woman candidate and the woman officeholder.[11] For Carol Berman of Long Island, concern for community expanded into the environmental issue of noise pollution, and became the signature issue of her candidacy for the Senate in 1978. Though she initially ran as someone concerned with mental health issues, Assemblywoman Connelly also took up the challenge to her district's environment when she pursued legal action to shut down Fresh Kills on Staten Island, New York City's only remaining landfill by the 1980s.[12] Nationally, regardless of where women legislators focus their attention, they continue to show that they prioritize issues over personal political advancement more so than male colleagues.[13] This was one way women overtly used the gendered constraints existing in society. They maximized their leverage in traditional areas by broadening the definition of those areas.

Women have brought more attention to women's issues big and small. From Genesta Strong's battle for oleo margarine to Constance Cook's crusade for abortion reform, women's presence has meant that issues stayed alive from session to session. The Legislative Women's Caucus has added its collective voice on some issues, giving greater weight to women's concerns. At the same time, women have had to face up to divisions within their ranks that undercut the idea that women speak with one voice. Political scientist Cindy Simon Rosenthal sees an upside to these divisions. From the 1980s on, as women became a larger presence in state legislatures, these differences represent women's increased ability to be seen as individuals rather than as symbols of their gender.[14] The balance sought then becomes one of maintaining the idea of a group voice on issues, even as individuals stand out from within the whole.

The most effective women legislators from the pioneer generation on have been those who acclimated to the legislative and political dynamics in New York and acquired a reputation for maneuvering within them to go along with their passion on issues. In the activist era, some women came to the New York legislature primed for action on issues, but faltered as they came up against the drive to professionalize and bureaucratize the legislative process. In contrast, legislators like Graves, Connelly, and Cook stand as success stories in terms of their leadership on issues and their political acumen. There is a correlation between the changing nature of the legislature itself and women's self-image as politicians. Nationally, research shows that women in highly professionalized legislatures are more likely to embrace the idea of politics as a career. As of the 1980s, more of New York's women have carved out careers in elective office. Many of those women's career résumés began at the local level and/or continued there after their terms in the state legislature.

Longer tenure in office has also given women access to leadership opportunities. As I write this, the New York State Senate is currently led by a Black woman, Andrea Stewart-Cousins, who was first elected in 2006 from a district encompassing much of Westchester County. The 1992 shift of Westchester's Assembly delegation to Democrat coupled with the heightened influence overall for the county in state politics contributed to Stewart-Cousin's elevation to Senate Majority Leader following a Democratic takeover of the chamber in the 2018 election. Like the women profiled in chapter 8, Stewart-Cousins's career began in Westchester, where she served for ten years, 1996–2006, in the county legislature. Widowed since 2007, Stewart-Cousins is a mother and a grandmother. Emblematic of that lingering tension between career and family, she only began here elective career at the county level at age forty-five and won the Senate seat at age fifty-six.

Becoming part of the legislative system has also meant that women have had deal with the ways that gender stereotypes have constrained their careers. One such stereotype has been the image of the woman as reformer. To be a reformer means to be on the outside looking in, which allows you to claim the moral high ground. This idea that women should be above the seamier side of politics has lingered and can negatively affect perceptions of the woman politician. Party loyalty, prized and expected for members, can be seen in a woman as the surrender of her integrity. Women politicians, from Ida Sammis to Joni Yoswein, have had to deal with accusations of their prioritizing politics over principle. The irony for women is that to win elections and have influence in office, they need to be inside one or the other major party. As women reach the leadership level in New York, their ability to be a voice for women competes with the requirements of party. Politicians all make compromises among competing interests. Women politicians have done so as well, even as they tried not to lose the high ground as issues warriors.

Finally, New York's women are a product of the state's own political history and dynamics. Women legislators, like their male counterparts, experienced marginalization when in the minority and achieved successes when in the majority. In the first half of the twentieth century, Republican women had more legislative successes because of that party's control of both houses. Even though New York State's population increases fueled urban and suburban growth, politicians from rural areas had influence disproportionately higher than demographics warranted. That manufactured influence plus a moderate form of Republicanism on social issues enabled the party to compete for the governorship and hold off the growing influence of the Democratic Party until the 1970s. Republican women legislators thus had more successful careers up until population shifts and court decrees stripped the party of its electoral advantages. Since then, women from the cities and suburbs, especially around New York City, have had the more influential legislative careers. By 1992, a hefty majority of female legislators were Democrats. Republican women like Mary Goodhue and Cecile Singer represented moderate Republicanism in decline. Goodhue was out as of 1992 and Singer in 1994.

This study, and others like it from states around the country, put to bed the idea that you can generalize about women or overlook their diversity. In 1992, there were 1,373 women in the legislatures of the fifty states. That number reveals that women have everywhere successfully embraced and embedded themselves in the political process. I have tried to show how that process unfolded for New York's political women. These women worked hard to open the legislature to women, as well as win broad acceptance of both their presence and their contributions to the well-being of the state. They are part of the New York story that, if overlooked, leaves that story unfinished.

officials in both parties supported a woman's right to choose, though there were differences in the degree to which they supported limits on public financing or notification requirements. The antiabortion sentiment that existed was concentrated in the relatively new Right to Life Party, which fielded candidates in all the races but was not a factor in any. Because of the overall consensus in the county, it was harder for the women to own that issue. Only Matusow aggressively tied her 1992 campaign to it, and that seems to have been necessary more to secure enough financial support to run than reflecting a passionate commitment to a single women's issue. For her part, Republican Singer in no way identified herself with the women's movement. She saw it as a problematic force for legislative politics. In her eyes, the movement was too strident in its positions and unwilling to compromise.[70]

Hints of Division to Come

The Goodhue campaign talked about the unfairness of a male-led party trying to force out one of its few women officeholders. That strategy highlights a key element in New York elections and one that supporters of the "Year of the Woman" mostly avoided: differences by party. As far as Westchester was concerned, party differences among the women candidates were not all that significant in 1992. Goodhue and Singer were both considered moderate Republicans. They were relatively liberal on social issues and more inclined to support government programs to address those issues. To a degree, these Republican women won elections by drawing support from independents and even some Democrats. The Goodhue campaign should then have been able to generate broad cross-party attention and support as a "Year of the Woman" battleground contest. However, nationally there were signals that the parties were becoming more polarized along a liberal-conservative continuum. Nationally, issue polarization appeared early over women's rights.[71] In the 1950s and early 1960s, both parties had agreed on a women's rights agenda that stressed equality of treatment. By the late 1960s and into the 1970s, Democrats adopted a more strident rhetoric of liberation, while Republican support for traditionalism was derided by feminists as the embrace of inequality. Women at the state level in New York were beginning to exhibit some of the same inability to find common ground around gender. None of the women in the Westchester delegation saw a clear role for the Women's Legislative Caucus in Albany to play in their campaigns.[72] This

Notes

Introduction

1. "Women Run Legislature, but Men Have Last Word," *New York Times*, March 12, 1954, 29.

2. "Mystery of Murray Hall," *New York Tribune*, January 19, 1901, 5; "Murray Hall Fooled Many Shrewd Men," *New York Times*, January 18, 1901, 2. Hall's story is recounted in a series of *Times* stories from 1901, January 19, 3; January 20, 7; January 24, 16; January 29, 16. The story is also reported in the *New York Tribune* on January 18, 1901, 1; January 20, 6; January 29, 2.

3. For information on Senator Martin, see his obituary. *New York Times*, August 11, 1914, 9. *New York Times*, January 18, 1901, 2.

4. "Senator Martin Amazed," *Brooklyn Eagle*, January 18, 1901, 1.

5. Kristi Anderson, *After Suffrage: Women in Partisan and Electoral Politics before the New Deal* (Chicago: University of Chicago Press, 1996), 116; Sophonisba Preston Breckinridge, *Women in the Twentieth Century: A Study of Their Political, Social, and Economic Activities* (New York: McGraw-Hill, 1933), 324.

6. Gerald Benjamin and Robert Nakamura, eds., *The Modern New York State Legislature: Redressing the Balance* (NY: Rockefeller Institute of Government, 1991), 195–96. The three were Carol Bellamy, Karen Burstein, and Mary Ann Krupsak.

7. Anne Marie Cammisa and Beth Reingold, "Women in State Legislatures and State Legislative Research: Beyond Sameness and Difference," *State Politics & Policy Quarterly* 4, no. 2 (Summer 2004): 183.

8. Jeane Kirkpatrick, *Political Woman* (New York: Basic Books, 1974), 5, 17, 21–22.

9. Irene Diamond, "Female Legislators: Where Are They?" and "Both Woman and Legislator," in *Sex Roles in the State House* (New Haven: Yale University Press, 1977).

10. Suzanne O. Schenken, *Legislators and Politicians: Iowa's Women Lawmakers* (Ames: Iowa State University Press, 1995); Nancy Baker Jones and Ruth Winegarten, *Capitol Women: Texas Female Legislators 1923–1999* (Austin: University of

Texas Press, 2000); Beth Reingold, *Representing Women: Sex, Gender and Legislative Behavior in Arizona and California* (Chapel Hill: University of North Carolina Press, 2003); Heidi Osselaer, *Winning Their Place: Arizona Women in Politics 1883–1950* (Tucson: University of Arizona Press, 2009); Van Ingen, Linda, *Gendered Politics: Campaign Strategies in California Women Candidates 1912–1970* (Lanham: Lexington Books, 2017).

11. This approach has its limitations for I am well aware that individual women's careers straddled more than one era, and women's individual careers are more than the sum of a few characteristics.

12. Jones and Winegarten, *Capitol Women: Texas Female Legislators 1923–1999*, 17.

13. Michel-Rolph Trouillot, *Silencing the Past: Power and the Production of History* (Boston: Beacon Press, 2015), 26, 46, 48–49.

Chapter 1

1. Edward Schneier and John Brian Murtaugh, *New York Politics a Tale of Two Cities* (New York: M. E. Sharpe, 2001), xiii.

2. Ray Gunn, "Antebellum Society and Politics 1824–1860," in Milton M. Klein, ed., *The Empire State: A History of New York* (Ithaca: Cornell University Press, 2001), 317.

3. Schneier and Murtaugh, *New York Politics a Tale of Two Cities*, 9.

4. Gerald Benjamin, "The New York State Legislature," in Peter Eisenstadt, ed., *Encyclopedia of New York State* (Syracuse: Syracuse University Press, 2005), 878–80.

5. Jeffery Stonecash, "Introduction: the Sources of Conflict," in Robert Pecorella and Jeffrey Stonecash, eds., *Governing New York State Fifth Edition* (Albany: State University of New York Press, 2006): 11–15.

6. Benjamin and Nakamura, *The Modern New York State Legislature: Redressing the Balance*, 85–88.

7. See Richard Zacks, *Island of Vice: Theodore Roosevelt's Doomed Quest to Clean Up Sin-Loving New York* (New York: Doubleday, 2012).

8. Herbert Mitgang, *Once Upon a Time in New York: Jimmy Walker, Franklin Roosevelt, and the Last Great Battle of the Jazz Age* (New York: The Free Press, 2000), 168–69, 202–4.

9. S. Sara Monsoon, "The Lady and the Tiger: Women's Electoral activism in New York City before Suffrage," *Journal of Women's History* 2, no. 2 (Fall 1990): 100–35; Jo Freeman, "'One Man, One Vote; One Woman, One Throat': Women in NYC Politics 1890–1910," *American Nineteenth Century History* 1, no. 3 (Autumn 2000): 101–23.

10. Shirley Chisholm, *Unbought and Unbossed* (New York: Houghton Mifflin, 1970), 45, 65–68.

11. John C. Walter, ed., *The Harlem Fox: J. Raymond Jones and Tammany 1920–1970* (New York: State University of New York Press, 1989), 12, 128.

12. Schneier and Murtaugh, 66, 67, 106. The authors note that parties in New York have the ability to cross-endorse candidates, which allows them to claim some measure of any victories. Third parties that have more or less achieved stability in New York State are limited to Conservative, Liberal, Right to Life, and Working Families.

13. Jeffrey Stonecash and Amy Widestrom, "Political Parties and Elections," in *Governing New York State*, 50, 67.

14. Allan Nevins, *Herbert Lehman and His Era* (New York: Charles Scribner, 1963): 154–69.

15. Richard Norton Smith, *Thomas E. Dewey and His Times* (New York: Touchstone, 1962), 360

16. Joel Schwartz, "The Empire State in a Changing World," in Milton M. Klein, ed., *The Empire State: A History of New York*, 660–61.

17. Richard Norton Smith, *On His Own Terms: A Life of Nelson Rockefeller* (New York: Random House, 2014), 459–60.

18. Daniel C. Kramer, *The Days of Wine and Roses Are Over: Governor Hugh Carey and New York State* (Lanham: University of America Press, 1997); Schwartz, "The Empire State in a Changing World," in *Empire State*, 699, 703–5.

19. Jeffery Stonecash and Amy Widestrom, "Political Parties and Elections," in *Governing New York State*, 52.

20. Timothy J. Sullivan, *New York State and the Rise of Modern Conservatism: Redrawing Party Lines* (Albany: State University of New York Press, 2009), 122.

21. John W. Davis, the Democratic nominee in 1920, had West Virginia listed as his home state, but Davis's career was spent in New York as a Wall Street lawyer. Franklin Roosevelt was the VP nominee that year.

22. Between 1894 and 1938, the governor's term of office was two years. The constitutional reforms of 1938 extended the term to four years.

23. Gerald Benjamin and Elizabeth Benjamin, "New York's Governorship," in *Governing New York State*, 157.

24. Gerald Benjamin and Elizabeth Benjamin, "New York's Governorship," in *Governing New York State*, 142; John J. Pitney Jr., "Leaders and Rules in the New York State Senate," *Legislative Studies Quarter* 7, no. 4 (November 1982): 492: Schneier and Murtaugh: 150–58.

25. Jeffery Stonecash and Amy Widestrom, "Political Parties and Elections," in *Governing New York State*, 52.

26. Robert Pecorella, "The Two New Yorks in the Twenty-First Century," in *Governing New York State*, 8, 15.

27. Clark Ahlberg and Daniel P. Moynihan, "Changing Governors-and Policies," *Public Administration Review* 20. no. 4 (Autumn, 1960): 196.

28. Stonecash and Widestrom, "Political Parties and Elections," in *Governing New York State*, 54.

29. Ray Gunn, "Antebellum Society and Politics, in Milton M. Klein, ed., *The Empire State: A History of New York* (New York: New York State Historical Association, 2001): 357–58.

30. Paula Baker, "The Gilded Age," in Milton M. Klein, ed., *The Empire State: A History of New York*, 472–75.

31. Vincent Cannato, *The Ungovernable City John Lindsay and His Struggle to Save New York* (New York: Basic Books, 2001): chapter 8, "From Integration to Decentralization to Community Control: Reforming New York City Public Schools" and chapter 9, "Community Control and the 1968 Teachers Strike," esp. 348–50. Lindsay determined to redo the education system to decentralize its administration by creating locally elected boards. The resultant clash between the Black community and the teachers' unions doomed the larger goal of decentralization. But the precedent of community board involvement remained. A number of women who served in the legislature spent some time on these boards prior to and/or during their terms in the legislature.

32. "Albany Creates 7 Member Board for City Schools," *New York Times*, May 28, 1973, 1. The Legislature was forced to act after the framework for the elective board was successfully challenged in the courts on the grounds it did not meet the "one person one vote" standard. Each borough was to elect a member of the board but the boroughs had very different population. Also "Education Panel Is Urged to Alter Decentralization," *New York Times*, October 10, 1973, 51.

33. Roger Sanjek, *The Future of Us All: Race and Neighborhood Politics in NYC* (Ithaca: Cornell University Press, 1998), 3.

34. Roger Sanjek, "Color-Full before Color Blind: the Emergence of Multiracial Neighborhood Politics in Queens, New York City," *American Anthropologist* 102, no. 4: 763. See also Sanjek, *The Future of Us All*, 375 and chapters 10–15. Mayor Lindsey had earlier in 1967 experimented with the community board concept, which he dubbed "little city halls." See Cannato, *The Ungovernable City*, 111–12.

35. *The Modern New York Legislature*, interview with Stanley Steingut, 110–14; interview with Arthur Kremer, 140; interview with Albert Abrams, 197–207; interview with Robert Herman, 225.

36. Schneier and Murtaugh, *New York Politics a Tale of Two States*, 133; *The Modern New York Legislature*, xxiv, 42–44; Schneier and Murtaugh, 162–69; Stonecash and Widestrom, "Political Parties and Elections," in *Governing New York State*, 64–65.

37. Republicans had temporarily lost control of the Assembly between 1965 and 1968, as the result of both a Democratic presidential wave election in 1964 and court-ordered redistricting. Before that the Democrats were in the majority only in the single years of 1911, 1913, and 1935.

38. *WMCA v. Lomenzo*, Oyez website, accessed July 2, 2020, https://www.oyez.org/cases/1963/20.

39. Edward Schneier and John Brian Murtaugh, *New York Politics a Tale of Two Cities*, 85–88.

40. Schneier and Murtaugh, *New York Politics a Tale of Two States*, 133; *The Modern New York Legislature*, xxiv, 42–44; Schneier and Murtaugh, 162–69; Stonecash and Widestrom, "Political Parties and Elections," in *Governing New York State*, 64–65.

41. Schneier and Murtaugh, *New York Politics a Tale of Two States*, 24.

Chapter 2

1. Susan Goodier and Karen Pastorello, *Women Will Vote: Winning Suffrage in New York State* (Ithaca: Cornell University Press, 2017), 3.

2. The arguments and sources presented in this section on partisanship are taken from Lauren Kozakiewicz, "Political Episodes 1890–1960: Three Republican Women in Twentieth Century New York State Politics" (PhD diss., University at Albany, 2006), chapter 1, "The Partisan Dilemma: Womanhood and Politics, Historically Hard to Mix" and chapter 2, "Helen Varick Boswell 1890–1912, Winning Attention for Women in the World of Late Nineteenth Century Politics."

3. Richard McCormick, *The Party Period and Public History* (New York: Oxford University Press, 1986), 162–64, 201–4.

4. Paula Baker, "The Domestication of Politics: Women and the American Political System 1789–1920, *American Historical Review* 89 (June 1984): 628.

5. Michael McGerr, *The Decline of Popular Politics the American North 1865–1928* (Oxford: Oxford University Press, 1986): 14. For additional references to the masculine aspect of party politics in the nineteenth century, see also Mark L. Kornbluh, *Why America Stopped Voting* (New York: New York University Press, 2000), 18; Paula Baker, *The Moral Frameworks of Public Life: Gender Politics and the State in Rural New York 1830–1920* (New York: Oxford University Press, 1991), xiii.

6. For a discussion of partisanship in practice, see Kornbluh, *Why America Stopped Voting*, chapter 2, "Party Rule," 36–62.

7. Melanie Susan Gustafson. *Women and the Republican Party 1854–1924* (Urbana: University of Illinois Press, 2001), 3

8. Baker, "Domestication of Politics," 629–630. Baker argues that government in the nineteenth century largely relinquished economic regulation to business and the courts. As for social legislation, there was little history of government leadership in this area. Governments in the nineteenth century had limited goals revolving around distributory activities. This position is reiterated Seth Koven and Sonya Michel, "Womanly Duties: Maternalist Politics and the Origins of the Welfare States in France, Germany, Great Britain and the United States, 1880–1920," *American Historical Review* 95, no. 4 (October 1990): 1093.

9. Theda Skocpol, *Protecting Soldiers and Mothers: the Political Origins of Social Policy in the United States* (Boston: Harvard University Press, 1995), 2.

10. Elizabeth York Enstam, "They Called It 'Motherhood' Dallas Women and Public Life 1895–1918," in *Hidden Histories of Women in the New South*, ed.

Virginia Bernhard, B. Brandon, E. Fox-Genovese, T. Perdue, and E. Hayes Tunes (Columbia: University of Missouri Press, 1994), 73.

11. Jack Blocker, *"Give to the Winds Thy Fears": The Women's Temperance Crusade, 1873–74* (Westport: Greenwood Press, 1985), 3, 9–11.

12. Blocker, *"Give to the Winds Thy Fears,"* 223, 229. Blocker actually argues that the Women's Crusade, to which organizers of what became the WCTU referred as the point of origin, was based more on claims of direct individual harm from drink rather than a broader kind of feminist empowerment.

13. For a full discussion of the first generation WCTU organization and its activities, see Ruth Bordin, *Women and Temperance* (Philadelphia: Temple University Press, 1981) and *Frances Willard a Biography* (Chapel Hill: University of North Carolina Press, 1986). For a discussion of how WCTU reform activity persisted into the twentieth century see Alison Parker, *Purifying America Women, Cultural Reform, and Pro-Censorship Activism 1873–1933* (Urbana: University of Illinois Press, 1997).

14. Epstein credits Willard with helping refashion feminist politics into a broad-based movement that included support for suffrage by conventional mainstream women. By 1881 WCTU members felt comfortable enough with home protection arguments to endorse the "home protection" ballot. See Barbara Epstein, *The Politics of Domesticity: Women, Evangelism, and Temperance in the Nineteenth Century* (Middletown: Wesleyan Press, 1981), 9, 121, 147, and Bordin, *Women and Temperance*, 119. Willard had first publicly called for a suffrage commitment from the WCTU in 1876.

15. For a sense of the broadening application of those ideas see Molly Ladd-Taylor, *Mother-work, Women Child Welfare and the State 1890–1930* (Urbana: University of Illinois, 1994); Elizabeth J. Clapp, *Mothers of All Children Women Reformers and the Rise of Juvenile Courts in Progressive Era America* (University Park: Penn State University Press, 1998); Kathryn Kish Sklar, "Two Political Cultures in the Progressive Era: The National Consumer's Leagues and the American Association for Labor Legislation," in *US History as Women's History*; Maureen Flanagan, "The Predicament of New Rights: Suffrage and Women's Political Power from a Local Perspective," *Social Politics* (1995): 305–330.

16. Paula Baker, "The Gilded Age," in Milton M. Klein, ed., *The Empire State: A History of New York*, 472–73.

17. Baker, "The Gilded Age," 474.

18. Rebecca Edwards, *Angels in the Machinery Gender in American Party Politics from the Civil War to the Progressive Era* (New York: Oxford University Press, 1997).

19. Melanie Gustafson, "Florence Collins Porter and the Concept of the Principled Partisan Woman," *Frontiers: a Journal of Women's Studies* 18, no. 1 (Summer 1997): 10.

20. Gustafson, "Florence Collins Porter": 10.

21. Goodier and Pastorello, *Women Will Vote*, 14, 16.

22. Goodier and Pastorello, *Women Will Vote*, 25.

23. Lisa Tetrault, *The Myth of Seneca Falls: Memory and the Women's Suffrage Movement, 1848–1898* (Chapel Hill: University of North Carolina Press, 2017).

24. Tetrault, *The Myth of Seneca Falls*, 35.

25. Tetrault, *The Myth of Seneca Falls*, 45.

26. With regard to the WCTU, Leslie Epstein has shown the connection was not based on the equal rights feminism so characteristic of the suffrage movement from the 1850s through the 1870s. Epstein credits Willard with helping refashion feminist politics into a broad-based movement that included support for suffrage by conventional mainstream women. By 1881 WCTU members felt comfortable enough with home protection arguments to endorse the "home protection" ballot. See Leslie Epstein, *The Politics of Domesticity: Women, Evangelism, and Domesticity in Nineteen-Century America* (Middletown: Wesleyan University Press, 1981), 9, 121, 147, and Bordin, *Women and Temperance*, 119. Willard had first publicly called for a suffrage commitment from the WCTU in 1876.

27. For the evolution of the single issue perspective within the suffrage movement see Jean H. Baker, ed. *Votes for Women the Struggle for Suffrage Revisited*. Viewpoints on American Culture Series (Oxford: Oxford University Press, 2002).

28. Baker, "Domestication of Politics," 638.

29. S. Sara Monsoon, "The Lady and the Tiger: Women's Electoral activism in New York City before Suffrage, *Journal of Women's History* 2, no. 2 (Fall 1990): 100–35.

30. Goodier and Pastorello, *Women Will Vote*, 50.

31. Jo-Ann Argersinger, ed., *The Triangle Fire: A Brief History with Documents* (Boston: Bedford St. Martins, 2016), 3–4.

32. Ellen Carol Dubois, "The Next Generation of Suffragists: Harriot Stanton Blatch and Grassroots Politics," in Linda Kerber, Jane de Hart, Cornelia Hugh Dayton, eds., *Women's America: Refocusing the Past*, 7th ed. (New York: Oxford University Press, 2011), 421.

33. Goodier and Pastorello, *Women Will Vote*, 164.

34. Elisabeth Israels Perry, *After the Vote: Feminist Politics in La Guardia's New York* (New York: Oxford Press, 2019), 27–28.

35. Perry, *After the Vote*, 28.

36. Material and sources for the campaign train are taken from Lauren Kozakiewicz, "To Pure for Politics? Women, Non-Partisanship and the Hughes Campaign Train of 1916," unpublished paper, part of the panel Women and Electoral Politics in the Long 1920s, American Historical Association 125th Annual Conference, January 8, 2011.

37. *New York Times*, October 3, 1916, 10.

38. There were daily newspaper reports on the progress of the train in both the *New York Times* and *New York Tribune*.

39. Maude Elliott, "The Golden Special," Maude Howe Elliott Papers Ms.89.13 (Box 19, Folders 1–13), Brown University Special Collection Department, 64, 142.

Historians generally describe the women on the train as having reform backgrounds and associations with the Progressive Party in 1912. Examples of secondary analysis include Molly Wood, "Mapping a Campaign Strategy: Partisan Women in the Presidential Election of 1916," in Gustafson, et al., *We Have Come to Stay: American Women in Political Parties* (Albuquerque: University of New Mexico Press, 1999), 81; incomplete profiles of some leaders in J. Leonard Bates and Vanette M. Schwartz, "Golden Special Campaign Train," *Montana, the Magazine of Western History* (Summer 1987): 26–35; and short biographies of several participants in Edward T. James, et al., *Notable American Women 1607–1950*, 3 vols. (Cambridge: Harvard University Press, 1971). Maude Howe Elliott began a memoir, never published, about the train.

40. Elliott, "The Golden Special," 6. *New York Times*, August 2, 1916, 1; Jo Freeman, *We Will Be Heard: Women's Struggles for Political Power in the United States* (New York: Rowman & Littlefield, 2008), 73.

41. *New York Times*, October 17, 1916, 4; Elliott "The Golden Special," 38.

42. Kellor, *Women in National Politics*, 25.

43. For a broader look at women's party-centered organizing presuffrage that includes Foster's activities, see Kozakiewicz, "Political Episodes"; chapter 2, 73–92.

44. Jo Freeman, *A Room at a Time: How Women Entered Party Politics* (Lanham: Rowman & Littlefield, 2000), 82, 86–88, 96–98.

45. Freeman, *A Room at a Time*, 114–122.

46. Freeman, *A Room at a Time*, 167–68.

47. William Riordon, ed., *Plunkitt of Tammany Hall* (Boston: Bedford Books, 1994 ed.), 58. The collection of interviews with Plunkitt was first published in 1905.

48. "Urges Suffragists Not to Stand Alone," *New York Times*, December 17, 1917, 12.

49. Mary Boyd Sumner, *The Woman Citizen: A General Handbook of Civics, with Special Consideration of Women's Citizenship* (New York: Frederick A. Stokes, 1918), 137. Sumner was a specialist in suffrage education. This was meant as a civics handbook, explaining the mechanics of government operation and voting. It also featured chapters on each of the national parties. Those chapters were written by women party supporters.

50. Anna Harvey, *Votes without Leverage* (Cambridge: Cambridge University Press, 1998), 155.

51. "Rules of Republican County Committee Changed to Admit More Women," *New York Times*, June 21, 1918, 8.

52. Kate M. Bostwick, "Women's Political Clubs," the *Monthly Illustrator* (December 1896), 304.

53. *New York Times*, June 26, 1918, 6.

54. *New York Times*, June 16, 1928, 18.

55. Harvey, *Votes without Leverage*, 155, 160.

56. Harvey, *Votes without Leverage*, 2. Several examples of the failed issues advocacy of women at this time include the failed Women's Joint Congressional

Committee of the 1920s and the League of Women Voters decision to withdraw from issues advocacy in favor of civic education. See also Freeman, *A Room at a Time*: 124–29, 203–5.

57. Harvey, *Votes without Leverage*, 66.

58. Irene Diamond, *Sex Roles in the State House* (New Haven: Yale University Press, 1977), 1, 36, 38, 45; Richard Fox and Jennifer Lawless, "Gendered Perceptions and Political Candidates: A Central Barrier to Women's Equality in Electoral Politics," *American Journal of Political Science* 55, no. 1 (January 2011): 60, 70; J. Miller McPherson and Lynn Smith-Lovin, "Sex Segregation in Voluntary Associations," *American Sociological Review* 51, no. 1 (February 1986): 75.

59. Perry, *After the Vote*, 47.

60. "Women in State Legislatures for 2017," National Conference of State Legislators website, published 11/7/2017, http://www.ncsl.org/legislators-staff/legislators/womens-legislative-network/women-in-state-legislatures-for-2017.aspx.

61. Quoted in Diamond, *Sex Roles in the Statehouse*, 30.

62. Michelle Saint-Germain, "Does Their Difference Make a Difference? The Impact of Women on Public Policy in the Arizona Legislature," *Social Science Quarterly* 70, no. 4 (1989): 958.

63. Kathleen Dolan and Lynne E. Ford, "Are All Women State Legislators Alike?," in *Women and Elective Office: Past, Present, and Future*, Sue Thomas and Clyde Wilcox, eds. (New York: Oxford University Press, 1998), 75.

Chapter 3

1. *New York Times*, April 23, 1966, 43. As Aileen Ryan left the legislature to assume a seat on the New York City Council, a debate broke out about the legality of calling someone a councilwoman. Several members thought the legal title had to be councilman.

2. "Two Women Legislators Making Their Presence Felt in Albany," *Brooklyn Daily Eagle*, January 19, 1919, 7.

3. *Syracuse Journal*, January 10, 1919, 8.

4. Through 1937, elections for the Assembly were held annually. Since 1938, elections have been held every two years with two-year terms for the Assembly and two-year terms for the Senate. Voters rejected four-year Senate terms in 1938 and 1941, and for all legislators in 1965. See Gerald Benjamin and Henrik N. Dullea, eds., *Decision 1997* (Albany, State University of New York Press, 1997), 73–74.

5. While Assemblywoman Cook began her legislative career in 1963, the majority of her time falls into the next era considered in chapter 4.

6. Jeane Kirkpatrick, *Political Woman* (New York: Basic Books, 1974), 219.

7. Jo Freeman, *A Room at a Time: How Women Entered Party Politics* (New York: Rowman & Littlefield, 2002).

8. Kristi Anderson, *After Suffrage*, 2, 15, 150.

9. "Widow Nominated for Assembly, *New York Times*, February 14, 1942, 10; *New York Times*, February 17, 1942, 10; *Brooklyn Daily Eagle*, March 10, 1942, 1.

10. "First Assemblywoman Takes Honor Modestly," *Brooklyn Daily Eagle*, February 20, 1942, 4.

11. "Politics and People," *Brooklyn Daily Eagle*, July 22, 1954, 2.

12. Aileen Ryan Obituary, *New York Times*, August 10, 1987; "Woman Politician Began in Scouts," *New York Times*, July 20, 1958, 24.

13. "Dorothy Bell Lawrence Campaigns," *New Pittsburgh Courier*, September 9, 1961, 6; "Woman Opposes Dudley for Post," *New York Times*, October 30, 1961, 20.

14. "Woman Opposes Dudley for Post," *New York Times*, October 30, 1961, 20.

15. "Newcomer Mines Legislative Gold," *New York Times*, March 24, 1959, 27.

16. Jane Mathews, "The Woman Suffrage Movement in Suffolk County New York 1911–1917: A Case Study of the Tactical Differences between Two Prominent Long Island Suffragists: Mrs. Ida Bunce Sammis and Miss Rosalie Jones" (master's thesis, Adelphi University, 1988), 10, 12, 16.

17. "Mrs. Sammis to Seek Nomination," *Brooklyn Daily Eagle*, June 17, 1918, 5.

18. Biographical entry for Marguerite Smith in the *New York Red Book: An Illustrated State Manual for 1920* (Albany: J. B. Lyons, 1925).

19. "Assemblyman Miss Smith of Harlem," *New York Times*, November 9, 1919, XXI.

20. "Negro to Oppose Woman," *New York Times*, August 30, 1919, 18.

21. "Assemblyman Miss Smith of Harlem," *New York Times*, November 9, 1919, XXI.

22. Jane Mathews, *The Woman Suffrage Movement*, 82.

23. *Brooklyn Standard Union*, November 15, 1919, 3.

24. *Auburn Citizen Advertiser*, January 12, 1934, 2.

25. *Syracuse Post Standard*, April 20, 1919, 5.

26. "Women must Organize New Party 'Asserts Ida B. Sammis Satchwell,'" *New York Sun*, June 20, 1934, 27.

27. "Republicans Gain Eleven Seats," *New York Times*, November 5, 1919, 1.

28. *Huntington Long Islander*, November 10, 1933; December 8, 1933, II:5; January 19, 1934, II:1; August 10, 1934; July 27, 1935, II:6.

29. Kristi Anderson. *After Suffrage*, 25, cites the persistence of the association of women with piety and domesticity as a factor in women's slow path to electoral success; Jeane Kirkpatrick, "Participant Woman: Values, Life Styles, and Personalities," in *Political Woman*, 45–50, observes women legislators mid-twentieth century and notes they have a history of mirroring traditional ideas about womanhood in their behavior and values; Daniel Hayes, "When Gender and Party Collide: Stereotyping in Candidate Trait Attribution," *Politics and Gender* 7 (2011): 135, begins a present-day assessment of the persistence gender stereotyping by citing a long line of research supporting the thesis that gender attributes had historically been regularly applied to women candidates.

30. "Acting Speaker Smith," *New York Times*, April 23, 1920, 1 and April 26, 1920, 12. The article used the term *parliamentary* when referring to Smith's actions, suggesting it was her ability to use the rules to keep the other legislators in line.

31. New York approved a fifty-four-hour-a-week work limit for women and minors in 1912. The law also included a prohibition on late-night work. Critics argued that the prohibition on night work effectively barred women from certain, potentially more lucrative, kinds of employment. During this period the WTUL was pushing for a lower threshold with a forty-eight-hour bill. The forty-eight-hour bill would become law in 1927.

32. "Assembly Proposal A190 to Amend the Labor Law on Women Workers and Maximum Work Hours," chapter 489 of *The Laws of 1921*, New York State Library, Albany, NY; "League Would Defeat City Assemblywoman," *New York Times*, October 31, 1921, 2.

33. The divide is covered here in Nancy Cott, "Equal Rights and Economic Roles: The Conflict Over the Equal Rights Amendment in the 1920s," in *Women's America: Refocusing the Past*, 8th ed., Linda Kerber, Sharon De Hart, Cornelia Dayton, and Judy Wu, eds. (New York: Oxford University Press, 2015), 503–12.

34. *The Red Book: An Illustrated State Manual for 1919* (Albany: J. B. Lyons, 1919), "Amendment to the State Labor Law," chapter 544 of *The Laws of 1919*; *Watkins New York Express*, March 26, 1919, 1.

35. "Women Fail to Agree on Welfare Measures," *New York Times*, March 6, 1919, 7.

36. "B.R.T. Women Beg Smith for Aid," *New York Times*, May 25, 1919, 1

37. Edward Schneier and John Brian Murtaugh, eds., *New York Politics a Tale of Two States*, 23–24.

38. The exceptions were the Senate in the 1932 election and both houses in the 1964 election. In 1933 Republicans lost the Senate for one two-year period when Democrats held a slim majority with twenty-six out of fifty-one seats. 1964 was another Democratic wave year nationally. But due to the outcome of disputes over representation, the winners of the 1964 election received only one-year terms and a special off year election took place in 1965, under new apportionment rules.

39. "New York State Legislature," in *the Encyclopedia of New York*, 877–80.

40. *New York Evening Post*, March 4, 1926, 5; *New York Times*, January 18, 1928, 11; *Hammond New York Advertiser*, September 11, 1924, 2.

41. Lauren Kozakiewicz, "Political Episodes 1890–1960: Three Republican Women In Twentieth Century in Twentieth-Century New York State Politics," 290–295.

42. *New York Times*, March 12, 1952, 19.

43. *New York Times*, March 25, 1955, 18; *New York Times*, February 25, 1957, 1.

44. Scheneier, *New York Politics*, 23.

45. *New York Times*, December 1, 1933, 16.

46. *New York Times*, May 30, 1964. 13; *New York Times*, August 2, 1965, 26.

47. *Brooklyn Daily Eagle*, February 20, 1942, 4.

48. "Legislature's Youngest Member is a Mother Now, *New York Herald Tribune*, June 14, 1950; Obituary, *New York Times*, September 19, 1990, B6.

49. "Support Mrs. Lilly," *Brooklyn Daily Eagle*, September 30, 1918, 16.

50. "Woman Politician Began in Scouts," *New York Times*, July 20, 1958, 42.

51. Julie Gallagher, *Black Women and Politics in New York City* (Urbana: University Illinois Press, 2012), 60.

52. Gallagher, *Black Women*: 104–5; articles in the *New York Age* that show her vying for "Best Dressed Woman" in Harlem, February 21, 1953, 5 and February 26, 1953, 5.

53. "Two Women Legislators Making Their Presence Felt in Albany," *Brooklyn Daily Eagle*, January 19, 1919, 7.

54. Senate Resolution 917 of the Laws of 1942.

55. "Albany Bill to Ask State Arts Council," *New York Times*, February 14, 1960, 59; "Candid Candidate," *New York Times,* July 18, 1961, 18; "Vote on Hammarskjold Tribute," *New York Times*, March 21, 1962, 30; "State Votes Tribute to Hammarskjold, *New York Times*, March 22, 1962, 27.

56. *Red Book* entry; *New York Times*, January 10, 1919, 6.

57. *Buffalo Evening News*, January 11, 1926, 14.

58. *New York Times*, February 20, 1936, 4.

59. "Enter the Woman," *Commercial Advertiser*, May 27, 1924, 4.

60. *Hammond NY Advertiser*, May 29, 1924, 1; *Gloversville Morning Herald*, November 3, 1924, 9.

61. *New York Times*, March 3, 1928, 3.

62. Letter from Rhoda Fox Graves to Harold Johnson, Publisher of the *Watertown Daily Times*, April 3, 1940, in the Papers of Rhoda Fox Graves, Gouverneur Museum, Gouverneur, NY. These materials currently reside at the M. E. Grenander Department of Special Collections and Archives, University Libraries, University at Albany SUNY (hereafter known as Graves Papers).

63. *New York Times*, May 16, 1944, 14.

64. "Extension of Bridge Commission," in the Legislative Jacket for "An Act to Amend the Motor Vehicle Law," chapter 94 of *The Laws of 1935*; Legislative Jacket for "An Act to Amend the Tax Law, in Relation to Personal Income Tax Exemptions," chapter 319 of *The Laws of 1929*, microfilm, New York State Library, Albany, NY; "Rural Areas Fight for the School Law," *New York Times*, March 30, 1939, 14; Letter from Rhoda Fox Graves to Mrs. Charles McArthur, February 1, 1931, on supporting rural school concerns, in the Graves Papers.

65. "Press Release Announcing Senatorial Candidacy," July 7, 1932, in the Graves Papers.

66. "Relieves His Party of Load," *New York Times*, June 12, 1934, 5. From 1926 through 1932, Thayer had received 27,000 dollars from the Associated Gas

and Electric Company, supposedly as compensation for his interests in a power company purchased by Associated Gas. In addition to a number of irregularities in the arrangement itself, payments ceased abruptly when the Democrats won a Senate Majority in 1932, and Thayer was no longer chair of the Senate Public Service Committee.

67. Letter from Rhoda Fox Graves to George McIntyre, July 20, 1927, letter to Mr. and Mrs. James Moor, February 11, 1926, Graves Papers.

68. Letter from Rhoda Fox Graves to Harold Johnson, editor of the *Watertown Daily Times*, April 3, 1940, Graves Papers.

69. "Seeks Milk Price Inquiry," *New York Times*, February 24, 1931, 34.

70. Text of the Statement by Rhoda Fox Graves to the State Senate, March 28, 1936, Graves Papers.

71. "Milk Audit Draws Labor Party Fire," *New York Times*, February 9, 1938, 4.

72. Legislative Jacket for "An Act to Suspend for a Limited Period of Time the Effectiveness of Sections Sixty-Five and Sixty-Six of the Agriculture and Markets Law," chapter 9 of *The Laws of 1948*, microfilm, New York State Library, Albany, NY.

73. Letter from Kenneth Fake, Legislative Representative of the New York Grange to Charles Breitel, Counsel to the Governor," Legislative jacket for "An Act to Suspend for a Limited Period of Time the Effectiveness of Sections Sixty-Five and Sixty-Six of the Agriculture and Markets Law," chapter 9 of *The Laws of 1948* microfilm, New York State Library, Albany, NY.

74. "Agricultural and Environmental Issues," in Suzanne O. Schenken, *Legislators and Politicians: Iowa's Women Lawmakers*, 136–140.

75. "Oleo Under Federal Law 1886–1949," *Congressional Digest* 28, no. 5 (May 1949): 135–36.

76. "Colored Oleo Bill Put Off in Albany," *New York Times*, February 24, 1949, 17.

77. "Dewey Attempts to Save Oleo Bill," *New York Times*, February 21, 1950, 5.

78. "Oleo Bills Killed by Assembly Unit," *New York Times*, February 2, 1950, 18.

79. *Binghamton Press*, March 22, 1946, 20.

80. "State Is Unlikely to End Oleo Curb," *New York Times*, January 20, 1950, 15.

81. "State Is Unlikely to End Oleo Curb," 15.

82. "Senate Group Bars Yellow Oleo Sale," *New York Times*, February 22, 1950, 22.

83. "Fight Ebbs in State on legalizing Oleo," *New York Times*, January 10, 1951, 29.

84. "Storm Claims Bill Passed by Senate," *New York Times*, February 16, 1951, 27.

85. "'Messy' Oleo Coloring Job Displayed in Assembly," *New York Times*, February 12, 1952, 12.

86. "Yellow Oleo Wins in Assembly Test," *New York Times*, February 28, 1952, 1, 16, 17.

87. "Oleo Ban Ended by the State, *New York Times*, March 7, 1952, 21. Legislative Jackets for "An Act to Amend the Agriculture and Markets Law in Relation to the Manufacture and Sale of Oleomargarine, Butterine, and Similar Substances," chapter 97 of *The Laws of 192*, microfilm, New York State Library, Albany, NY.

88. *New York Times*, March 9, 1952, 58.

89. *New York Times*, March 7, 1958. 25; *Jamestown Post Journal*, March 7, 1958, 3.

90. "Assembly Votes School Spanking," *New York Times*, March 12, 1959, 18.

91. *New York Times*, April 23, 1959, 13.

92. "Woman Suffrage Amendment Wind in Legislature," *New York Times*, June 17, 1919, 1.

93. Chapter 1, "An Act to Amend and Repeal the Conservation Law with Respect to Duck Hunting," and chapter 39, "An Act to Amend the Conservation Law to Regulate the Catching of Scallops," chapters 1 and 39 of *The Laws of 1919*; *Syracuse Post Standard*, April 20, 1919, 5.

94. In 1937, twenty-one states allowed women to serve on juries; in nine states it was mandatory and in ten states plus the District of Columbia it was permissive. See "States that Admit Jurors," *New York Times*, January 17, 1937, VI 9.

95. "Assembly Passes Women Jury Bills," *New York Times*, March 27, 1935, 23.

96. "Assembly Passes Women Jury Bills," 23.

97. "Women Jury Bill in Test Tomorrow," *New York Times*, February 9, 1936, N7. As early as 1934, the Republican state chairman, W. Kingsland Macy, had expressed public support for women's jury service. See "Woman Jurors' Law Is Favored by Macy," *New York Times*, March 4, 1934, 29.

98. Kozakiewicz, "Political Episodes": 300; Elisabeth Israels Perry, "Rhetoric Strategy, and Politics in the New York Campaign for Women's Jury Service, 1917–1975," *New York History* (Winter 2001): 67–69.

99. Kozakiewicz, "Political Episodes": 300–1.

100. Perry, "Rhetoric, Strategy, and Politics," 65–66.

101. "Albany Bills End Jury Duty Option, *New York Times*, January 27, 1950, 14; "Jury Duty Is Voted for State's Women," *New York Times*, February 28, 1950, 7; "Vote on Jury Duty for Women Is Set," *New York Times*, March 2, 1951, 20.

102. "An Act to Amend the Judiciary Law in Relation to Repealing the Provisions Exempting a Woman from Jury Duty," chapter 4 of *The Laws of 1975*; Perry, "Rhetoric, Strategy, and Politics," 77.

103. "Divorce Reform Miracle," *New York Times*, April 30, 1966, 25. The history of New York's divorce law is laid out in Hendrik Hartog, *Man and Wife in America a History* (Cambridge: Harvard University Press, 2000): 71–74 and 244–57, and in Nelson Blake *The Road to Reno a History of Divorce in the United States* (Westport: Greenwood Press, 1962), 64–66, 119, 189–202, 203–25. Blake devotes two chapters to New York State specifically. Even in 1787, New York legislators

refused to consider a bill written by Alexander Hamilton to expand divorce criteria and make punishments less harsh (Blake, 64). Instead, New York adhered to an approach to divorce that classified the action as more criminal than anything else. There had to be a guilty and innocent party in each decision. The state felt justified in "punishing" the guilty party by denying the person the freedom to remarry (Hartog, 66, 72). Over time, the state did modify this prohibition, allowing the divorced party to remarry after a period of time.

104. Blake, *Road to Reno*, 190.

105. Blake, *Road to Reno*, 66.

106. Blake, *Road to Reno*, 194.

107. "Divorce Reform Killed in State This Year," *New York Times*, March 25, 1949, 16; "Albany Seeks Divorce Law Study," *New York Times*, February 12, 1951, 34; "State Divorce Law Is Attacked Again," *New York Times*, January 28, 1943, 19; "Albany Gets Bill on Divorce Study: Measure Identical to One Defeated in 1953—It Seeks to Set Up a Commission," *New York Times*, January 29, 1954, 14; "Bill Urges Study of Divorce Laws," *New York Times*, January 21, 1955, 15; "Divorce Reform Beaten in Albany, *New York Times*, March 30, 1955, 24.

108. "Divorce Reform Beaten in Albany," *New York Times*, March 30, 1955, 24.

109. Transcript, Public Hearing on Assembly Bill 972, March 5, 1953, *Janet Gordon Papers*, Box 5, New York State Archives, Albany, New York, 8, 27, 47–48.

110. Resolution Establishing a Special Joint Committee, *Janet Gordon Papers*, Box 5, New York State Archives, Albany, New York, 3.

111. "Assembly Votes Annulment Bill," *New York Times*, March 13, 1958, 22; Veto Message on S2779, *Janet Gordon Papers*, Box 12, New York State Archives, Albany, New York.

112. "New York's Antique Divorce Law," *New York Times*, January 17, 2010, WK7.

113. "No-Fault Divorce Finally in Sight for New York," *New York Times*, June 16, 2010, A1. The law went into effect on October 12, 2010.

114. "Only Woman Negro Legislator in State Guided by Brotherhood," *Tonawanda News*, February 16, 1961, 4.

115. Gallagher, *Black Women in New York City Politics*, 105.

116. "The Vanishing Coattail," *New York Times*, February 22, 1960, 18.

117. "Subway Safety Urged," *New York Times*, September 6, 1960, 37; "Fare in Danger," *New York Times*, October 18, 1960: 41; "Subway Testing a Talking System," *New York Times*, September 7, 1960, 43; "Legislator Seeks Subway Crime Cut," *New York Times*, January 18, 1964, 13; "City Is Advised to Guard Subway," *New York Times*, June 2, 1964, 1. Ryan Letter to the Editor, *New York Times*, July 9, 1964, 2.

118. Kirkpatrick, *Political Woman*, 214–15.

119. Anne Marie Cammisa and Beth Reingold, "Review Essay Women in State Legislatures and State legislative Research: Beyond Sameness and difference," *State Politics and Policy Quarterly* 4, no. 2 (Summer 2004): 194.

120. "New Local Taxes Finally Approved," *New York Times*, March 14, 1947, 15.

121. *Mt. Vernon Daily Argus*, December 21, 1944.

122. *New York Times*, February 3, 1949, 1; New York Times, March 18, 1953, 1; *New York Times*, November 19, 1953, 35.

123. *New York Times*, August 22, 1948, 5.

124. *New York Times*, August 22, 1948, 5.

125. The discussion of Todd's political career is taken from Lauren Kozakiewicz, "Political Episodes . . . ," "Jane Hedges Todd: Transitions and Legacies, the New Generation," chapter 6, 278–331.

126. "Candidates Ready for a Final Spurt," *New York Times*, October 31, 1937, VI 6.

127. Handwritten and typed text of statement by Miss Todd, undated. Scrapbook II, Box 10 # 2783, in the *Jane Todd Papers*, Department of Manuscripts and University Archives, Cornell University, Ithaca, New York. Todd then convinced the women of Westchester County not to wage an insurgency and nominate her anyway. See "Republicans Fail to Nominate Miss Todd," *New York Times*, May 25, 1944, 14.

128. Obituary, *New York Times*, May 8, 1977, 32; "RNC Delegate for Dewey," *New York Times*, February 17, 1944, 34.

129. "Democrats Gain 14 Albany Seats," *New York Times*, November 3, 1954, 12. The total NYC delegation in 1955 numbered 67—48 Democrats and 19 Republicans.

130. "Mrs. Ten Eyck Appointed," *New York Times*, January 12, 1955, 19. This position is part of the Office of the Clerk of the Assembly, the unit charged with maintaining the Assembly's records. Appointments to positions here are made by the majority party in the Assembly. This specific position had previously been occupied by Natalie Couch who had run unsuccessfully as the Republican nominee for US representative at large against Democrat Caroline O'Day in 1934. Representative at large seats existed from 1933 to 1945, when NYS gained seats due to the census but the legislature could not agree on reapportionment.

131. *New York Times*, January 1, 1967, 44.

132. "Republicans Favor Mrs. Gordon," *New York Times*, May 6, 1962, 62; "Stratton Loses Upstate County to Party Regulars," *New York Times*, September 7, 1962, 17.

133. Stratton would serve in Congress through 1988. In the mid-1970s the Legislature acknowledged Stratton's staying power and redistricted him back closer to the Capital District, which was heavily Democratic.

Chapter 4

1. "Assemblymen Ok a 'Good Slap' as an Aid to Learning," *The Saratogian*, March 12, 1959, 20.

2. "Is a Woman's Handbag a Luxury or a Necessity?," *Pittsburgh Courier*, November 10, 1962, 13; "Legislator Seeks Subway Crime Cut," *New York Times*, January 18, 1964, 13; "How Can We Be Heard?," *Albany Times Union* clipping, May 20, 1965, 21.

3. Though Cook was technically elected in the pioneer era, I include her with the activist cohort, given that the majority of her service from 1965 to 1974 occurred there, and that she advocated for women's issues on a scale similar to what is found in the activist era.

4. Constance E. Cook Obituary, *New York Times*, January 24, 2009, A14.

5. Michele Swers, "Research on Women in Legislatures: What Have We Learned, Where Are We Going?," *Women & Politics* 23, no. 1/2 (2001): 173.

6. Two of the women senators, Mary Anne Krupsak and Mary Goodhue, were first elected to the Assembly.

7. The broader contours of this pattern, which emerged in the 1960s, were evident outside New York as well. See Suzanne Schenken, *Legislators and Politicians: Iowa's Women Lawmakers*, 13–14.

8. Jen Fifield, "State Legislatures Have Fewer Farmers, Lawyers; But Higher Education Level," *Stateline Article*, December 10, 2015, https://www.pewtrusts.org/en/research-and-analysis/blogs/stateline/2015/12/10/state-legislatures-have-fewer-farmers-lawyers-but-higher-education-level.

9. The lawyers were Constance Cook, Constance Motley, Rosemary Gunning, Mary Anne Krupsak, Carol Bellamy, Karen Burstein, Mary Goodhue, May Newburger, and Florence Sullivan.

10. Gail Hellenbrand was married to a judge; Jean Amatucci Fox's father was a judge; Jeanette Gadsen was an executive assistant for a law firm; Mary Rose McGee was a deputy in an attorney's office; Estella Diggs had been a confidential aide to Supreme Court Judge Donald J. Sullivan; Antonia Rettaliata was an administrative assistant in the Suffolk County Court System; Joan Hague Smith was the commissioner of juries in Warren County.

11. Kathleen Dolan and Lynne E. Ford, "Are All Women State Legislators Alike?," in *Women in Elective Office: Past, Present and Future*, ed. Sue Thomas and Clyde Wilcox (New York: Oxford University Press, 1998), 76; Cindy Simon Rosenthal, *When Women Lead: Integrative Leadership in State Legislatures* (New York: Oxford University Press, 1998), 35.

12. Jeane Kirkpatrick, *Political Woman* (New York: Basic Books, 1974), 73, 83.

13. Irene Diamond, *Sex Roles in the State House*, 41.

14. "Nassau Dems Meet to Pick Federal and State Candidates," *New York Times*, April 7, 1980, 37; "Woman 28 Is Fighting for Wydler's Long Island House Seat, *New York Times*, October 24, 1970, 39.

15. Mary Ann Krupsak, Transcript of Oral Interview, May 3, 1994, *New York State Legislative Women's Caucus Oral History Project*, New York State Archives, Albany, NY, 2.

16. "Three Women in State Senator Race," *New York Times*, October 29, 1972, 47.

17. "Abortion Bill Advocate: Constance Eberhardt Cook," *New York Times*, April 9, 1970, 46.

18. Rosemary Gunning, Transcript of Oral Interview, *New York State Legislative Women's Caucus Oral History Project*, recorded New York State Archives, Albany, NY, 2.

19. Diamond, *Sex Roles in the State House*, 110.

20. Diamond, *Sex Roles in the State House*, 79.

21. "Speaker Steingut Loses . . . ," *New York Times*, November 8, 1970, B5; "The Two Men Who Waged War on Stanley Steingut," *New York Times*, November 9, 1978, B8; *New York Jewish Weekly*, September 17, 1978, 20.

22. Helene Weinstein Biography, New York State Assembly Member Official Website, https://nyassembly.gov/mem/Helene-E-Weinstein/bio/.

23. Rosenthal, *When Women Lead: Integrative Leadership in State Legislatures*, 35

24. "Steingut's Vote against Death Penalty May Help a Challenger, 26, in Primary," New York Times, July 10, 1978, B3.

25. "Fear and Loathing on Long Island," *New York Times*, March 15, 1977, 39; "About New York: The Rising Decibels of the Concorde Debate," *New York Times*, April 4, 1977, 44; "Kennedy Neighbors Vow to Continue Fight," *New York Times*, August 8, 1977, 50; "Ruling Allows Concorde Landings at JFK Upheld by Appeals Court, *New York Times*, September 3, 1977, 1; "SST Foes Roll at the Speed of a Snail . . . ," *New York Times*, October 10, 1977, 56; "Opponents and Fans See Concorde Land, *New York Times*, October 24, 1977, 1; "Concorde Protest Attracts 250 Cars," *New York Times*, November 21, 1977.

26. "A Happy Landing in the Senate," *New York Times*, February 4, 1979, LI 4.

27. Gerdi Lipschutz, Elizabeth Connelly, and Gail Hellenbrand did not have four-year degrees. It is likely but not completely clear that Carol Berman also had no degree. Shirley Chisholm began her career as a preschool teacher. Dorothy Rose was both a teacher and librarian. Audre Cooke was a social worker.

28. "Script in Albany: A Touch of Levity and Many New Characters," *New York Times*, January 4, 1973, 29.

29. "Three Women in Senate Race," *New York Times*, October 29, 1972, 47; *New York Times*, January 4, 1973, 29.

30. "State Senate Gets an Antiwar Feminist from L.I.," *New York Times*, November 12, 1972, 138.

31. "2 Women Senators Stand Together," *New York Times*, April 28, 1974, 106.

32. Gunning, Transcript of Oral Interview, 10.

33. Gunning, Transcript of Oral Interview, 10.

34. Chisholm, *Unbought and Unbossed*, 79.

35. "Good for Her District but What Lies Ahead?," *Yonkers Herald Statesman*, June 16, 1981, 7; "Legislators Find Ennui, Not Whoopee, in Albany," *New York Times*, January 30, 1975, 36.

36. Elizabeth Connelly, Transcript of Oral Interview, *New York State Legislative Women's Caucus Oral History Project*, New York State Archives, 15.

37. Kirkpatrick, *Political Woman*, 106, 116, 120.

38. "Tribute to the Distinguished Life and Career of Renowned Trailblazer Estella B. Diggs," New York State Senate Resolution, adopted April 23, 2013.

39. Author interview with Joyce Diggs, daughter and campaign manager of Estella Diggs, September 24, 2013.

40. Gunning, Transcript of Oral Interview, 7–8.

41. "Legislature Fails to Pass Tax Package for City . . . ," *New York Times*, November 23, 1975, 1, 54.

42. "Assemblymen Locked in to Keep Them Working, *New York Times*, June 6, 1971, 64.

43. Author Interview with Aurelia Greene, May 30, 2013; Elizabeth Connelly, Transcript of Oral Interview, 4; "Emotional Speeches Mark Closing of the SIDC," clipping from the *Staten Island Observer*, September 24, 1987, 1, *Elizabeth Connelly Papers*, Box 78, Folder 7, Archives and Special Collections, College of Staten Island, Staten Island, New York.

"In Legislature, Women Make Quiet Strides," *New York Times*, January 28, 1987, B1.

44. "Ban on Pay Toilets Passes . . . ," *New York Times*, July 11, 1975, 27.

45. Clipping from the *Flatbush News*, December 1978, 5 *Papers of Assemblywoman Rhoda Jacobs*, Box 1, Series 1, File 1, Brooklyn College Library Archives and Special collections.

46. Clipping from the *Flatbush News*, *Papers of Assemblywoman Rhoda Jacobs*, 4.

47. Press Release announcing 1976 challenge, *Papers of Assemblywoman Rhoda Jacobs*, Brooklyn College Library Archives and Special collections, Box 1, Series 1, File 1; "Under the Influence," Flatbush Life column undated 1978, *Papers of Assemblywoman Rhoda Jacobs*, Brooklyn College Library Archives and Special collections, Box 1, Series 1, File 1; Biographical Statement, *Papers Assemblywoman Rhoda Jacobs*, Brooklyn College Library Archives and Special collections, Box 1, Series 1, File 2.

48. Interview in the *Legislative Gazette*, June 12, 1986, 3A, *Papers of Assemblywoman Rhoda Jacobs*, Brooklyn College Library Archives and Special collections, Box 3, Series 1, File 3.

49. Diamond, *Sex Roles in the State House*, 90.

50. Stacie Taranto, *Kitchen Table Politics: Conservative Women and Family Values in New York* (Philadelphia: University of Pennsylvania Press, 2017), 102–3.

51. John Pitney Jr., "Leaders and Rulers in the New York Senate, *Legislative Quarterly* 7, no. 4 (November 1982): 494–95.

52. "Voting in Albany: A Test of Loyalty and Endurance," *New York Times*, July 10, 1981, B2.

53. "Legislature Passes MTA Tax Package, *Nyack Journal News*, July 19, 1981, A7.

54. David Hill, "Women State Legislators and Party Voting on the ERA," *Social Science Quarterly* 64 (June 1983): 318.

55. Michelle Barnello, "Gender and Roll Call Voting in the New York State Assembly," *Women & Politics* 20, no. 4 (2001): 82, 87.

56. Benjamin and Nakamura, *The Modern New York Legislature: Redressing the Balance*, 114.

57. Benjamin and Nakamura, *Modern New York Legislature*, xxii, xxiv, 44, 207, 213, 225.

58. David B. Hill, "Political Culture and Female Political Representation," *Journal of Politics* 43, no. 1 (February 1981): 159.

59. Diamond, *Sex Roles in the State House*, 3, 7; John Carey, Richard Niemi Lynda Powell, "Are Women State Legislators Different?," in Sue Thomas and Clyde Wilcox, eds., *Women and Elective Office: Past, Present, and Future* (New York: Oxford University Press, 199), 88–89.

60. Suzanne Schenken, *Legislators and Politicians: Iowa's Women Lawmakers*, xiv, 27.

61. "Candidate for Gordon Seat," *New York Times*, May 18, 1978, B6; "Politics, Lights, Camera, Politics," May 28, 1978, WC16.

62. "This Year Goodhue Faces Opponent," *New York Times*, August 12, 1990, 16.

63. "Mrs. Goodhue's Role in Joint Custody Bill, *New York Times*, June 21, 1981, WCI.

64. Women with children still at home when they ran: Cook, Winikow, Connelly, Jacobs, and Hellenbrand.

65. Chisholm, *Unbought and Unbossed*, 72.

66. Chisholm, Shirley. *Unbought and Unbossed 40th Anniversary Edition* (Washington, DC: Media Take Root, 1970 and 2009), 65–68.

67. Chisholm, *Unbought and Unbossed*, 70–72; Julie Gallagher, *Black Women and Politics in New York City*, 164–65.

68. NYS Black, Puerto Rican, Hispanic and Asian Legislative Caucus, *1917–2014 A Look at the History of Legislators of Color*, 14, 16, accessed July 8, 2020, https://www.nysenate.gov/newsroom/articles/1917-2014-look-history-legislators-color.

69. Constance Baker Motley, Transcript of Oral Interview, April 13, 1994, *New York State Legislative Women's Caucus Oral History Project*, New York State Archives, Albany, NY, 2.

70. Constance Bake Motley Obituary, *New York Times*, September 29, 2005, B10.

71. Constance Baker Motley, Transcript of Oral Interview, April 13, 1994, *New York State Legislative Women's Caucus Oral History Project*, 3–4.

72. Chisholm, *Unbought and Unbossed*, 86.

73. Chisholm, *Unbought and Unbossed*, 92.

74. Constance Baker Motley, Transcript of Oral Interview, April 13, 1994, 5.

75. Jones, *The Harlem Fox*, 166–69. See also "Harlem Democrats Pick Ellison for Special Senate Race," *New York Times*, January 5, 1964, 20; "Mayor Tells Ellison to Quit Race because of Policy Convictions," *New York Times*, January 17, 1964, 17; "Democrats Ask Election Board to void Nomination of Ellison," *New York Times*, January 18, 1964, 10; "Ellison Is Replaced by Mrs. Motley," *New York Times*, January 24, 1964, 13.

76. "Ellison Opponent Receives G.O.P. Bid," *New York Times*, January 16, 1964, 21; *New York Times*, January 25, 1964, 19.

77. Jones, *The Harlem Fox*, 167.

78. Jones, *The Harlem Fox*, 190.

79. Jones, *The Harlem Fox*, 194.

80. Author interview with Joyce Diggs, daughter and campaign manager of Estella Diggs, September 24, 2013.

81. "Tribute to the Distinguished Life and Career of Renowned Trailblazer Estella B. Diggs," New York State Senate Resolution, adopted April 23, 2013.

82. He also briefly spoke by phone with Diggs on March 24, 1980. President Carter call to Estella Diggs, 4:07 p.m., Daily Diary for March 24, 1980, Jimmy Carter Presidential Library, https://www.jimmycarterlibrary.gov/assets/documents/diary/1980/.

83. *New York Times*, October 19, 1980, 37.

84. *The Olga A. Mendez Senatorial Papers*, Archives of the Puerto Rican Diaspora, Centro de Estudios Puertorriquenos, Hunter College, Box 20, Folder 54, "Press Clippings 1970s–2000s," n.d., unattributed column by Miguel Perez.

85. Mendez switched from Democrat to Republican in 2002. *The Olga A. Mendez Senatorial Papers*, CUNY, Box 15, Folder 22, Statement announcing switch of parties.

86. *The Olga A. Mendez Senatorial Papers*, Box 20, Folder 54, "Press Clippings 1970s–2000s," n.d., unattributed column by Miguel Perez.

87. "Letter to the Editor," *Amsterdam News*, September 22, 1984, 12; Op-Ed, *Amsterdam News*, June 3, 1984, 13; *Amsterdam News*, June 12, 1982, 20.

88. *The Olga A. Mendez Senatorial Papers*, Box 20, Folder 54, press release, n.d., announcing her resignation from the Black and Puerto Rican Caucus; "Governor's Speech Stirs Hope," *Amsterdam News*, February 23, 1985, 3.

89. *The Olga A. Mendez Senatorial Papers*, Box 20, Folder 53, *New York Daily News* clipping, February 22, 1985, n.p.

90. *The Olga A. Mendez Senatorial Papers*, Biographical Notes.

91. *Amsterdam News*, June 3, 1984, 13; *Amsterdam News*, September 22, 1984, 12; *Amsterdam News*, June 6, 1982, 15; Amsterdam News, September 18, 1982, 15; *The Olga A. Mendez Senatorial Papers*, Box 6, Folder 21, "Job-Hunting through the Times," *New York Post*, September 6, 2000, 1.

92. *The Olga A. Mendez Senatorial Papers*, Box 6, Folder 14, press statement on switch to Republican Party.

93. *The Olga A. Mendez Senatorial Papers*, Box 20, Folder 54, n.d. unattributed press clipping.

94. *The Olga A. Mendez Senatorial Papers*, Biographical Notes; Box 20, Folder 54, 2004, unattributed press clipping.

95. *New York Amsterdam News*, October 1, 1977, B7.

96. Biographical entry for Geraldine Daniels in the *New York Red Book: An Illustrated State Manual #87 1983–84* (Albany: Williams Press, 1983), 211.

97. "Key Battles in the Primary," *Brooklyn World Telegram*, September 9, 1965, B1.

98. *New York Recorder*, April 4, 1970, 5.

99. "West Side Democrats Again Ensnared in Political Wars over Nominations," *New York Times*, July 1, 1976, 15.

100. "Mrs. Runyon Faces Six Challengers . . . ," *New York Times*, August 27, 1976, 18.

101. "Voting in Primaries . . . ," *New York Times*, September 16, 1976, 34–35.

102. "Assembly to Get Black Woman," *New York Times*, November 19, 1972, 42.

103. "Assembly to Get Black Woman," *New York Times*, November 19, 1972, 42.

104. "3 in the Assembly Face a New Vote in the City," *New York Times*, October 19, 1980, 37; *New York Times*, October 23, 1980, D18.

105. "Assemblywoman Expected to Plead Guilty to Bribery," *New York Times*, January 6, 2003, B4.

106. "Leading Bronx Politics Like the Bosses of Old," *New York Times*, August 8, 1998, B1.

107. "Former State Assemblywoman Gloria Davis: A Wasted Life," *New York Amsterdam News*, January 9, 2003, 12.

108. After 1927 the position was constitutionally changed to be appointive. The arguments and sources presented in this section on Knapp's trial for graft in office are taken from Lauren Kozakiewicz, "Political Episodes," chapter 4, "Florence E. S. Knapp: Suffrage, Politics, and Missteps."

109. "The Census Scandal," *New York Times*, October 4, 1927, 28.

110. "Albany Speaker's Aide Indicted on Mail Fraud and Tax Charges, *New York Times*, October 22, 1986, A1; "U.S. Trial Starts for Ex-Official of Queens Party," *New York Times*, January 16, 1987, B3; "In the Wind," *New York Times*, January 21, 1987, A30.

111. Alan Chartock, "Did Gerdi Take a Fall for Everyone Else," *Washington County Post*, April 1, 1987, n.p. readable.

112. "Ethics Legislation Faulted by Cuomo; He Warns of Veto," *New York Times*, April 15, 1987, A1.

113. "Ethics Legislation Faulted by Cuomo," B4.

114. *Rockland Journal News*, October 31, 1980, 1B; *Yonkers Herald Statesman*, June 6, 1981, 7, 9.

115. *Yonkers Herald Statesman*, June 6, 1981, 7.

116. "A Winikow Shift on Death Penalty," *New York Times*, May 23, 1982, 61.

117. "Law Restricts Use of Campaign Gifts," *New York Times*, June 9, 1985, 42; "Running for Public Office and Private Profit," *New York Times*, September 29, 1985, E8.

118. "Ex-State Senator is at Center of Embezzlement Charges," *New York Times*, August 29, 1993, 33; "Former State Senator Admits Illegal Use of Money," *New York Times*, October 7, 1993, B8.

119. Chisholm, *Unbought and Unbossed*, 74–75.

120. *Amsterdam News*, April 9, 1977, B1.

121. "Ocean Hill Faction Calls for Election on Board Vacancy," *New York Times*, December 6, 1973, 31; "Wright Quits Ocean-Hill Board; Aide Named to Fill School Post," *New York Times*, December 6, 1973; 98; "Miss Gadson Is Named over Anker Objection," *Amsterdam News*, December 22, 1973, C1.

122. I have seen one reference to Gadson as Wright's niece but was not able to corroborate that relationship.

123. *The Villager*, October 5, 1978, n.p.; "Gadson Seeking City Council Seat . . . ," *Amsterdam News*, August 5, 1978, B4.

124. "Albert Blumenthal to Retire," *New York Times*, June 10, 1976, 78; *New York Times*, June 11, 1976, 46; Biographical Entry, *The New York State Red Book #85 for 1979–1980* (Albany: Williams Press), 203–4.

125. *Greece NY Post*, May 29–30, 1985, n.p.; *Greece NY Post*, March 18, 1986, 7; *Greece NY Post*, March 21–23, 1989, n.p.

126. Letter to the Editor, *Greece NY Post*, September 25, 1984, 9.

127. "Republican Women's Legislative Network Announced," *Mt. Morris NY Enterprise*, 1979, n.d., n.p.

128. "Albany Freshmen's Key Goal: Tax Relief," *New York Times*, November 26, 1978, LI7.

129. "Suffolk Gains Equal Strength in Redistricting," New York Times, May 16, 1982, LI1.

130. "GOP Minority Elevates Four," *New York Times*, February 6, 1983, LI8.

131. "Dems Give the Number Two Spot Top Attention," *New York Times*, May 21, 1986, B28; "An L.I. Cast for State G.O.P.," *New York Times*, May 25, 1986, LI4.

Chapter 5

1. "Women Find Albany a Male World," *New York Times*, March 18, 1980, B1, B4; Anne Marie Cammisa and Beth Reingold, "Women in State Legislatures and State Legislative Research: Beyond Sameness and Difference, *State Politics & Policy Quarterly* 4, no. 2 (Summer 2004): 182.

2. Diamond, *Sex Roles in the State House*: 47; "Women Find Albany a Male World," *New York Times*, March 18, 1980; B1, B4.

3. Kirkpatrick, *Political Woman*; 144, 215.

4. Mary Ann Krupsak, Transcript of Oral Interview, May 3, 1994, 1, 6.

5. "1st Statewide Political Convention of Women Draws 400 Political Activists," *New York Times*, February 18, 1974, 21.

6. "Assembly Spurns Woman's Appeal . . . ," *New York Times*, March 6, 1969, 45.

7. Mary Ann Krupsak, Transcript of Oral Interview, May 3, 1994, 6, 8–9.

8. Krupsak, Transcript of Oral Interview, 9.

9. *New York Times*, November 29, 1973, 39.

10. "Two Women Senators Stand Together," *New York Times*, April 28, 1974, 106; "Carey Appoints Burstein to PSC," *New York Times*, December 16, 1977, 47.

11. Diamond, *Sex Roles in the Statehouse*, 155.

12. *New York Times*, July 1, 1974, 14; July 27, 1974, 20; August 17, 1974, 25.

13. *New York Times*, August 17, 1974, 35.

14. *New York Times*, September 15, 1974; Daniel C. Kramer, *The Days of Wine and Roses Are Over: Governor Hugh Carey and New York State* (Lanham: University Press of America, 1997), 157.

15. "For Women in Politics, Stamp Lickin' Is Over," *New York Times*, September 15, 1974, 196.

16. Kramer, *Days of Wine and Roses*, 158.

17. Kramer, *Days of Wine and Roses*, 159.

18. "Three Women in State Senator Race," *New York Times*, October 29, 1972, 47; Kramer, *Days of Wine and Roses*, 159–60; *New York Times* January 26, 1975, 40.

19. "Carey with Miss Krupsak at His Side vows 'Less Chauvinism' to Women," *New York Times*, March 21, 1975, 34.

20. "Miss Krupsak Settling into New Albany Role," *New York Times*, January 6, 1976, 1; "Carey Expressed Preference for Krupsak . . . ," *New York Times*, December 19, 1977, 19.

21. "Senate Challenges Krupsak's Power in Presiding over the Senate," *New York Times*, January 15, 1975, 54; "Judge Rules Out Regent Election," *New York Times*, January 15, 1976, 20; New York High Court Upholds Disputed Election of Three Regents," *New York Times*, July 7, 1976, 32.

22. "Carey with Miss Krupsak at His Side Vows 'Less Chauvinism' to Women," *New York Times*, March 21, 1975, 34; "Carey-Krupsak 'Togetherness' Is Doubted by Insiders," *New York Times*, March 31, 1975, 22; "A Salary Cut Set by Miss Krupsak . . ." *New York Times*, January 26, 1975, 40; *New York Times*, January 29, 1975, 15; "State Delegates Challenged on Women . . . ," *New York Times*, May 3, 1976, 12.

23. *New York Times*, August 28, 1977: 36; Jonathan Mahler, *The Bronx Is Burning* (New York: Farrar & Straus, 2005), 102.

24. *New York Times*, March 9, 1975, 1; "Women's Caucus Ends on Cheering Note," New York Times, March 17, 1975, 20; "Miss Krupsak Bids Women Save Parley," *New York Times*, June 6, 1975, 73; "For Women, Gains and Losses in 1975 . . ." *New York Times*, January 2, 1976, 46; "Krupsak Supports New York Women's Lobby . . . ," *New York Times*, February 19, 1975, 36; "For Women in Politics, Stamp Lickin' Is Over," *New York Times*, September 15, 1974, 196.

25. Mary Ann Krupsak, Transcript of Oral Interview, May 3, 1994, 13; Kramer, *The Days of Wine and Roses*, 160–61; "Krupsak Splits with Carey," *New York Times*, June 13, 1978, A1; "Hurt Pride, Misunderstandings at Heart of Carey-Krupsak Split," *New York Times*, June 30, 1978, A1.

26. "Carey Seen as Vulnerable on Eve of Re-Election Campaign," *New York Times*, June 12, 1978, B5.

27. *New York Times*, June 15, 1978, B12.

28. Kramer, *The Days of Wine and Roses*, 162–63; "Krupsak Splits with Carey," June 13, 1978, A1, B12; "Krupsak Campaign to Open Today with Theme of Distant Government," *New York Times*, June 26, 1978, NJ13.

29. Mary Ann Krupsak, Transcript of Oral Interview, May 3, 1994, 13–15.

30. "Krupsak Campaign so Far in Disarray," *New York Times*, July 7, 1978, 16.

31. "Feminists Say Carey Reneged in Campaign Pledges to Women," *New York Times*, March 28, 1976, 52; "Connelly an Ally of Carey . . . ," *New York Times*, July 12, 1978, B3.

32. *New York Times*, July 17, 1978, B3.

33. "Krupsak Bandwagon Rolling against the Odds, *New York Times*, July 31, 1978, NJ 12.

34. "Strong-Minded Candidate," *New York Times*, June 27, 1978, B4.

35. *New York Times*, June 25, 1978, 29.

36. There had been a third Democrat in the primary race, Jeremiah Bloom who got 14 percent of the vote.

37. "The Krupsak-Martin House Campaign: As Slow as Upstate New York Is Vast," *New York Times*, October 28, 1980, A26.

38. "Cellar and Holtzman Staff Dig for Errors," *New York Times*, August 4, 1972, 37.

39. *New York Times*, January 17, 1973, 29.

40. *New York Times*, January 11, 1974, 36

41. "New Law on Rape Signed by Wilson, *New York Times*, February 20, 1974, 34; "Legislators Say Changes in Rape Law Are Likely, *New York Times*, November 16, 1973, 45.

42. "Women's Caucus Plans Fund Drive Benefit," *New York Times*, September 4, 1972, 16.

43. "In Albany, the Women Show Their Strength," *New York Times*, January 29, 1974, 28.

44. "Women's Rights Faces Snag in Albany," *New York Times*, May 1, 1975, 45.

45. "Equal Rights Amendment Gets Final Albany Passage," *New York Times*, May 22, 1975, 1.

46. "Defeat of Equal Rights Bills Traced to Women's Votes," *New York Times*, November 6, 1975, 1.

47. "Albany Meets Wednesday on Brooklyn Redistricting," *New York Times*, May 25, 1974, 79; "Political Hopefuls Are Squaring Off . . . ," *New York Times*, June 9, 1974, 101.

48. "Sutton and Wright Say Districting Plan Is Possibly Harmful," *New York Times*, May 29, 1974, 85.

49. "Chairmanship Lost for Lack of Vital Vote," *New York Times*, January 16, 1977, 46.

50. "Council Post Sought by Senator Bellamy," *New York Times*, March 3, 1977, 38.

51. "Carol Bellamy Wins a Place in the Runoff . . . ," *New York Times*, September 9, 1977: 1, B7; "Sketches of Three Winners in Citywide Elections," *New York Times*, November 9, 1977, 30.

52. "Albany Pace: Slow Motion," *New York Times*, July 17, 1977, L1.

53. "Carol Bellamy Vows She'll Be Noticed," *New York Times*, January 8, 1978.

54. "State Senate Gets an Antiwar Feminist from L.I.," *New York Times*, November 12, 1972, 138.

55. "Women Play Major Election Role," *New York Times*, November 2, 1975, 130.

56. "Carey Appoints Karen Burstein to Public Service Commission," *New York Times*, December 16, 1977, 47.

57. Author interview with Marie Runyon, November 21, 2013; "Legislature Welcomes 46 New Freshman," *New York Times*, 40.

58. The majority of the recounting of Runyon's background, path to office, and time in the Assembly comes from the author interview with Runyon, November 21, 2013.

59. Author interview with Runyon, November 21, 2013.

60. Author interview with Runyon, November 21, 2013. Runyon recalled that Columbia wanted to erect a new school, though she was not sure if it was to have been a College of Pharmacy or Social Work.

61. *Constance Cook Papers*, Notes for reelection campaign, Box 28, Folder labeled 1967 Legislation—Family I, Kroch Library of Manuscripts and University Archives, Cornell University, Ithaca, New York.

62. *Constance Cook Papers*, Testimony before the Temporary State Commission on the Constitution, Box 29, Folder labeled 1967 Legislative Reform.

63. *Constance Cook Papers*, Press Release dated November 6, 1967, Box 29, Folder labeled 1967 Legislative Reform.

64. *New York Times*, February 24, 1970, 1, 34; February 15, 1970, 36; March 27, 1970, 29; April 1, 1970, 1.

65. *New York Times*, January 1, 1972, E3; January 30, 1972, 48.

66. *Watertown Daily Times*, January 5, 1973, 2; "Assembly Tables School Post Bill," *New York Times*, May 24, 1973, 19.

67. "Three Women in State Assembly Seek Feminist Reforms, Gently," *New York Times*, January 22, 1971, 24.

68. *Constance Cook Papers*, Concurrent Resolution of the Senate and Assembly proposing the ERA amendment and a letter to the Judiciary Committee chair pressing to have it reported out to the floor; Assembly Bill 3777 to Make Illegal Discrimination by Sex as Practiced by Employment Agencies, Box 37, Folder labeled Legislation.

69. Elizabeth Connelly, Transcript of Oral Interview, March 3, 1994, 2–3, 6; *New York Times*, November 4, 1973, 70; *Elizabeth Connelly Papers*, Box 79, Folder 2, "Volunteer of the Year at Staten Island Hospital," "Dems Ok Woman for Albany Post," clippings dated May 7, 1973 and September 11, 1972, no papers attributed.

70. Elizabeth Connelly, Transcript of Oral Interview, March 3, 1994, 5–6.

71. Connelly, Transcript of Oral Interview, 6.

72. "'Home Rule' Factor May Block S.I. Secession," *New York Times*, March 5, 1994, 27.

73. "'Home Rule' Factor," 10.

74. *Elizabeth Connelly Papers*, Biographical Sketch in the Online Finding Aid; Elizabeth Connelly, Transcript of Oral Interview, March 3, 1994, 12–14.

75. *Elizabeth Connelly Papers*, Box 79, Folder 7, "Island Polls Fit Overall Vote Pattern," *Staten Island Advance*, November 15, 1987, A1, A18.

76. Elizabeth Connelly, Transcript of Oral Interview, March 3, 1994, 14.

77. *Elizabeth Connelly Papers*, Box 79, Folder 6, "In 1985, Connelly Got Top Billing," *Staten Island Advance*, April 13, 1986, 1, 7.

78. *Elizabeth Connelly Papers*, Box 79, Folder 3, "Assemblywoman Connelly Relocates to Willowbrook," *New York Association for Retarded Children* 23, no. 3 (September 1977): front cover.

79. "Revisiting the Atrocities that Once Consumed the Halls of What Was the Willowbrook State School in Staten Island," *New York Daily News*, April 9, 2017, https://www.nydailynews.com/news/national/atrocities-consumed-halls-willowbrook-school-article-1.3030716.

80. *Elizabeth Connelly Papers*, Box 65, Folder 12, District Newsletter dated March 1978 that discussed changes in the 1975 consent decree; Media Statement dated May 7, 1982 expresses disagreement with appointment of a special master to oversee the consent decree.

81. *Elizabeth Connelly Papers*, Box 79, Folder 3, Editorial, "Some Very Important Questions," *Staten Island Advance*, December 16, 1979.

82. *Elizabeth Connelly Papers*, Box 79, Folder 4, "Building Named for Connelly," *Staten Island Advance*, October 3, 1981, A8.

83. *Elizabeth Connelly Papers*, Box 79, Folder 7, "Emotional Speeches Mark Closing of the SIDC," *State Island Register*, September 24, 1987, 1, 6, 14.

84. Elizabeth Connelly, Transcript of Oral Interview, March 3, 1994, 15.

85. *Elizabeth Connelly Papers*, Box 16, Folder 6, Bound Report Drunk Driving Reform in New York State 1980–1984.

86. Elizabeth Connelly, Transcript of Oral Interview, March 3, 1994, 4.

Chapter 6

1. Anna Mitchell Mahoney, *Women Take Their Place in State Legislatures: The Creation of Women's Caucuses* (Philadelphia: Temple University Press, 2018), 8.

2. Mahoney, *Women Take Their Place*, 11.

3. Mahoney, *Women Take Their Place*, 23.

4. Mahoney, *Women Take Their Place*, 29, 176.

5. Mahoney, *Women Take Their Place*, 41, 43.

6. For support for the importance of the "critical mass" theory, see Michelle Saint-Germain, "Does Their Difference Make a Difference? The Impact of Women on Public Policy in the Arizona Legislature," *Social Science Quarterly* 70 (December): 956–68; Sue Thomas and Susan Welch, "The Impact of Gender on Activities and Priorities of State Legislators," *Western Political Quarterly* (1990): 447; Linda Witt, Karen Paget, and Glenna Matthews, *Running as a Woman Gender and Power in American Politics* (New York: The Free Press, 1994), 18. For analysis that suggests the critical mass theory should be modified or qualified by the addition of other factors, see Beth Reingold, *Representing Women: Sex, Gender and Legislative Behavior in Arizona and California* (Chapel Hill: University of North Carolina Press, 2003), 3.

7. W. L. George, "Women in Politics," *Harper's Magazine*, June 1919, 85–92. He did hold out some hope that there would be those women who could overcome male prejudice against women politician and thus exhibit some independence.

8. "Women Gain in Legislature," *New York Times*, April 29, 1984, CN12. Information on the Connecticut OWL's history in this paragraph comes from the article.

9. Letter of Invitation reprinted in Emma Poeter, editor, *History of the National Order of Women Legislators* (Las Vegas: Hanes Thomas Printers, 1981). This work is a collection of documents covering OWL history and does not include page numbers.

10. Abstract of the Minutes of the First Annual Meeting, April 21–April 24, 1939, reprinted in *History of the National Order of Women Legislators*.

11. NOWL Constitution Article II–Objectives in the 1946–49 Scrapbook, *National Order of Women Legislators collection*, Sophia Smith Collection: 85S-2 Box 3, Smith College Special Collections, Smith College, Northampton, MA.

12. Letter from NOWL president to membership, March 18, 1943, in the *Papers of Rhoda Fox Graves*, Gouverneur Museum, Gouverneur, NY.

13. "School Aid Called Inadequate," *Binghamton Press*, May 24, 1947, 3.

14. Report on 1949 Convention Highlights, reprinted in *History of the National Order of Women Legislators*.

15. Membership records are not available for every year. However in the 1970s records show the following New York women as multiple year members: Cook (71–77); Krupsak (71–79); Gunning (71–73, 76–85); and Frick Taylor (71–77).

16. Membership Rosters from the 1970s and 1980, reprinted in *History of the National Order of Women Legislators*; "Krupsak Participates in Recent OWL Convention," *St. Johnsville NY Enterprise*, December 3, 1970, 2; *Ridgewood Times*, December 7, 1978, 20.

17. Report of the 1948 convention listing Todd's election as first vice president, Report of Annual Convention 1950 listing Gillette's election as second vice president, reprinted in *History of the National Order of Women Legislators*; List of NOWL officers, Scrapbook 1950–1960, *National Order of Women Legislators collection*, Sophia Smith Collection, Box 3, 85S-2.

18. Reports of the 1974 and 1975 conventions, reprinted in *History of the National Order of Women Legislators*.

19. Reports of the 1978 and 1982 conventions, reprinted in *History of the National Order of Women Legislators*.

20. The OWL records preserved in the Sophia Smith Special Collections cover limited years of its existence. Individual records within given years or for publications like the *OWLetter* are incomplete.

21. "Women Legislators Activities throughout the States, *OWLetter* 3, no. 3 (1973); 5, no. 3 (September 1975); 6, no. 1 (December 1975), *National Order of Women Legislators Collection*, Sophia Smith Collection, Box 1, 85S-1/86S-7.

22. "Women Legislators Activities throughout the States," *OWLetter* 1, no. 3 (September 1971), *National Order of Women Legislators collection*, Sophia Smith Collection, Box 1, 85S-1/86S-7.

23. "Doris Byrne, First Woman Justice of City Court," *New York Herald Tribune*, June 30, 1950; "Legislature's Youngest Member Is a Mother Now," *New York Herald Tribune*, January 14, 1950; "Rhoda Fox Graves Dies at 75," *New York Herald Tribune*, January 24, 1950; Nonattributed article on Strong, dated March 5, 1952; "Legislator Sifts Phoned in Bills," *New York Times*, January 24, 1954; all are in the *National Order of Women Legislators collection*, Sophia Smith Collection, Box 3, 85S-2.

24. Letter from OWL president dated June 24, 1953, announcing site for next year's convention, *National Order of Women Legislators collection*, Sophia Smith Collection, Box 3, 85S-2; "50 from 14 States," *Knickerbocker News*, September 23, 1953, 2B.

25. Report of the 1952 and 1953 Conventions, reprinted in *History of the National Order of Women Legislators*.

26. Letter from Elizabeth Belen, Recording Secretary, OWL, to Mildred Taylor, dated May 26, 1954, Series 1, Box 5, *Mildred Taylor Papers 1921–1974*, M. E. Grenander Department of Special Collections and Archives, University Libraries, University at Albany, State University of New York.

27. Letter from Mildred Frick Taylor to Clara Jarvis, OWL president, Series 1, Box 5, *Taylor Papers*.

28. Letter from Mildred Frick Taylor to the Honorable Mayme Collins, Crisfield, MD, Series 1, Box 5, *Taylor Papers*.

29. Press Release on Election as OWL president, Series 1, Box 5, *Taylor Papers*.

30. Letter from Mildred Frick Taylor to the Honorable Myrtle Trube Hahn, dated November 22, 1954, Box 1, Series 5, *Taylor Papers*.

31. Minutes of the 1956 convention, Box 1, Series 5, *Taylor Papers*.

32. Liz Carpenter in Suzanne Braun Levine and Mary Thom, *Bella Abzug an Oral History* (New York: Farrar, Straus & Giroux, 2007), 136–38.

33. Liz Abzug in *Bella Abzug an Oral History*, 83.

34. "Women's Caucus Has New Rallying Cry: 'Make Policy Not Coffee,'" *New York Times*, February 6, 1972, 60.

35. Margot Polivy in *Bella Abzug an Oral History*, 141.

36. "Votes by Women in GOP Attacked," *New York Times*, July 12, 1981, 16.

37. Mission Statement, National Women's Political Caucus, accessed July 28, 2020, https://www.nwpc.org/.

38. History Statement, Congressional Caucus for Women's Issues, accessed July 29, 2020, https://www.wcpinst.org/our-work/the-womens-caucus/caucus-history-and-accomplishments/.

39. "Women's Caucus: Eight Years of Progress," *New York Times*, May 27, 1985, 20.

40. "First Statewide Political Convention of Women . . . ," *New York Times*, February 18, 1974, 21.

41. "First Statewide Political Convention of Women . . ."

42. "For Women in Politics, Stamp Lickin' Is Over," *New York Times*, September 15, 1974, 196.

43. Anne Marie Cammisa and Beth Reingold, "Review Essay: Women in State Legislatures and State Legislative Research: Beyond Sameness and Difference," *State Politics and Policy Quarterly* 4, no 2 (Summer 2004): 185.

44. "Women's Political Caucus Votes to Alter Membership Structure . . . ," *New York Times*, July 1, 1974, 14.

45. "Women's Caucus Ends on Cheering Note," *New York Times*, March 17, 1975, 20.

46. "Brooklyn Women's Political Caucus Is Back on Electoral Scene" *New York Times*, July 28, 1974, 80.

47. Mission Statement, Legislative Women's Caucus, accessed July 30, 2020, https://www.nysenate.gov/newsroom/articles/2019/legislative-womens-caucus-mission-statement.

48. Author interview with Shirley Tranholm, Executive Director, LWC, June 2017.

49. *Utica Valley News*, September 14, 1995, 5; *Fulton NY Patriot*, October–December, 1992, n.p. visible.

50. Author interview with Aurelia Greene, May 30, 2013.

51. *Village Voice*, February 11, 2005, B1.

52. Author interview with Francine Delmonte, May 21, 2013.

Chapter 7

1. Drude Dahlerup, "The Story of the Theory of Critical Mass" in a special section, Rethinking the Critical Mass Debate," *Politics and Gender* 1 (December 2005): 514, 519.

2. Kristi Anderson, *After Suffrage*, 155, 157.

3. For a full articulation of the "Republican Mother" construct see "The Republican Mother: Female Political Imagination in the Early Republic," chapter 9 of Linda Kerber, *Women of the Republic: Intellect and Ideology in Revolutionary America* (Chapel Hill: University of North Carolina Press, 1997), 265–88.

4. Gallagher, *Black Women and Politics in New York City*, 162. Gallagher notes that Chisholm's childlessness may have been health related or a by-product of her political aspirations.

5. Chisholm, *Unbought and Unbossed*, 37.

6. Chisholm, *Unbought and Unbossed*, 34–36, 38.

7. Chisholm, *Unbought and Unbossed*, 78.

8. "Assembly Passes School Book Plan . . . ," *New York Times*, May 17, 1966, 33; Chisholm, *Unbought and Unbossed*, 79.

9. "Assembly Passes School Book Plan . . . ," *New York Times*, May 17, 1966, 33.

10. Diane Ravitch, *The Great School Wars: A History of New York City Public Schools* (Baltimore: Johns Hopkins University Press, 2000), 55–66; Gunn, "Antebellum Society and Politics 1825–1860," 342–43.

11. Joel Schwartz, "The Empire State in a Changing World," in Milton M. Klein, editor, *The Empire State: a History of New York* (Ithaca: Cornell University Press, 2001), 658.

12. *Constance Cook Papers*, "Mrs. Cook Pledges to Examine State Bus Law," *Ithaca Journal*, December 8, 1966; Box 37, Legislation.

13. *Constance Cook Papers*, "Schools Aid Northeast Parents," *Ithaca Journal*, November 30, 1966; "Court Orders School to Continue Bus Service," *Ithaca Journal*, November 28, 1966; "Signs Will Be Up, Response in the Question," *Ithaca Journal*, November 24, 1966, 3; Box 37, Legislation.

14. *Constance Cook Papers*, Assembly Bill 3272, "An Act to Amend the Education Law in Relation to the Transportation of School Children in Tompkins

County," and Assembly Bill 1220, "An Act to Amend the Education Law in Relation to the Transportation of School Children in Hazardous Zones," Box 37, Legislation.

15. *Constance Cook Papers*, "Cook's Bill on Busing Vetoed," *Ithaca Journal*, May 5, 1967, Box 37, Legislation.

16. "Albany Aims Rhetoric at Voters," *New York Times*, April 29, 1972, 35. In 1972 Nixon's antibusing stance was part of a broader overture to Southern Democrats who opposed mandatory bussing laws for racial balancing purposes.

17. *Constance Cook Papers*, Letter from CUNY Women's Coalition, January 4, 1972, Box 87, Folder 9. The letter references the Chancellor's announcement of the Committee formation and the quoted language refers to that earlier document.

18. *Constance Cook Papers*, summary of phone message from Carol Greitzer dated December 2, 1971; copy of letter from Greitzer to CUNY Chancellor Kibbee dated January 3, 1972, Box 87, Folder 9.

19. *Constance Cook Papers*, Letter from CUNY Women's Coalition, January 4, 1972, Box 87, Folder 9.

20. *Constance Cook Papers*, Minutes of the Advisory Committee Meeting of January 7, 1972, Box 87, Folder 9.

21. *Constance Cook Papers*, "Minutes of Advisory Committee Meeting of January 7, 1972," "Notice of Upcoming Hearing to Collect Information on Inequality," n.d., Box 87, Folder 9; US Department of Health, Education, and Welfare, National Institute of Education, Public Hearings Testimony, an Edited Summary and Evaluation, Doc ED 071 560 HE 003 681, September 1972, https://files.eric.ed.gov/fulltext/ED071560.pdf.

22. U.S. Department of Health, Education, and Welfare, National Institute of Education, *The Status of Women at the City University of New York: A Report to the Chancellor*, Doc ED 081 347 HE 004 507, December 1972: iii, https://files.eric.ed.gov/fulltext/ED081347.pdf.

23. *Constance Cook Papers*, Forwarding Notice of Sexual Discrimination Complaint to Fellow Committee Member Zelda Jones, dated March 17, 1972; letter from Ruth Cowan, February 1, 1972, Box 87, Folder 9.

24. Others whose service ended before submission of the final report: Dean Gladys Correa, Professor Elizabeth Wickendon, Shana Alexander, NYC Councilwoman Aileen Ryan, and Professor Lillian Weber.

25. "Cornell Criticized in Hiring Politics," *New York Times*, January 31, 1973, 65.

26. Rosemary Gunning, Transcript of Oral Interview, Albany, NY, 5.

27. Rosemary Gunning, Transcript of Oral Interview, Albany, NY, 5.

28. "New Group Fights Mass Pupil Shifts," *New York Times*, October 3, 1963, 20. Gunning is not listed as having a leadership role in the creation of PAT out of fifteen separate groups. The figure quoted in the article is Bernard Kessler, counsel to one of the merging groups.

29. "NAACP Seeking Talk on Housing," *New York Times*, February 20, 1965, 26 (350,000); Ravitch, *The Great School Wars*, 271 (300,000); "State to Review Integration Plan for City Schools," *New York Times*, February 25, 1964, 1 (500,000).

30. Gunning's acknowledged leadership is consistently reported in the press throughout 1964. Beginning *New York Times*, February 16, 1964, 1, until she resigned to run for president of the City Council in 1965 on the Conservative Party line, *New York Times*, July 2, 1965, 15. She is first credited as executive secretary of PAT, but by August she is called "the undisputed leader of the anti-busing forces." See "New York Schools Face a Boycott: Busing Opposed by Whites," *Chicago Tribune*, August 30, 1964, A3. A profile on Gunning when she announced her retirement from the legislature called her the "chairman" of PAT. See "Rosemary Gunning, at 71, Ends Legislative Career," *New York Times*, June 8, 1976, 24.

31. New York City's battle over integration in 1963–1964 is covered in Diane Ravitch, "Boycotts and Demonstrations," chapter 24 and "The Allen Report," chapter 25, in *The Great School Wars: A History of the New York City Public Schools*, 267–86; "Allen to Offer School Plan for Easing Tension Here, *New York Times*, February 16, 1964, 1.

32. "Allen to Offer School Plan for Easing Tension Here, *New York Times*, February 16, 1964, 1.

33. Ravitch, *The Great School Wars*, 268.

34. Rosemary Gunning, Transcript of Oral Interview, Albany, NY, 5; "Boycott Organizers Plan Own Schools," *New York Times*, August 12, 1964, 1.

35. "Integration Furor, White Parent in New York Protest Plan to 'Pair' Schools," *Wall Street Journal*, April 23, 1964, 16.

36. Robert Snyder, *Crossing Broadway: Washington Heights and the Promise of New York City* (Ithaca: Cornell University Press, 2015), 82; Ravitch, *The Great School Wars*, 271. Both authors suggest an extreme militancy existed among the white membership.

37. Snyder, *Crossing Broadway*, 70.

38. Snyder, *Crossing Broadway*, 84–85.

39. Snyder, *Crossing Broadway*, 69.

40. Snyder, *Crossing Broadway*, 81.

41. "Planner of White Boycott: Rosemary Gunning," *New York Times*, August 12, 1964, 23.

42. "Planner of White Boycott: Rosemary Gunning," *New York Times*, August 12, 1964, 23.

43. "Parents to Stage Protest Today," *New York Times*, March 12, 1964, 26.

44. "State to Review Integration Plan for City Schools," *New York Times*, February 25, 1964, 1; "Wide Opposition Is Found to Pupil Transfers Here," *New York Times*, March 12, 1965, 1; "Parents to State Protest Today," *New York Times*, March 12, 1964, 26; "NAACP & CORE Map Joint Action," *New York Times*, April

4, 1964, 1; "School Plan Foes Map Bitter Fight," *New York Times*, June 5, 1964, 1; "Schools Consider Transfer Plan," *New York Times*, July 11, 1964, 52.

45. Obituary, George Cott, *New York Times*, July 10, 1972, 34.

46. "Wagner to Meet School Plan Foes," *New York Times*, August 19, 1964, 26; "Council Defeats Four Moves to Block Pupil Transfers," *New York Times*, September 25, 1964, 1. At first the City claimed the petition did not have enough valid signatures, which turned out not to be true. The City then shifted its challenge to process grounds, claiming the petition was filed after the deadline to qualify for the fall election. See "Whites Here Plan a School Boycott, *New York Times*, August 11, 1964, 1.

47. "Court Says Allen Has Power to Pair Schools," *New York Times*, July 23, 1964, 1.

48. "Boycott Is Hinted on School Pairing," *New York Times*, June 22, 1964, 14; "Whites Here Plan a School Boycott," *New York Times*, August 11, 1964, 1; "Boycott Organizers Plan Own Schools," *New York Times*, August 12, 1964, 1; "Planner of the White Boycott," *New York Times*, August 12, 1964, 23. Press reports cite two organizations planning the boycott, PAT, and the Joint Council for Better Education. At the same time, the press identifies Gunning as "the undisputed leader of the anti-busing forces."

49. "Absences Drop 2d Day of School Boycott in N.Y.," *Chicago Tribune*, September 16, 1964, 16.

50. "New Laws Urged by Boycott Groups," *New York Times*, September 16, 1964, 21.

51. "Slate Completed by Conservatives," *New York Times*, July 2, 1965, 15.

52. Timothy Sullivan, *New York State and the Rise of Modern Conservatism: Redrawing Party Lines* (Albany: State University of New York Press, 2009), 56–57.

53. Rosemary Gunning, Transcript of Oral Interview, Albany, NY, 5; Sullivan, *Rise of Modern Conservatism*, 88.

54. Rosemary Gunning, Transcript of Oral Interview, Albany, NY, 5. Gunning said she was not the first choice of the party, but replaced the other candidate late in the summer. It was feared the other person would not meet residency requirements in the district.

55. "Conservatives to Enter All Major City Races in State in 1969," *New York Times*, November 1 5, 1968, 31.

56. "Conservative Party's Influence on State Politics Expected to Grow," *New York Times*, May 25, 1970, 22.

57. "43 Freshmen Members of the Legislature . . . ," *New York Times*, January 9, 1969, 19.

58. Ravitch, *The Great School Wars*, 308; Cannato, *The Ungovernable City*, 309.

59. Ravitch, *The Great School Wars*, 310.

60. Ravitch, *The Great School Wars*, 308.

61. "The Elusive School-Reform Compromise," *New York Times*, April 29, 1969, 32.

62. Cannato, *The Ungovernable City*, 348–49.

63. "Albany Creates 7-Member Board for City Schools," *New York Times*, May 28, 1973, 1; Ravitch, *The Great School Wars*, 386–87.

64. Ravitch, *The Great School Wars*, 386.

65. "The Elusive School-Reform Compromise," *New York Times*, April 29, 1969, 32.

66. Rosemary Gunning, Transcript of Oral Interview, Albany, NY, 10.

67. "Assembly Rejects Move to License Lay Analysts," *New York Times*, April 13, 1973, 52. In 1973 when she introduced a resolution supporting the calling of a constitutional convention to amend the US Constitution to prohibit busing for integration of schools. Though passed by the Assembly 86 to 36, the resolution and the idea went nowhere after that.

68. Wilbur Rich, *David Dinkins and New York City Politics: Race, Images, and the Media* (Albany: State University of New York Press, 2007), 168–70.

69. Kim Phillips-Fein and Ester Cyna, "Harlem Schools and the Fiscal Crisis," in Ansley T. Erickson and Ernest Morrell, eds., *Educating Harlem: A Century of Schooling and Resistance in a Black Community* (New York: Columbia University Press, 2019), 257–59.

70. Phillips-Fein and Cyna, "Harlem Schools and the Fiscal Crisis," 261.

71. Brittney Lewer, "Pursuing 'Real Power to Parents,'" in Ansley T. Erickson and Ernest Morrell, editors, *Educating Harlem: A Century of Schooling and Resistance in a Black Community* (New York: Columbia University Press, 2019), 278.

72. Phillips-Fein and Cyna, "Harlem Schools and the Fiscal Crisis," 284–85.

73. The word *reform* in this context specifically references legislation that would provide for specific legal exemptions to the existing ban on abortions in New York State. That is to be distinguished from calls and proposals to "repeal" the ban on abortion.

74. *Constance Cook Papers*, Dear Colleague Letter authored by Richard Blumenthal, dated January 9, 1967; Copy of "An Act to Amend the Public Health Law in Relation to Therapeutic Abortions," Box 28, Folder labeled 1967 Legislation Health–Abortion.

75. *Constance Cook Papers*, Letter from Cook to Mrs. Daniel Frey dated April 12, 1967, Box 28, Folder labeled 1967 Legislation Health–Abortion.

76. "Legislature Voids Birth Control Ban in Effect 84 Years," *New York Times*, June 17, 1 1965, 1. The existing language had been in effect since 1881. While the language banning birth control was removed, the prohibition on information designed to cause an unlawful abortion remained. Cook noted in her remarks that this legislation was in keeping with the 1965 Supreme Court decision in *Griswold v. Connecticut*, which laid out a right to privacy (in this case for married couples).

It actually went further in that licensed pharmacies could provide those materials to any adult.

77. Stacie Taranto, *Kitchen Table Politics: Conservative Women & Family Values in New York* (Philadelphia: University of Pennsylvania, 2017), 63.

78. *Constance Cook Papers*, "How Women Feel about Abortion," *Ithaca Sentinel*, March 11, 1967, Box 28, Folder labeled 1967 Legislation Health–Abortion. Positions of the legislators are taken directly from interviews with them in the article.

79. *Constance Cook Papers*, undated press clipping, Box 28, Folder labeled 1967 Legislation Health–Abortion.

80. *Constance Cook Papers*, clipping from the *Knickerbocker News*, February 13, 1967, 5B, Box 28, Folder labeled 1967 Legislation Health–Abortion.

81. Committee Reports and Public Hearing Transcripts, *NYS Governor's Committee Appointed to Review New York State's Abortion Law*, 1968, Series 10996, New York State Archives, Albany, New York. The recommended areas of approved abortion would be preserving the mother's life; grave danger to the mother's physical or mental health; permanent physical or mental condition rendering the mother incapable of caring for the child; substantial risk of major birth defects or physical or mental abnormalities in the child; pregnancy resulting from an act of rape or incest; pregnancy commenced when the mother was single and under age sixteen and is still unmarried; and female has at least four living children (under certain conditions).

82. "States Are Pressing for Repeal of Abortion Laws," *New York Times*, March 12, 1970, 21.

83. "Sponsors in Albany Optimistic on Reform of Abortion Laws," *New York Times*, November 23, 1969, 78; Taranto, Kitchen *Table Politics*, 65. The Blumenthal bill was defeated in the Assembly seventy-eight to sixty-nine.

84. "Albany's Year: From Abortion to Redistricting," *New York Times*, January 5, 1970, 36.

85. "Brydges Easing Opposition to New Abortion Law," *New York Times*, February 19, 1970, 51.

86. "Abortion Bill Advocate: Constance Eberhardt Cook," *New York Times*, April 9, 1970, 46.

87. "Abortion Reform Beaten in the Assembly by 3 Votes," *New York Times*, March 31, 1970, 1; *Constance Cook Papers*, "How Women Feel about Abortion," *Ithaca Sentinel*, March 11, 1967, Box 28, Folder labeled 1967 Legislation Health–Abortion; "Duryea Vote Ban Kills Abortion Bill," *The Saratogian*, March 31, 1970, 2A.

88. Taranto, *Kitchen Table Politics*, 66.

89. Mary Ann Krupsak, Transcript of Oral Interview, May 3, 1994, 7.

90. "Duryea Vote Ban Kills Abortion," *The Saratogian*, March 31, 1970, 2A.

91. "Duryea Vote Ban Kills Abortion," 2A.

92. "Abortion Reform Beaten in the Assembly by 3 Votes," *New York Times*, March 31, 1970, 1.

93. "New Vote Due Next Week," *New York Times*, April 1, 1970, 1. Duryea was seen as being in bind. He was personally in favor of reform, but the majority of the opposition came from his own Republican Party.

94. "Abortion Reform Is Voted by the Assembly, 76 to 73; Final Approval Expected," *New York Times*, April 10, 1970, 1.

95. *Connie Cook: A Documentary*, Sue Perlgut producer, 2016; "Abortion Reform Is Voted . . . ," *New York Times*, April 10, 1970, 1, 42.

96. *Connie Cook: A Documentary*, Sue Perlgut producer, 2016.

97. *Constance Cook Papers*, Editorial, *New York Times*, February 18, 1972, 94, Box 85, Folder 85, labeled 1972 Abortion Clippings. The Cook bill was the response to a four-to-three New York State Appeals Court decision supporting the withholding of Medicaid dollars from funding abortions.

98. "Aborting Abortions," *New York Times*, February 18, 1972, 34; Taranto, *Kitchen Table Politics*, 75. Congress passed the Hyde Amendment in 1976 that blocked the use of those funds for abortion nationwide.

99. *Constance Cook Papers*, untitled clipping, *Knickerbocker News*, May 8, 1972, 53, "Abortion Dispute in State Accentuated by Nixon's letter," *New York Times*, May 8, 1972, 1, Box 85, Folder labeled 1972 Abortion Clippings; "Nixon Weighed in for State Repeal," *New York Times*, May 7, 1972, 1.

100. Taranto, *Kitchen Table Politics*, 73–75; *Constance Cook Papers*, "Women Protesting Easier Abortions Storm Assembly and Halt Proceedings, *New York Times*, April 19, 1972, 94, Box 85, Folder labeled 1972 Abortion Clippings.

101. Taranto, *Kitchen Table Politics*, 77.

102. Taranto, *Kitchen Table Politics*, 82.

103. There is speculation that some of the votes lost were political calculations and nothing more. Members from conservative or even moderate districts supported the bill on the floor because they knew the governor would veto it.

104. *Constance Cook Papers*, "Abortion Reform Upheld," *New York Post*, July 7, 1972, n.p. visible, Box 85, Folder labeled 1972 Abortion Clippings. The vote was five-to-two.

105. *Constance Cook Papers*, Assembly Bill 11647, Box 103, Contraceptives, Folder 1972.

106. *Constance Cook Papers*, "Lobbying at Its Peak" and "Sponsors 18 Week Bill," *Ithaca Journal*, May 9, 1972, n.p. visible, Box 85, Folder labeled 1972 Abortion Clippings.

107. *Constance Cook Papers*, Editorial, *Atlanta Journal Constitution*, May 18, 1972, n.p. visible, Box 85, Folder labeled 1972 Abortion Clippings.

108. *Constance Cook Papers*, *Newsday*, June 2, 1972, n.p. visible, Box 85, Folder labeled 1972 Abortion Clippings.

109. *Constance Cook Papers*, *Syracuse Post Standard*, May 10, 1972, 1, 14, Box 85, Folder labeled 1972 Abortion Clippings. She repeated the statement in the fall; see "Objectivity Urged for Abortion Foes," *New York Times*, September 28, 1972, 34.

110. "Objectivity Urged for Abortion Foes," *New York Times*, September 28, 1972, 34.

111. *Constance Cook Papers*, Assembly Bills A10047, A10048, A10050, A10051, Box 103, Contraceptives, Folder 1972. These are the bills Cook introduced in the Assembly.

112. *Constance Cook Papers*, Box 86, undated news release, Folder labeled 1972 News Releases.

113. "Assemblywoman Goads Women to Try for Policy Making Jobs, *Times Union*, May 20, 1965, 21. This article appeared on the "Features for Women" page.

114. *Waterville Times*, May 28, 1971, 8, February 17, 1972, 4. The bill was nicknamed the "McSorley Bill" after the famous New York City bar that was sued in 1969 for refusing to serve women. The bar only opened its doors after the City passed an ordinance making it illegal to discriminate because of sex.

115. "Constance Cook, 89; Wrote Abortion Law," *New York Times*, January 24, 2009; *Connie Cook: A Documentary*, Sue Perlgut producer, 2016.

116. Taranto, *Kitchen Table Politics*; 63–64. Here I differ with how Taranto's frames Cook's feminism. She sees it tied more explicitly to abortion as an issue than I do.

117. "Assembly to Get Black Woman," *New York Times*, November 19, 1972, 42

118. Author interview with Joyce Diggs, daughter and campaign manager of Estella Diggs, September 24, 2013.

119. *Elizabeth Connelly Papers*, various pieces of correspondence showing Connelly's support for banning partial birth abortion, including a Letter from Kathleen Lawson, executive director of the New York State Right to Life Committee, dated January 14, 1997; letter from Connelly to Michael Merlino, June 8, 1998, outlining the pro-life legislation she was supporting; Box 1, Folder 1, labeled Abortion.

120. *Elizabeth Connelly Papers*, letter from Connelly to Mr. and Mrs. Gene Cosgriff, Staten Island Right to Life Committee, January 14, 1997, Box 1, Folder 1, labeled Abortion.

121. *Elizabeth Connelly Papers*, Legislative Women's Caucus, Inc. New York State, "Caucus Programs," Box 56, Folder 4, labeled Women's Caucus.

122. *Elizabeth Connelly Papers*, Annual Summary of LWC activities from Devra Nusbaum to Elizabeth Connelly, dated May 30, 1995, Box 56, Folder 4, labeled Women's Caucus.

Chapter 8

1. "In Albany, Women Make Quiet Strikes," *New York Times*, January 28, 1987, B1. The references, information, and quotations in this paragraph and the one after it are taken from this article.

2. "Women in New York Find Fast Track Has Slowed," *New York Times*, August 12, 1986, A1.

3. Suzi Oppenheimer, Transcript of Oral Interview, *New York State Legislative Women's Caucus Oral History Project*, April 8, 1994, New York State Archives, Albany, NY, 5. There was not the same level of unity among women in the Senate. That was partly because of lack of power. Both efforts to start a Senate Task for on Women's Issues came from Democratic women who were in the minority.

4. "County's Influence in the State Assembly," *New York Times*, December 27, 1992, WC1.

5. Ten women were elected to the Assembly (7 Democrats and 3 Republicans). Three women were elected to the Senate (3 Democrats and 1 Republican).

6. *New York Times*, April 30, 1992, A1.

7. Linda DiVall, "More Females Are Running for Office," *New York Times*, May 14, 1992, A25.

8. See, for example, S. Roberts and G. Cohen, "Will 1992 Be the Year of the Woman?" *U.S. News & World Report*, April 27, 1992, 37; E. Salholz and E. Clift, "Women on the Run," *Newsweek* May 4, 1992, 18.

9. Timothy Krebs and Michael Walsh, "Nonincumbent Female Candidate Success in the 1992 U.S. House Elections," *Social Science Quarterly* 77, no. 3 (September 1996): 697–707; Jennifer Lawless and Richard Fox, *It Takes a Candidate: Why Women Don't Run for Office* (New York: Cambridge University Press, 2005), 25.

10. Linda Witt, Karen Paget, and Glenna Matthews, *Running as a Woman: Gender and Power in American Politics* (New York: Free Press, 1994), 5.

11. "'Year of the Woman' Becomes Reality as Record Number Win Seats," *Washington Post*, November 4, 1992, CA30.

12. Kira Sanbonmatsu and Susan Carrol, "Gender and Elections to the State Legislature: Then and Now," delivered at the Ninth Annual State Politics and Policy Conference (Chapel Hill, May 22–23, 2009), 11; Lawless and Fox, *It Takes a Candidate*, 96.

13. Witt, *Running as a Woman*, 6. See also "Women Advance in Politics by Evolution, Not Revolution," *New York Times*, October 21, 1992, A1.

14. Pamela Paxton, "Year of the Woman, Decade of the Man: Trajectories of Growth in Women's State Legislative Representation," *Social Science Research* 38 (2009): 87.

15. For an early example of both the use of the term and the impact of the Hill-Thomas hearings, see "The Year of the Woman," *New York Times*, April 30, 1992, A1. In addition to those two women, Patty Murray of Washington and Jean Lloyd-Jones of Iowa tied their campaigns directly to the hearings. For an academic validation of the impact of the hearings on the 1992 election, see Michael Delli Carpini and Bruce Williams, "The Year of the Woman? Candidates, Votes and the 1992 Elections," *Political Science Quarterly* 108 (1993): 31, 34.

16. Yeakel lost a close race to Specter 49-to-46 percent, a difference of 13,149 votes.

17. Elizabeth Holtzman, *Who Said It Would Be Easy? One Woman's Life in the Political Arena* (New York: Arcade Publishing, 1996), 246–47.

18. "Bus Tour for Votes; Holtzman Hits Road to Attack Ferraro," *New York Times*, August 14, 1992, 21; "Holtzman Draws Criticism from Feminists over Ads," *New York Times*, August 27, 1992, B4; "Ferraro's About-Face," *New York Times*, September 11, 1992, B7; Holtzman, *Who Said It Would Be Easy*, 248.

19. Holtzman, *Who Said It Would Be Easy*, 247.

20. "For Feminists, It Wasn't What They Had in Mind." *New York Times*, September 17, 1992; B5.

21. Richard Norton Smith, *On His Own Terms: A Life of Nelson Rockefeller* (New York: Random House, 2014); 459–60.

22. Timothy J. Sullivan, *New York State and the Rise of Modern Conservatism*, 2, 8.

23. "Albany Democrats Hope Clinton's Coattails Will Help Them Take Back Senate," *New York Times*, October 18, 1992, 50.

24. Suzi Oppenheimer, Transcript of Oral Interview, Albany, NY, 2.

25. "County's Influence in the State Assembly," *New York Times*, December 27, 1992, WCI.

26. Interview with Cecile Singer, August 12, 2015.

27. Interview with Naomi Matusow, February 15, 2014.

28. *New York Times*, May 6, 1990, WCI.

29. "New County Lineup for State Assembly," *New York Times*, October 18, 1992, WCI.

30. Edward Schneier and John Brian Murtaugh, *New York Politics a Tale of Two States*, 133; *The Modern New York Legislature*, XXIV, 42–44.

31. "A New County Lineup for State Assembly," *New York Times*, October 19, 1992, WC4.

32. "County's Influence in State Assembly, *New York Times*, December 27, 1992, WCI.

33. Interview with Sandra Galef, June 5, 2015.

34. Galef interview, June 5, 2015.

35. Galef interview, June 5, 2015.

36. Galef interview, June 5, 2015.

37. Galef interview, June5, 2015.

38. "A New City Lineup for State Assembly," *New York Times*, October 18, 1992, WC1

39. Galef interview, June 5, 2015.

40. David McKay Wilson newspaper column, *Audrey Hochberg Papers*, Box 2, Folder 1, Westchester County Historical Society.

41. "A New County Lineup for the State Assembly," *New York Times*, October 18, 1992, WC1.

42. 1992 Campaign Flyer "For Some-Commitment Begins Early in Life," *Audrey Hochberg Papers*, Box 3, Folder 11, Westchester County Historical Society.

43. Campaign postcard, *Audrey Hochberg Papers*.

44. David McKay Wilson newspaper column, *Audrey Hochberg Papers*, Box 2, Folder 1.

45. Gannett *Inquirer* article, *Audrey Hochberg Papers*, Box 2, Folder 1.

46. Singer interview, August 12, 2015.

47. "Singer Wins G.O.P.'s Assembly Contest," *New York Times*, October 1988, WC1.

48. Cecile Singer, Transcript of Oral Interview, *New York State Legislative Women's Caucus Oral History Project*, April 4, 1994, New York State Archives, Albany, NY, 5.

49. Singer interview, August 12, 2015.

50. "Ticket Formation Proves Difficult," *New York Times*, June 18, 1992, WC16.

51. "Democrats See Uphill State Senate Battle," *New York Times*, September 26, 1982, WC1; "Democrats Concede Seat to Goodhue," *New York Times*, August 21, 1988, WC6.

52. George Marlin, *Fighting the Good Fight: A History of the New York Conservative Party* (South Bend: St. Augustine's Press, 2002), 293.

53. "Taking on the Change-NY Challenge," *New York Times*, May 24, 1992, 41.

54. Senate Majority Leader Marino opposed much of what Change-NY was trying to do. One interpretation is that Marino liked the current arrangement where he dominated the party and could cut deals with a Democratic Governor that benefited his own district on Long Island. See Marlin, *Fighting the Good Fight*: 292–93.

55. Galef interview, June 5, 2015.

56. "Taking on the Change-NY Challenge," *New York Times*, May 24, 1992, 41; "GOP Fears It May Lose Goodhue's Safe Seat," *New York Times*, May 31, 1992, WC1; "Upset by Pataki Leaves a Conservative Message," *New York Times*, September 20, 1992, WC1.

57. "GOP Fears It May Lose Goodhue's Safe Seat," *New York Times*, May 31, 1992, WC1.

58. "Race for New York Senate Signifies Republican' Turmoil," *New York Times*, August 13, 1992, B1.

59. "Race for New York Senate," August 13, 1992.

60. "Upset by Pataki Leaves a Conservative Message," *New York Times*, September 20, 1992, WC1.

61. Witt, *Running as a Woman*, 19.

62. "An 11 Member Force in Albany," *New York Times*, June 18, 2000, WE1.

63. Matusow interview, February 15, 2015; Singer interview, August 12, 2015.

64. Galef interview, June 8, 2015.

65. "An 11 Member Force in Albany," *New York Times*, June 18, 2000, WE1.

66. Nancy Baker Jones and Ruthe Winegarten, *Capitol Women*, 15.

67. "The Voice of Women in Politics," *New York Times*, September 15, 1996, WC1.

68. "County's Influence in the State Assembly," *New York Times*, December 27, 1992, WC13.

69. Cecile Singer, Transcript of Oral Interview, 11.

70. Singer interview, August 12, 2015.

71. Christina Wolbrecht, *The Politics of Women's Rights: Parties, Positions and Change* (Princeton: Princeton University Press, 2000), 11 and chapter 5, "Equilibrium, Disruption, and Issue Redefinition."

72. Galef interview, June 5, 2015; Matusow interview February 5, 2014; Singer interview August 12, 2015.

73. As recently as 2008 the Caucus commissioned a study by the University at Albany Center for Women in Government and Civil Society focused to identify ways to better address its mission. The final report noted that the Caucus identity remained undefined and there were unresolved tensions around bipartisanship. Judith Saidel and Dina Refki, "Assessment of Legislative Women's Caucus Executive Committee Members' Priorities," Center for Women in Government and Civil Society (Nelson A. Rockefeller College of Public Affairs & Policy, 2008), 3.

74. Marlin, *Fighting the Good Fight*, 318.

75. "Cuomo's G.O.P. Rival Faces Biggest Challenge, *New York Times*, May 24, 1994, B4.

76. Marlin, *Fighting the Good Fight*, 331–32.

77. Craig L. Brians, "Women for Women?: Gender and Party Bias in voting for Female Candidates," *American Politics Research* 33 (2005): 368.

78. Anne Marie Cammisa and Beth Reingold, "Women in State Legislatures and State Legislative Research: Beyond Sameness and Difference," *State Politics and Policy Quarterly* 4, no. 2 (Summer 2004): 192, 197.

79. Pamela Paxton, "Year of the Woman, Decade of the Man . . . ," 98.

80. Interview with Joni Yoswein, October 3, 2013. Yoswein was also campaign manager for State Senator Martin Markowitz's unsuccessful campaign for Brooklyn Borough president in 1985, and a Democratic state committeewoman.

81. Yoswein Interview, October 3, 2013; "With Miller Gone, Brooklynites Brawl for Power," *New York Times*, December 29, 1991, 23. Miller received probation for his conviction.

82. Yoswein Interview, October 3, 2013.

83. "This Race Is the Nastiest of the Season," *New York Times*, September 11, 1992, A34; Yoswein interview, October 3, 2013. Yowein ran in the general election on the Liberal line but lost again to the Democrat Brennan.

84. Green interview, May 30, 2013.

85. "Assembly Passes Nation's Toughest Legislation against Predatory Lending," *Voice of Harlem*, July 25, 2001, 9; Greene interview, May 30, 2013.

Conclusion

1. Kira Sanbonmatsu and Susan Carroll, "Gender and Election to the State Legislatures: Then and Now," paper delivered at the 9th Annual State Politics and Policy Conference, May 22–23, 2009, Chapel Hill, NC, 4.

2. John Carey, Richard Niemi, and Lynda Powell, "Are Women State Legislators Different?," in Sue Thomas and Clyde Wilcox, eds., *Women and Elective Office: Past, Present, and Future* (New York: Oxford University Press, 1998), 87–88.

3. Kira Sanbonmatsu, "Gender Pools and Puzzles: Charting a "Woman's Path" to the Legislature," *Politics and Gender* 2, no. 3 (2006); Kira Sanbonmatsu and Susan Carroll, "Gender and Election to the State Legislatures: Then and Now," paper delivered at the 9th Annual State Politics and Policy Conference, May 22–23, 2009, Chapel Hill, NC.

4. Kira Sanbonmatsu, "Gender Pools and Puzzles," 387.

5. Kira Sanbonmatsu, "Gender Pools and Puzzles," 396. See also Kathleen Dolan and Lynne Ford, "Are All Women State Legislators Alike? In Sue Thomas and Clyde Wilcox, ed., *Women and Elective Office: Past, Present, and Future* (New York: Oxford University Press, 1998), 76.

6. Sanbonmatsu and Carroll, "Gender and Election to State Legislatures . . . ," 8.

7. "Assemblyman Miss Smith of Harlem," *New York Times*, November 9, 1919, XXI.

8. Kathleen Dolan and Lynne Ford, "Change and Continuity among Women Legislators: Evidence from Three Decades," *Political Research Quarterly* 50, no. 1 (March 1997): 143.

9. Kathleen Dolan and Lynne Ford, "Change and Continuity among Women Legislators," 143.

10. Sanbonmatsu and Carroll, "Gender and Election to State Legislatures . . . ," 10.

11. Cindy Simon Rosenthal, *When Women Lead: Integrative Leadership in State Legislatures* (New York: Oxford University Press, 1998), 36, 46, 119; Paul Herrnson, J. Celest Lay, and Atiya Kai Stokes, "Women Running 'as Women': Candidate Gender, Campaign Issues, and Voter-Targeting Strategies," *Journal of Politics* 65, no. 1 (February 2003): 246; Dolan and Ford, "Change and Continuity among Women Legislators . . . ," 144, 148.

12. Martin Melosi, *Fresh Kills: A History of Consuming and Discarding in New York City* (New York: Columbia University Press, 2020), 310–11.

13. Rosenthal, *When Women Lead*, 48, 61, 71.
14. Rosenthal, *When Women Lead*, 120.

Bibliography

Government Publications

Biographical Sketches of the Women of the New York State Legislature 1918–1988, New York State Library, Albany, NY. There were editions published in 1988 and 1998.
New York Red Book: An Illustrated State Manual, New York State Library, Albany, NY. Printed by year.
New York State Black, Puerto Rican, Hispanic and Asian Legislative Caucus, *1917–2014: A Look at the History of Legislators of Color.*
New York State Legislature Bill Jackets Collection, NYS Archives, Albany, NY.
New York State Legislature, Member Introduction Books, NYS Archives, Albany, NY.
The Status of Women at the City University of New York: A Report to the Chancellor, US Department of Health, Education, and Welfare, Washington, DC.

Manuscript Collections

Connelly, Elizabeth. Papers. Archives and Special Collections, College of Staten Island, Staten Island, NY.
Cook, Constance. Papers, Department of Manuscripts and Archives, Cornell University, Ithaca, NY.
Elliott, Maude. Papers. Special Collections, Brown University, Providence, RI.
Gordon, Janet. Papers. New York State Archives, Albany, NY.
Graves, Rhoda Fox. Papers. Modern Political Archive, M. E. Grenander Department of Special Collections and Archives, University Libraries, University at Albany, State University of New York, Albany, NY
Hay, Mary Garrett. Scrapbook. New York Public Library, NY.
Hochberg, Audrey. Papers. Westchester County Archives, Elmsford, NY.
Jacobs, Rhoda. Papers. Brooklyn College Library Archives and Special Collections, Brooklyn College, Brooklyn, NY.

Mendez, Olga. Senatorial Papers. Archives of the Puerto Rican Diaspora, Centro de Estudios Puertorriquenos, Hunter College, CUNY, NY.
National Order of Women Legislators Collection. Smith College Special Collections, Smith College, Northampton, MA.
Smith, Alfred E. Papers. New York State Library, Albany, NY.
Taylor, Mildred Frick, Papers, Modern Political Archive, M. E. Grenander Department of Special Collections and Archives, University Libraries, University at Albany, State University of New York, Albany, NY.
Todd, Jane Hedges. Reminiscences. 1952. Columbia Oral History Project, Columbia University, New York.
———. Papers. Department of Manuscripts and Archives, Cornell University, Ithaca, NY.

Oral Histories and Interviews

Connelly, Elizabeth. Transcript of Oral Interview, *Legislative Women's Caucus Oral History Project*, New York State Archives, Albany, NY.
Delmonte, Francine. Author interview, May 2013.
Diggs, Joyce. Author interview, September 2013.
Galef, Sandra. Author interview, June 2015.
Greene, Aurelia. Author interview, May 2013.
Gunning, Rosemary. Transcript of Oral Interview, *Legislative Women's Caucus Oral History Project*, New York State Archives, Albany, NY.
Krupsak, Mary Ann. Transcript of Oral Interview, *Legislative Women's Caucus Oral History Project*, New York State Archives, Albany, NY.
Matusow, Naomi. Author Interview. February 2014.
Motley, Constance Baker. Transcript of Oral Interview, *Legislative Women's Caucus Oral History Project*, New York State Archives, Albany, NY.
Oppenheimer, Suzi. Transcript of Oral Interview, *Legislative Women's Caucus Oral History Project*, New York State Archives, Albany, NY.
Runyon, Marie. Author interview, November 2013.
Singer, Cecile. Author interview, August 2015.
———. Transcript of Oral Interview, *Legislative Women's Caucus Oral History Project*, New York State Archives, Albany, NY.
Tranholm, Shirley. Author interview May 2017.
Yoswein, Joni. Author interview, October 2013.

Newspapers

Brooklyn Daily Eagle.
National Republican, New York State Library, Albany, NY.

New York Times.
Woman Republican, New York Public Library, New York City, NY.
Miscellaneous news outlets around New York State, https://fultonhistory.com/Fulton.html.

Articles, Dissertations, Unpublished Papers

Ahlberg, Clark, and Daniel P. Moynihan. "Changing Governors and Politics." *Public Administration Review* 20, no. 4 (Autumn 1960): 195–204.

Baker, Jean. "Getting Right with Women's Suffrage." *Journal of the Gilded Age and Progressive Era* 5, no. 1 (January 2006): 7–18.

Baker, Paula. "The Domestication of Politics: Women and American Political Society 1780–1920." *American Historical Review* 89 (June 1984): 620–47.

Barnello, Michelle. "Gender and Roll Call Voting in the New York State Assembly." *Women and Politics* 20, no. 4 (2001): 77–94.

Becker, Susan. "International Feminism between the Wars: The National Woman's Party Versus the League of Women Voters." In Scharf and Jensen, eds., *Decades of Discontent the Women's Movement 1920–40.* Westport, CT: Greenwood Press, 1983, 223–42.

Blair, Emily Newell. "Women in the Political Parties." *Annals of American Academy of Political and Social Science* 143 (May 1929): 220.

Bostwick, Kate M. "Women's Political Clubs." *Monthly Illustrator* (December 1896): 304–8.

Butler, Sarah Schuyler. "Women Who Do not Vote." *Scribner's Magazine* 76, November 1924, 529–33.

Cammisa, Anne Marie, and Beth Reingold. "Women in State Legislatures and State Legislative Research: Beyond Sameness and Difference." *State Politics and Policy Quarterly* 4, no. 2 (Summer 2004): 181–210.

Carpini, Michael Delli, and Bruce Williams. "The Year of the Woman? Candidates, Votes, and the 1992 Elections." *Political Science Quarterly* 108 (1993): 29–36.

Fisher, Marguerite J., "Women in the Political Parties," *Annals of the American Academy of Political Science and Social Sciences* 251 (May 1947): 87–93.

Fox, Richard, and Jennifer Lawless. "Gendered Perceptions and Political Candidates: A Central Barrier to Women's Equality in Electoral Politics." *America Journal of Political Science* 55, no. 1 (January 2011): 59–73.

Freeman, Jo, " 'One Man, One Vote; One Woman, One Throat.' " Women in New York City Politics, 1890–1910." *American Nineteenth Century History* 1, no. 3 (Autumn 2000): 101–23.

Gustafson, Melanie. "Florence Collins Porter and the Concept of the Principled Partisan Woman." *Frontiers: A Journal of Women's Studies* 18, no. 1 (Summer 1997): 7–30.

Hill, David. "Political Culture and Female Political Representation. *Journal of Politics* 43, no. 1 (February 1981): 159–68.

———. "Women State Legislators and Party Voting on the ERA." *Social Science Quarterly* 64 (June 1983): 318–26.

Kleppner, Paul. "Were Women to Blame? Female Suffrage and Voter Turnout." *Journal of Interdisciplinary History* 12, no. 4 (Spring 1982): 621–43.

Koven, Seth, and Sonya Michel. "Womanly Duties: Maternalist Politics and the Origins of the Welfare States in France, Germany, Great Britain and the United States, 1880–1920." *American Historical Review* 95, no. 4 (October 1990): 1076–108.

Kozakiewicz, Lauren. "Political Episodes 1890–1960: Three Republican Women in Twentieth Century New York State Politics." PhD diss., University at Albany, State University of New York, 2006.

———. "Too Pure for Politics: Women, Non-Partisanship and the Hughes Campaign Train of 1916," Delivered at the American Historical Association 125th Annual Conference, January 8, 2011.

Krebs, Timothy, and Michael Walsh. "Nonincumbent Female Candidate Success in the 1992 U.S. House Elections." *Social Science Quarterly* 77, no. 3 (September 1996): 697–707.

McGerr, Michael. "Political Style and Women's Power, 1830–1930." *Journal of American History* 77, no. 3 (December 1990): 864–85.

McPherson, J. Miller, and Lynn Smith-Lovin. "Sex Segregation in Voluntary Associations." *American Sociological Review* 51, no. 1 (February 1986): 61–79.

Monsoon, S. "The Lady and the Tiger: Electoral Activism in New York City before Suffrage." *Journal of Women's History* (fall 1990): 100–35.

Morrison, Glenda E. "Women's Participation in the 1928 Presidential Campaign." PhD diss., University of Kansas, 1978.

"Oleo under Federal Law 1886–1949." *Congressional Digest* 28, no. 5 (May 1949): 135–36.

Paxton, Pamela. "Year of the Woman, Decade of the Man: Trajectories of Growth in Women's State Legislative Representation." *Social Science Research* 38 (2009): 86–102.

Perry, Elisabeth Israels. "Men Are from the Gilded Age, Women Are from the Progressive Era." *Journal of the Gilded Age and Progressive Era* 1, no. 1 (January 2002): 25–48.

Perry, Elisabeth Israels. "Rhetoric, Strategy, and Politics in the New York Campaign for Women's Jury Service." *New York History* (Winter 2001): 53–78.

Perry, Elisabeth Israels. "Women's Political Choices after Suffrage: The Women's City Club of New York 1915–1990." *New York History* (October 1990): 417–34.

Pitney, John, Jr. "Leaders and Rules in the New York State Senate." *Legislative Studies Quarterly* 7, no. 4 (November 1982).

Roberts, S. V., and S. Cohen. "Will 1992 Be the Year of the Woman?" *U.S. News & World Report* 112, no. 16 (April 27, 1992): 2–5.
Roosevelt, Theodore. "Machine Politics in New York City. *The Century* 33, no. 1 (November 1886): 74–82.
Saidel, Judith, and Dina Refki. "Assessment of Legislative Women's Caucus Executive Committee Members' Priorities." *University at Albany, Center for Women in Government and Civil Society*. Nelson A. Rockefeller College of Public Affairs and Policy, 2008.
Saint-Germain, Michelle. "Does Their Difference Make a Difference? The Impact of Women on Public Policy in the Arizona Legislature." *Social Science Quarterly* 70, no. 4 (1989): 956–68.
Sanjek, Roger. "Color-Full before Color Blind: the Emergence of Multiracial Neighborhood Politics in Queens, New York City." *American Anthropologist* 102, no. 4 (2000): 762–72.
Stein, Judith. "The Impact of the New Deal on New York Politics: Kenneth Simpson and the Republican Party." *New York Historical Quarterly* 56 (January 1972): 29–53.
Swers, Michele. "Research on Women in Legislatures: What Have We Learned, Where Are We Going?" *Women & Politics* 23, no. 1/2 (2001): 167–85.
Thomas, Sue, and Susan Welch. "The Impact of Gender on Activities and Priorities of State Legislators." *Western Political Quarterly* (1990): 445–56.
Wilkerson-Freeman, Sarah. *Women and the Transformation of American Politics: North Carolina, 1898–1940*. PhD diss., University of North Carolina at Chapel Hill, 1995.
Zimmerman, Joseph. "Can the 'Year of the Woman' Be Repeated?" *National Civic Review* 85, no. 2 (Spring 1995): 5–6.

Books and Book Chapters

Anderson, Kristi. *After Suffrage Women in Partisan and Electoral Politics before the New Deal*. Chicago: University of Chicago Press, 1996.
Argersinger, Jo-Ann, ed. *The Triangle Fire: A Brief History with Documents*. Boston: Bedford/St. Martin's, 2016.
Baker, Jean, ed. *Votes for Women: The Struggle for Suffrage Revisited*. Oxford, UK: Oxford University Press, 2002.
Baker, Paula. "The Gilded Age." In Milton Klein, ed., *The Empire State: A History of New York*. New York: New York State Historical Association, 2001.
———. *The Moral Frameworks of Public Life: Gender Politics and the State in Rural New York 1830–1920*. New York: Oxford University Press, 1991.
———. "'She Is the Best Man on the Ward Committee': Women in Grassroots Party Organizations, 1930s–1950s." In Melanie Gustafson, Kristie Miller,

and Elisabeth Israels Perry, eds., *We Have Come to Stay: Women and Political Parties 1880–1860*. Albuquerque: University of New Mexico Press, 1999.

Benjamin, Gerald, and Robert Nakamura, eds. *The Modern New York State Legislature: Redressing the Balance*. New York: Rockefeller Institute of Government, 1991.

Blake, Nelson Manfred. *The Road to Reno: A History of Divorce in America*. Westport, CT: Greenwood Press, 1962

Blocker, Jack. *"Give to the Winds Thy Fears": The Women's Temperance Crusade 1873–1874*. Westport, CT: Greenwood Press, 1985.

Bordin, Ruth. *Frances Willard: A Biography*. Chapel Hill: University of North Carolina Press, 1986.

———. *Women and Temperance*. Philadelphia: Temple University Press, 1981.

Breckinridge, Sophonisba. *Women in the Twentieth Century: A Study of Their Political, Social, and Economic Activities*. New York: McGraw-Hill, 1933.

Brown, Arthur, Dan Collins, and Michael Goodwin. *I, Koch: A Decidedly Unauthorized Biography of the Mayor of New York City*. New York: Dodd, Mead, 1985.

Buell, Bill. *George Lunn the 1912 Socialist Victory in Schenectady*. Troy, NY: Troy Bookmakers, 2019.

Cannato, Vincent. *The Ungovernable City: John Lindsay and His Struggle to Save New York*. New York: Basic Books, 2001.

Carey, John, Richard Niemi, and Lynda Powell. "Are Women State Legislators Different?" In *Women and Elective Office: Past, Present and Future*. New York: Oxford University Press, 1998.

Caro, Robert A. *The Power Broker Robert Moses and the Fall of New York*. New York: Vintage Books, 1974.

Carter, Stephen. *Invisible: The Forgotten Story of the Black Woman Lawyer Who Took Down America's Most Powerful Mobster*. New York: Henry Holt, 2018.

Chessman, Wallace, G. *Governor Theodore Roosevelt: The Albany Apprenticeship 1898–1900*. Cambridge, MA: Harvard University Press, 1965.

Chiles, Robert. *The Revolution of '28: Al Smith, American Progressivism, and the Coming of the New Deal*. Ithaca, NY: Cornell University Press, 2018.

Chisholm, Shirley. *Unbought & Unbossed*. Boston: Houghton Mifflin, 1970.

Clapp, Elizabeth J. *Mothers of All Children: Women Reformers and the Rise of Juvenile Courts in Progressive Era America*. University Park: Pennsylvania State University Press, 1998.

Connery, Robert H., and Gerald Benjamin. *Rockefeller of New York: Executive Power in the Statehouse*. Ithaca, NY: Cornell University Press, 1979.

Cook, Elizabeth Adell, Sue Thomas, and Clyde Wilcox, eds. *The Year of the Woman: Myths and Realities*. Boulder, CO: Westview Press, 1994.

Cott, Nancy. "Equal Rights and Economic Roles: The Conflict over the Equal Rights Amendment in the 1920s." In Linda Kerber, Sharon De Hart, Cornelia Dayton, and Judy Wu, eds., *Women's America: Refocusing the Past*, 8th ed. New York: Oxford University Press, 2015, 503–12.

Cox, Elizabeth M. *Women State and Territorial Legislators: A State-by-State Analysis, with Rosters of 6,000 Women*. Jefferson, NC: McFarland, 1996.

Critchlow, Donald T. *Phyllis Schlafly and Grassroots Conservatism: A Woman's Crusade*. Princeton, NJ: Princeton University Press, 2005.

Dearstyne, Bruce W. *The Spirit of New York: Defining Events in the Empire State's History*. Albany: State University of New York Press, 2015.

Diamond, Irene. *Sex Roles in the State House*. New Haven, CT: Yale University Press, 1977.

Dolan, Kathleen, and Lynne E. Ford. "Are All Women State Legislators Alike?" In Sue Thomas and Clyde Wilcox, ed., *Women in Elective Office: Past, Present, and Future*. New York: Oxford University Press, 1998.

Dubois, Ellen Carol. "The Next Generation of Suffragists: Harriot Stanton Blatch and Grassroots Politics." In Linda Kerber, Jane de Hart, and Cornelia Hugh Dayton, eds., *Women's America: Refocusing the Past*, 7th ed. New York: Oxford University Press, 2011.

Edwards, Rebecca. *Angels in the Machinery: Gender in American Party Politics from the Civil War to the Progressive Era*. New York: Oxford University Press, 1997.

Enstam, Elizabeth, "They Called It 'Motherhood': Dallas Women and Public Life 1895–1918." In Virginia Bernhard, B. Brandon, E. Fox-Genovese, T. Perdue, and E. Hayes Tunes, eds., *Hidden Histories of Women in the New South*. Columbia: University of Missouri Press, 1994.

Epstein, Barbara. *The Politics of Domesticity: Women, Evangelism, and Temperance in the 19th Century*. Middletown, CT: Wesleyan Press, 1981.

Erickson, Ansley, and Ernest Morrell, eds. *Educating Harlem: A Century of Schooling and Resistance in a Black Community*. New York: Columbia University Press, 2019.

Ford, Gary L., Jr. *Constance Baker Motley: One Woman's Fight for Civil Rights and Equal Justice Under Law*. Tuscaloosa: University of Alabama Press, 2017.

Freeman, Jo. *A Room at a Time: How Women Entered Party Politics*. Lanham, MD: Rowman and Littlefield, 2000.

———. *We Will Be Heard: Women's Struggles for Political Power in the United States*. Lanham, MD: Rowman and Littlefield, 2008.

Gallagher, Julie. *Black Women and Politics in New York City*. Urbana: University of Illinois Press, 2012.

Gidlow, Liette. *The Big Vote: Gender, Consumer Culture, and the Politics of Exclusion 1890s–1920s*. Baltimore, MD: Johns Hopkins University Press, 2004.

Golway, Terry. *Machine Made: Tammany Hall and the Creation of Modern American Politics*. New York: W. W. Norton, 2014.

Goodier, Susan, and Karen Pastorello. *Women Will Vote: Winning Suffrage in New York State*. Ithaca, NY: Cornell University Press, 2017.

Gunn, Ray. "Antibellum Society and Politics 1815–1860." In Milton Klein, ed., *The Empire State: A History of New York*. Ithaca, NY: Cornell University Press, 2001.

Gustafson, Melanie. *Women and the Republican Party 1854–1924*. Urbana: University of Illinois Press, 2001.

Hartog, Hendrik. *Man and Wife in America a History*. Cambridge, MA: Harvard University Press, 2000.

Harvey, Anna. *Votes without Leverage: Women in Electoral Politics, 1920–1970*. Cambridge, UK: Cambridge University Press, 1998.

Holtzman, Elizabeth. *Who Said It Would Be Easy? One Woman's Life in the Political Arena*. New York: Arcade Publishing, 1996.

Kornbluh, Mark L. *Why America Stopped Voting: The Decline of Participatory Democracy and the Emergence of Modern American Politics*. New York: NYU Press, 2000.

Kramer, Daniel. *The Days of Wine and Roses Are Over: Governor Hugh Carey and New York State*. Lanham, MD: University of America Press, 1997.

Jones, Nancy Baker, and Ruth Weingarten. *Capitol Women: Texas Female Legislators 1923–1999*. Austin: University of Texas Press, 2000.

Kerber, Linda. *Women of the Republic: Intellect and Ideology in Revolutionary America*. Chapel Hill: University of North Carolina Press, 1997.

Kirkpatrick, Jeane. *Political Woman*. New York: Basic Books, 1974.

Kuhn, David Paul. *The Hardhat Riot: Nixon, New York City, and the Dawn of the White Working-Class Revolution*. New York: Oxford University Press, 2020.

Ladd-Taylor, Mollie. *Mother-Work: Children, Welfare and the State 1890–1930*. Urbana: University of Illinois Press, 1994.

Laas, Virginia Jeans. *Bridging Two Eras: The Autobiography of Emily Newell Blair 1877–1951*. Columbia: University of Missouri Press, 1999.

Lawless, Jennifer, and Richard Fox. *It Takes a Candidate: Why Women Don't Run for Office*. New York: Cambridge University Press, 2004.

Lemons, Stanley. *The Woman Citizen*. Urbana: University of Illinois Press, 1973.

Lever, Brittney, "Pushing 'Real Power to Parent': Babette Edwards' Activism from Community Control to Charter Schools." In Ansley Erickson and Ernest Morrell, eds., *Educating Harlem: A Century of Schooling and Resistance in a Black Community*. New York: Columbia University Press, 2019.

Levine, Suzanne Braun, and Mary Thom. *Bella Abzug: An Oral History*. New York: Farrar, Straus and Giroux, 2007.

Mahler, Jonathan. *The Bronx Is Burning*. New York: Farrar, Straus and Giroux, 2005.

Marlin, George. *Fighting the Good Fight: A History of the New York Conservative Party*. South Bend, IN: St. Augustine's Press, 2002.

Matthews, Jane. "The Woman Suffrage Movement in Suffolk County New York 1911–1917: A Case Study of the Tactical Difference Between Two Prominent Long Island Suffragists, Mrs. Ida Bunce Sammis and Miss Rosalie Jones." Master's thesis, Adelphi University, 1988.

McCormick, Richard. *The Party Period and Public History*. New York: Oxford University Press, 1986.

McGerr, Michael. *The Decline of Popular Politics in the American North 1865–1928*. New York: Oxford University Press, 1986.

Melosi, Martin V. *Fresh Kills: A History of Consuming and Discarding in New York City*. New York: Columbia University Press, 2020.

Miller, Kristie. *Ruth Hanna McCormick a Life in Politics 1880–1914*. Albuquerque: University of New Mexico Press, 1992.

Murray, Sylvie. *The Progressive Housewife: Community Activism in Suburban Queens, 1945–1965*. Philadelphia: University of Pennsylvania Press, 2003.

Osselaer, Heidi. *Winning Their Place: Arizona Women in Politics, 1883–1950*. Tucson: University of Arizona Press, 2009.

Parker, Allison. *Purifying America: Women Cultural Reform and Pro-Censorship Activism 1873–1933*. Urbana: University of Illinois Press, 1997.

Paxton, Annabel. *Women in Congress*. Richmond, VA: Dietz Press, 1945.

Pecorella, Robert, "The Two New Yorks in the Twenty-first Century," in Robert Peccarella and Jeffrey Stonecash, eds., *Governing New York State*. 5th ed. Albany: State University of New York Press, 2006.

Perry, Elisabeth. *After the Vote: Feminist Politics in La Guardia's New York*. New York: Oxford Press, 2019.

———. *Belle Moskowitz: Feminine Politics and the Exercise of Power in the Age of Alfred E. Smith*. New York: Oxford University Press, 1977.

Phillips-Fein, Kim. *Fear City: New York's Fiscal Crisis and the Rise of Austerity Politics*. New York: Metropolitan Books, 2017.

Phillips-Fein, Kim, and Esther Cyna, "Harlem Schools in the Fiscal Crisis." In Ansley Erickson and Ernest Morrell eds., *Educating Harlem: A Century of Schooling and Resistance in a Black Community*. New York: Columbia University Press, 2019.

Podair, Jerald, E. *The Strike That Changed New York: Blacks, Whites, and the Ocean-Hill Brownsville Crisis*. New Haven, CT: Yale University Press, 2004.

Poeter, Emma, ed. *History of the National Order of Women Legislators*. Las Vegas: Hanes Thomas Printers, 1981.

Ravitch, Diane. *The Great School Wars: A History of New York City Public Schools*. Baltimore, MD: Johns Hopkins University Press, 2000.

Reingold, Beth. *Representing Women: Sex Gender and Legislative Behavior in Arizona and California*. Chapel Hill: North Carolina University Press, 2003.

Reitano, Joanne. *New York State: People, Places and Priorities*. New York: Routledge, 2016.

———. *The Restless City: A Short History of New York from Colonial Times to the Present*, 2nd ed. New York: Routledge, 2010.

Rich, Wilbur C. *David Dinkins and New York City Politics: Race, Images and the Media*. Albany: State University of New York Press, 2007.

Riordan, William, ed. *Plunkitt of Tammany Hall*. Boston: Bedford/St. Martin's, 1994.

Rosen, Ruth. *The World Split Open: How the Modern Women's Movement Changed America*. New York: Penguin, 2000.

Rosenthal, Cindy Simon. *When Women Lead: Integrative Leadership in State Legislatures*. New York: Oxford University Press, 1998.

Rymph, Catherine E. *Republican Women: Feminism and Conservatism from Suffrage through the Rise of the New Right*. Chapel Hill: University of North Carolina Press, 2006.

Sanjek, Roger. *The Future of Us All: Race and Neighborhood Politics in New York City*. Ithaca, NY: Cornell University Press, 1998.

Schenken, Suzanne O. *Legislators and Politicians: Iowa's Women Lawmakers*. Ames: Iowa State University Press, 1995.

Schneier. Edward, and John Brian Murtaugh, *New York Politics a Tale of Two Cities*. New York: M. E. Sharpe, 2001.

Schwartz, Joel, "The Empire State in a Changing World." In Milton Klein, ed., *The Empire State: A History of New York,* New York: New York State Historical Association, 2001.

Skocpol, Theda. Protecting Soldiers and Mothers: *The Political Origins of Social Policy in the United States*. Cambridge: Harvard University Press, 1995.

Slayton, Robert A. *Empire Statesman the Rise and Redemption of Al Smith*. New York: Free Press, 2001.

Smith, Richard Norton. *Thomas E. Dewey and His Times*. New York: Touchstone Books, 1982.

———. *On His Own Terms: A Life of Nelson Rockefeller*. New York: Random House, 2014.

Snyder, Rob. *Crossing Broadway: Washington Heights and the Promise of New York City*. Ithaca, NY: Cornell University Press, 2015.

Soyer, Daniel. *Left in the Center: The Liberal Party of New York and the Rise and Fall of American Social Democracy*. Ithaca, NY: Cornell University Press, 2021.

Stonecash, Jeffrey, "Introduction: the Sources of Conflict." In Robert Peccarella and Jeffrey Stonecash, eds., *Governing New York State*, 5th ed. Albany: State University of New York Press, 2006.

Stonecash, Jeffrey, and Amy Widestrom, "Political Parties and Elections." In Robert Peccarella and Jeffrey Stonecash, eds., *Governing New York State*, 5th ed. Albany: State University of New York Press, 2006.

Sullivan, Timothy. *New York State and the Rise of Modern Conservatism: Redrawing Party Lines*. Albany: State University of New York Press, 2009.

Sumner, Mary Boyd. *The Woman Citizen: A General Handbook of Civics, with Special Consideration of the Women's Citizenship*. New York: Frederick A. Stokes, 1918.

Taranto, Stacie. *Kitchen Table Politics: Conservative Women and Family Values in New York*. Philadelphia: University of Pennsylvania Press, 2017.

Tetrault, Lisa. *The Myth of Seneca Falls: Memory and the Women's Suffrage Movement, 1848–1898*. Chapel Hill: University of North Carolina Press, 2017.

Trouillot, Michel-Rolph. *Silencing the Past: Power and the Production of History.* Boston: Beacon Press, 2015.
Underwood, James E., and William J. Daniels. *Governor Rockefeller in New York.* Westport CT: Greenwood Press, 1982.
Van Ingen, Linda. *Gendered Politics: Campaign Strategies of California Women Candidates 1912–1970.* Lanham, MD: Lexington Books, 2017.
Walter, John C., ed. *The Harlem Fox: J. Raymond Jones and Tammany 1920–1970.* New York: State University of New York Press, 1989.
Ware, Susan. *Beyond Suffrage: Women in the New Deal.* Cambridge, MA: Harvard University Press, 1981.
Williams, Clare. *History of the Founding and Development of the National Federation of Republican Women.* Washington, DC: Republican National Committee, 1963.
Winslow, Barbara. *Shirley Chisholm: Catalyst for Change.* Boulder, CO: Westview Press, 2014.
Witt, Linda, Karen Paget, and Glenna Matthews. *Running as a Woman: Gender and Power in American Politics.* New York: The Free Press, 1994.
Wolbrecht, Christina. *The Politics of Women's Rights: Parties, Positions and Change.* Princeton, NJ: Princeton University Press, 2000.
Wood, Molly, "Mapping a Campaign Strategy: Partisan Women in the 1916 Election." In Melanie Gustafson, Kristie Miller, and Elisabeth Perry, eds., *We Have Come to Stay: American Women and Political Parties, 1860–1960.* Albuquerque: University of New Mexico Press, 1999.
Young, Louise. *In the Public Interest: The League of Women Voters, 1920–70.* Westport, CT: Greenwood Press, 1989.
Zacks, Richard. *Island of Vice: Theodore Roosevelt's Doomed Quest to Clean Up Sin-Loving New York.* New York: Doubleday, 2012.

Index

abortion, 206n119
   Blumenthal bill, 135, 136–137
   law, 104, 135–136, 156, 157–158, 204n81
   reform, 138
Abrams, Albert, 2
Abrams, Robert, 150
Abzug, Bella, 97, 98, 101, 115
activist government, 8, 13–14, 46, 150–151
activist, woman legislator as, 4, 23, 64–68, 93–94
Activist-Era Legislators, 63t
Advisory Committee on the Status of Women in CUNY, 126
Albany, 76, 101, 172n32
Alexander, Cora, 82
Allen, James, 128
American Woman Suffrage Association, 25
archetypical woman legislator, 4
Argersinger, Jo-Ann, 26
Ashberry, Ray, 66, 103
Assembly District Democratic Club of Brooklyn, 12

Badillo, Herman, 83
Baker, Josephine, 45, 173n8
Baker, Paula, 22, 23
Baker v. Carr, 18

Banks, Gladys, 44, 57–58
Barnello, Michelle, 76
Bellamy, Carol, 70–72, 85, 95, 99–101
Benjamin, Gerald, 2, 57
Berman, Carol, 70–71, 165
big milk interests, 49
bill jackets, legislative, 5–6
bingo, legalization of, 42
biographies of women in legislature, of LWC, 119
bipartisanship, of LWC, 118
birth control, banning of, 135, 203n76
Black and Puerto Rican Legislative Caucus, of New York, 80, 83, 110
Black Democratic Leadership, 82
Blair, Emily Newell, 31
Blanco, Rita, 154
Blatch, Harriet Stanton, 26–27
Blatch, Nora Stanton, 41
Blumenthal, Albert, 90, 135–137
Boswell, Helen Varick, 28, 29
Braun, Carol Mosley, 149
breast cancer, public awareness for, 118
Brennan, James, 160
the Bronx, 57, 82–83
Bronx Citizens Committee, 82–83
Brooklyn Daily Eagle (newspaper), 37
Brooklyn Transit System, 41
Brooklyn Women's Club, 117

225

Brydges, Earl, 136, 138
Buchanan, Bessie, 43, 45, 56
Buchanan, Charles, 45
Buckley, Charles, 43
Buckley, Ray, 78
Buffalo Evening News (newspaper), 46
Burrows, Gordon, 154
Burstein, Karen, 68–69, 71–73, 85, 95
  highlights of career of, 101–102
  Krupsak and, 99
  on number of women in Assembly, 146
busing, 130–133
  eligibility for, 125
butter, price of, 51
Byrne, Doris, 43–44, 53–54, 58, 89, 113

Cammisa, Anne Marie, 3
Campbell, Donald, 94
candidates, women as
  children of, 37
  cross-endorsement of, 161n12
  minor parties role of, 12–13
  state-level, 2
  for "Year of the Woman," 149
Carey, Hugh, 14, 95–98, 103
Carroll, Susan, 163
Carter, Eunice Hunton, 45
Catholic Church, political power of, 55, 135–136, 140
Catt, Carrie Chapman, 28–29
caucuses, 109–110
  women's, 110, 116, 117, 142, 161, 165
change
  expectations for, 67, 74
  legislature as venue for immediate, 65–66
Change-NY, 155, 159
Chartock, Alan, 87
Cheney, Edith, 37–38, 44

children, of candidates, 37
children, women legislators and, 113, 164
Children's Bureau, 23
Chisholm, Shirley, 2, 12, 67, 72, 79–81
  assumptions about, 89
  Brooklyn Women's Club and, 117
  on education, 123–125
  "unbought and unbossed" slogan of, 81
Cincotta, George, 74
City Board of Education, 128, 130, 134
City Council president, Bellamy as, 101
City University of New York system (CUNY), 126
Citywide Committee for Integrated Schooling, 128
civil rights movement, 16, 79, 80, 82–83
Clark, Barbara, 118
clashing identities, of New York, 8–9
closure, of schools, 133–134
Cohen, David, 87
Colavita, Anthony, 155–156
Collins, Mayme, 114
colored oleo margarine, 50, 113
Columbia University, 102–103
community boards, neighborhood, 17
Congressional Caucus for Women's Issues, 116, 117
Congresswoman's Caucus, 116
Connecticut Order of Women Legislators (OWL), 111
Connelly, Elizabeth, 72, 77, 93, *105*, 105–108, 206n119
  abortion law and, 142
  committee chair as, 106
  Fresh Kills landfill and, 165
  LWC and, 118

on self-labelling as "politician," 147
Staten Island Secession effort, 106
Willowbrook reform of, 107–108
Conservative Party, 14, 75, 105, 130–133, 155
constituent service, focus on, 57
Constitutional Convention (1894), 10
contraception, 141
Cook, Constance, 35, 66, 69, 77, 93
abortion law and, 135–143, *137*, 165
advocacy of, *121*
on education, 123, 125–126
highlights of career of, 103–104, 177n5
pragmatic arguments for abortion and, 141
Cooke, Audre, 90–91
Cornell University, 126–127
corroboration requirements, in rape cases, 100
Van Cott, George, 130
Couch, Natalie, 184n130
county school commissioners, voting for, 24
cross-endorsement, of candidates, 171n12
CUNY. *See* City University of New York system
Cuomo, Andrew, 31
Cuomo, Mario, 87, 91–92, 95, 97, 106
Cyna, Esther, 134

DAC. *See* Democratic Assembly Committee
Dahlerup, Drude, 122
D'Amato, Alphonse, 91, 150
Daniels, Geraldine, 84, 147
Davis, Gloria, 85
Davis, John W., 171n21
Delmonte, Francine, 118–119

Democrat, immigrants as, 10
Democratic Assembly Committee (DAC), 152–153
Democratic Party
majority enrollment statewide, 42
minority status, 10, 42
takeover of Assembly, 10, 67–68, 91
takeover of Senate, 166
Democratic primary, for lieutenant governor, 95
democrats, downstate, 67
democrats, in New York City, 9
Department of Mental Hygiene, 107
Dewey, Thomas E., 13, 15, 57, 59, 60, 103
Diamond, Irene, 3, 69, 75, 93–94
Diggs, Estella, 72–73, 82–83, 85, 142, 185n10
Dinkins, David, 85
disability benefits, for pregnant workers, 101
disability issues, 107
discriminatory language, in state laws, 56–57
diversity issues
at Cornell, 126–127
at CUNY, 126
within women, 21, 30, 36, 52, 122
division, among women, 54, 122, 158–159
divorce reform, 42, 54–56, 112, 182n103
annulment, criteria of, 55
divorces, no-fault, 56
Downstate, Upstate *versus*, 8, 21–22, 51, 98
Dreier, Mary, 41
Dubois, Ellen Carol, 26–27
Dugan, Eileen, 147
DUI legislation, 108
Duryea, Perry, 104, 136, 137, 138–139

East Harlem, 83
education
  centralized control, 16
  compulsory, 16
  decentralization, 16–17, 132–133, 172n31
  The Decentralization Act, 17
  elementary and secondary education system reform, 104
  funding of, 123–125
  local community control, 131–132
  local schools, establishment of, 16
  of women legislators, 36–37, 68, 123
  policy, 15–16, 104, 123–134
  racial balance in schools, 128
  racial equity in schools, 127–128
  school boards, 17, 131–132, 143
  school closures, 133–134
  student transfers, 127–129
  textbook bill, 124–125
  vouchers, 134
Edwards, Babette, 134
elections (1992), 146, 149, 151, 159–160
Elizabeth Connelly Papers, 206n119
Ellison, Noel, 82
Emery, Julia, 111
Emily's List, 149
employment opportunities, 59
Epstein, Barbara, 174n14
Epstein, Leslie, 175n26
EQUAL, 129
Equal Rights Amendment (ERA), national, 41, 75, 112–113
Equal Rights Amendment (ERA), state, 75, 100, 122–123
Equality League of Self-Supporting Women, 26
ERA. *See* Equal Rights Amendment
Erie Canal, 9

expectations
  for change, 67, 74
  of early women legislators, 122
  post-suffrage, 30–31

Factory Investigating Commission (FIC), 13, 26
farmers, milk pricing and, 49–50, 63
female consciousness, 24–25
female-only dining room, of OWL, 111
feminism, of Bellamy, 99–100
feminism, of Burstein, 101
feminism, of Matusow, 152
Ferraro, Geraldine, 14, 150
FIC. *See* Factory Investigating Commission
Fifty-Four Hour Law, 41, 179n30
fight, for suffrage, 3–4, 25–26, 122
financial rescue package, for New York City, 101
Fink, Stanley, 73, 76, 99, 106
The Fleischman Commission, 104
Flynn, Edward, 89
Ford Foundation, 131
Ford, Gerald, 14
Foster, Judith Ellen, 28
Fox, Jean Amatucci, 79, 185n10
Friedan, Betty, 136

Gadson, Jeanette, 89–90, 185n10
Gage, Matilda Joslyn, 25
Galef, Sandra, 152, 153–154, 155
Galiber, Joseph, 134
geography, of New York, 8–9
George, Walter Lloyd, 110–111
Gillen, Mary, 37–38, 44
Gillette, Elizabeth, 43, 112
Goodhue, Mary, 77–79, 148, 154–156, 158–159
  moderate Republicanism, of, 78, 167

Goodier, Susan, 22
Gordon, Bernard, 77
Gordon, Janet, 42–43, 44, 51–52, 54–55, 57
  congressional campaign of, *60*, 60–61
  divorce reform and, 54–56
  NOWL and, 112, 113–114
government, activist, 8, 13–14, 46
government involvement, neighborhood-level, 17
government waste, Hochberg on, 153
governors' terms, 171n22
Grasso, Ella, 100
Graves, Rhoda Fox, 42–43, 45, 46–50, *47*, 53
  as individual woman politician, 110
  new opportunities for, 58
  obituary of in NOWL scrapbook, 113–114
Gray, Jesse, 102
Great Depression, 13
Greene, Aurelia, 118, 161, 165
Griswold v. Connecticut, 203n76
gubernatorial run, of Krupsak, 97, 98–99, 117
Gunning, Rosemary, 69–70, 112–113, *121*, 123, 127–128, 130–134
  abortion reform and, 138
  education policy achievements of, 143, 201n30
  gender stereotypes and, 129
Gustafson, Melanie, 23, 25

Hall, Murray, 1
Hamilton, Alexander, 182n103
Hamilton County, New York, 8
Hanniford, Elizabeth, 57–58
Harlem, 56–57, 102, 133–134
Harlem Parents Union, 134
Harper's Magazine (magazine), 110–111

Harriman, Averill, 56, 69
Harvey, Anna, 30, 176n56
Heckler, Margaret, 99
Hellenbrand, Gail, 84–85, 138, 185n10
Hill, Anita, 149
Hill, David, 77
Hochberg, Audrey, 152, 153–154, 156
Hochul, Kathy, 31
Holtzman, Elizabeth, 99, 150
housing, affordable, 102
Hughes Campaign Train, 27–28, 175n39
Hughes, Charles Evans, 27–28
Hughes, John, 124–125
Huntington Political Equality League, 39
Huntington Town Supervisor, 92
hydroelectric power, 48

immediate change, legislature as venue for, 65–66
immigrants, as mainly Democrat, 10
immigration, of Blacks and Hispanics, 10
industrialization, 9
  post-World War II, 8, 14
integration, of schools, 127
International Women's Day, 97
invisible, early legislators as, 31
Iowa, 77
Iroquois Political Club, 1
IS 201, 134
islands, pioneer generation as, 67
Ithaca, 125
Ithaca Sentinel (newspaper), 135

Jackson, Bernard, 85
Jacobs, Rhoda, 74–75, 108
Johnson, Lyndon, 82
joint custody, 78

Jones, J. Raymond, 12, 82
Jones, Nancy Baker, 4
junior license, for teens, 48
jury service, women and, 53–54, 141, 182n94

Kellor, Frances, 27–28
Kibbee, Robert, 126
Kirkpatrick, Jeanne, 3, 35, 57, 61, 93–94
Kleinfeld, Philip, 54
Knapp, Florence E., 86
Kramer, Daniel, 96
Krupsak, Mary Anne, 94–96, *96,* 100, 103, 112
   abortion reform and, 138
   Black maids in hotel and, 98
   gubernatorial run of, 97–99, 117
   lieutenant governor as, 95–97
   networks for women and, 116–117, *121*

La Guardia, Fiorello, 11, 151
labor laws, protective, 23
Laidlaw, Harriet, 27
law degrees, 68
Lawrence, Dorothy, 38, 44, 45
Lawson, Kathleen, 206n119
League of Women Voters, 111, 176n56
legal profession, 68, 163
legislative bill jackets, 5–6
legislative culture, 56, 71–74
legislative districts, majority minority, 18, 67, 79, 85
legislative environment, 61, 75
Legislative Office Building, 77
legislative record, of Sammis, 40
legislative structure
   committee Assembly Alcoholism & Drug Abuse, 91
   committee Assembly Child Care, 77–78
   committee Assembly Ethics, 87
   committee Assembly Rules, 75, 106
   committee Assembly Ways and Means, 46, 165
   committee Senate Agriculture, 46–47
   professionalization of, 89, 166
   seniority for committee service, 93
legislative style, of men and women, 163
legislative terms, 18, 36, 177n3
Legislative Women's Caucus (LWC), 110, 118–119, 142, 161, 165
Lehman, Herbert, 13, 43, 150–151
Leichter, Franz, 136–137
Lewis, Diocletian, 23
liberal republicanism, 117
liberalism, social, 8, 148, 150–151
lieutenant governor, responsibilities of, 94–97
Lilly, Mary, 35, 44–45, 52–53
limits, to pioneer generation, 58–61
Lindsay, John, 131, 151, 172n31
Lipshutz, Gerdi, 86–87
Long Island, political influence of, 91
Lowell, Josephine Shaw, 12
loyalties, partisan, 9–10, 22, 27, 38–39, 117, 166–167
Lurie, Irene, 129
LWC. *See* Legislative Women's Caucus

machine politics, 10–11
Maclay Bill, 124
Mahoney, Anna, 109–110
"make policy, not coffee" slogan of NWPC, 115
Manhattan Women's Political Caucus, 100
map, of New York, *7*
Marchi, John, 151
margarine, oleo, 50–52
Marlatt, Frances, 113–114
Martin, Barney, 1

Matusow, Naomi, 152, 156–157, 158
McCormick, Richard, 22
McGee, Mary Rose, 185n10
McGerr, Michael, 22
McMartin, Barbara, 77–78
McMartin Preschool, 77
  expert testimony unreliable, 78
McSorley Bill, 206n114
Mendez, Olga, 83–84
mental health issues, Connelly and, 107–108
Meredith, James, 80
Milk Control Act of 1933, 49
milk pricing
  farmers and, 49–50, 63
  official investigation into, 49
Miller, Mel, 106, 146, 160
Miller, Warner, 50
minor party candidates, 12–13
Minority Steering Committee, 91
minority women, 79–84
The Modern New York State Legislature (Benjamin and Nakamura), 2
Mondale, Walter, 150
Montgomery County, 94
Montgomery, Velmanette, 79, 145
Moses, Robert, 59
motherhood, authority of, 21
Motley, Constance, 67, 80–82, *81*
movement leaders, activist politicians as, 71
Ms., request to be called, 71
Municipal League, 12
Murtaugh, John, 8
Myerson, Bess, 150

NAACP. *See* National Association for the Advancement of Colored People
Nakamura, Robert, 2, 57
NARAL. *See* National Association for the Repeal of All Abortion Laws

Nassau County, 70, 102
National American Suffrage Association (NAWSA), 25
National Association for the Advancement of Colored People (NAACP), 80–81
National Association for the Repeal of All Abortion Laws (NARAL), 136
national gathering, of women legislators, 111
National Order of Women Legislators (NOWL), 110–115
National Organization for Women, 100
national party committees, Women's Division of, 28
National Woman Suffrage Association, 25
National Women's Party (NWP), 41
National Women's Political Caucus (NWPC), 115–116
NAWSA. *See* National American Suffrage Association
neighborhood-level involvement, in government, 17
New Way Democratic Club, 70
New York
  dichotomy, urban/rural, 15
  divides within, 8
  geography of, 8–9
  map, *7*
New York City, influence of, 79
New York City Police Department, 11
New York City Tammany machine, 1, 11, 86
New York County Republican Committee, 29
New York Court of Appeals, 24
New York governor, power of, 8, 15
New York Politics (Schneier and Murtaugh), 8
New York politics, corruption of, 10–11, 86

New York politics, key elements of, 8
The New York Red Book (government document), 5, 119
New York State Assembly, 1–2, 47–48
New York State Black and Puerto Rican Legislative Caucus, 80, 83, 110
New York State Census, 86
New York State Federation of Women's Clubs, 44
New York State Governor's Committee to Review New York State Abortion Law, 136
New York State Legislative Women's Caucus, 6, 110, 118–119, 210n73
New York State Legislature, 16, 18–19, 94
New York State Right to Life Party (RTLP), 140, 147
New York State Senate, 11, 18–19, 94–95, 166
New York State Woman Suffrage Association (NYSWSA), 25, 26
New York State Women's Political Caucus (NYSWPC), 116–117
New York Times (newspaper), 1, 38, 39, 51, 86
  on Conservative Party, 131
  on women in legislature, 145–146
  on "Year of the Woman," 148–149
New York-specific elements, in politics, 3, 9
Newburger, May, 89, 146
1919–1992 period, 2
nineteenth-century partisanship, 22
Nixon, Richard, 125, 140
no-fault divorces, 56
Nolan, Catherine, 145–146
noncitizen residents, inclusion in population base, 18
nonpartisanship, of women, 27–28, 115–116

NOWL. *See* National Order of Women Legislators
NOWL scrapbook, 113
NWP. *See* National Women's Party
NYSWPC. *See* New York State Women's Political Caucus
NYSWSA. *See* New York State Woman Suffrage Association

Ocean-Hill Brownsville school district, 17
O'Dwyer, William, 43
Office of the Clerk of the Assembly, 184n130
oleo margarine, 50–52, 165
Oppenheimer, Suzi, 151, 154, 157
oral history project, of New York State Legislative Women's Caucus, 6
Orange and Rockland Utilities, 88
organizations, unifying, of political women, 4–5, 109–110
Organizing to Win by the Political District Plan (Laidlaw), 27
O'Rourke, Andrew, 91–92
Owens, Major, 89
OWL. *See* Connecticut Order of Women Legislators
The OWLetter (newsletter), 112

Parent and Taxpayers Citywide Coordinating Council (PAT), 127–130
parochial schools, separation from state schools of, 124
partisan loyalties, 9–10, 22, 27, 38–39, 117, 166–167
partisanship. *See also* bipartisanship
  nineteenth-century, 22
  nonpartisanship, 27–28, 115–116
Pastorello, Karen, 22
PAT. *See* Parent and Taxpayers Citywide Coordinating Council

Pataki, George, 155–156, 159
Paul, Alice, 41
pay toilets, in public facilities, 73
permissive jury service, 53–54, 59
Perry, Elizabeth Israels, 27
Peterson, Dutton, 55–56
Phillips-Fein, Kim, 134
piety, women and, 178n29
pioneer women legislators, 4, 33t, *34*, 65
plain language, in memoranda, 106
Platt, Livingston, 59
Plunkitt, George Washington, 28–29
policy caucuses, 110
political ambition, 88
political competition, 9
political corruption, as cost of doing business, 10–11
political power, of Catholic church, 55, 135–136, 140
political process, exclusion of women from, 3–4
political scandals, 86
political system, opening of women to, 19
political tumult of 1920s, 36
The Political Voice (Buchanan, C.), 45
Political Woman (Kirkpatrick), 3
Polivy, Margot, 115
population
  noncitizen residents in, 18
  representation and, 10
  of rural New York, 8
positive, protégé as, 90
post-suffrage expectations, 30–31
post-World War II industrialization, 8, 14
power
  of Catholic Church, 55, 135–136, 140
  hydroelectric power, 48
  of New York governor, 8, 15

pragmatic arguments, for abortion, 141
pragmatism, 24
pre-office occupations, of women, 68–71, 163–164
presuffrage, 3–4, 19, 36, 65
pro-choice beliefs, of Hochberg, 154
"pro-choice," use of term in 1992 campaigns, 156
professional era, 89
professionalized legislature, 89, 166
Progressive Era, 23, 41
Prohibition Party, 40
property tax, proposed, 104
proposed separation, of Staten Island from New York City, 106
proposed statewide property tax, 104
protective labor laws, 23
protégé, as positive, 90
public awareness, for breast cancer, 118
Puerto Rican/Hispanic Task Force, 83
Pure Food and Drug Act, 50
Putnam County, 78–79, 155

Queens, 127

racial balance, in schools, 128
racial equality, in schools, 128
Ramirez, Roberto, 85–86
Rankin, Jeannette, 27–28
Ravitch, Diane, 132
record-keeping, women's careers of, 5
reform, 203n73
  abortion, 136–140
  divorce, 42, 54–56, 112, 182n103
  of elementary and secondary education system, 104, 132–134
reform package, of Senate Rules, 100
Reingold, Beth, 3
relief, tax, 91
representation, population and, 10
Republican dominance, in Upstate New York, 9. 42, 172n37, 179n38

Republican loss, of Assembly, 18
"Republican Mother," 123
Republican Party, 58, 91, 131, 167
Republican Senate leadership, 96–97
responsibilities, of lieutenant governor, 95–97
restrooms, in Assembly chamber, 73, 145
Rettaliata, Antonia, 90–92, 185n10
Reynolds v. Simms, 18
Rich, Mildred, 111–112
Rich, Wilbur, 133
Right to Life Committees (RTLC), 140
Right to Life movement, 135
Robinson, Corrine Roosevelt, 29
Rockefeller Drug Laws, 118
Rockefeller, Nelson, 14, 15, 38, 104, 127
  moderate views of, 161–162
  Smith, R., on, 151
Rockland County, 87
Roe v. Wade, 140, 147
roles, gender, 30–32
Roosevelt, Franklin, 11, 13, 14, 150–151
Roosevelt, Theodore, 14
Rose, Dorothy, 67, 135
Rosenthal, Cindy Simon, 165
Rothstein, Polly, 152, 156
RTLO. *See* New York State Right to Life Party
Rubin, Richard, 86
Rules Committee, 75, 106
Runyon, Marie, 85, 93, 101–103
rural New York, population of, 8
Ryan, Aileen, 35, 52, 57, 66, 177n1
Rylander, Isabelle, 115

Saint Germain, Michelle, 31
sales tax, 14
Sammis, Ida B., 35, 39, 41–42, 44, 53
  Marriages of, 40

Samuels, Howard, 95
Sanbonmatsu, Kira, 163
Sanjek, Roger, 17
scandals, political, 11, 40, 86–89, 160
Scheiss, Betty Bone, 141–142
Schenken, Suzanne, 77
Schlafly, Phyllis, 75
Schneier, Edward, 8, 14
school boards, 17
school closures, 133–134
school integration, 127
school vouchers, 134
scrapbook, of NOWL, 113
Search for Education, Elevation and Knowledge Bill (SEEK), 124
self-labeling, of Assembly members, as politicians, 147
Senate-approved administrative jobs, women and, 99–100
sex equity, 53
Sex Roles in the State House (Diamond), 3
Shaffer, Gail, 147
shared environment, group cohesion and, 117
SIDC. *See* Staten Island Development Center
Silencing the Past (Trouillot), 6
Silver, Sheldon, 106
Singer, Cecile, 152, 154, 157, 158, 167
Siwek, Carol, 147
Skocpol, Theda, 23
Smith, Al, 87
Smith, Joan, *146,* 185n10
Smith, Marguerite, 39, 40–42, 43–44, 46, 164
Smith, Richard Norton, 151
Snell, H. B., 48
social
  caucuses, 110
  expectations, 19

liberalism, 8, 148, 150–151
welfare, 15
social eligibility pool, for candidate selection, 163
Social Welfare and Education committee, 46
societal disadvantages, of women in politics, 5
spanking bill, 52, 66
Speaker Pro Tempore, Connelly as, 106–107
Specter, Arlen, 150
St. Lawrence River, 48
State Bar Association, 127
State Catholic Welfare Committee, 55–56
State Court of Appeals, 127
State Democratic Committee, 43
State Department of Agriculture and Markets, 51
state laws, discriminatory language in, 56–57
State Power Authority, 48
State Supreme Court, 130
state-level candidates, women as, 2
Staten Island, 105
Staten Island Development Center (SIDC), 107–108
Staten Island Hospital, 105
Steingut, Stanley, 70, 89
Stewart-Cousins, Andrea, 166
Stonecash, Jeffrey, 15
Stratton, Samuel, 60–61, 184n133
Strong, Genesta, 42, 50–51, 113–114
Strong, William, 11
suffrage fight, 3–4, 25–26, 122
Sullivan, Florence, 118
Sullivan, Peter, 152
support, for marginalized groups, 13
supportive networks, for women, 119
symposium, on marriage and divorce laws, 112

Syracuse Post Standard (newspaper), 141

Tammany machine, of New York City, 1, 11, 86
Taranto, Stacie, 135, 140
tax
on pocketbooks, 66
proposed statewide property tax, 104
relief, 91
Taylor, Mildred, 46, 114–115
Taylor v. Louisiana, 54
teaching, 123
teens, junior license for, 48
Temporary State Commission on the Constitution, 103
Ten Eyck, Maude, 44, 54–55, 59–60, 114, 184n130
terms
of governors, 171n22
legislative, 18, 36, 177n4
Tetrault, Lisa, 25
textbook bill, 124–125
Thayer, Warren, 48–49
third parties, 171n12
Thomas, Clarence, 149–150
thread the needle, between issues and party, 61–62
Tilden, Samuel, 12
Todd, Jane, 42, 58–60, 78, 112, 148
jury service women and, 53–54
tokenism, 31
Tompkins County, 105, 125
Triangle Shirtwaist Factory Fire, 13, 26
Trouillot, Michel-Rolph, 5
12th Congressional District, 81
27th Congressional District, 59

UDC. *See* Unity Democratic Club
UFT. *See* United Federation of Teachers
"unbought and unbossed," slogan of Chisholm, 81

undergarment bill, 161
United Federation of Teachers (UFT), 132
United States Equal Opportunity Commission (EEOC), 141–142
United War Relief Fund, 39
Unity Democratic Club (UDC), 80
Upper Manhattan, 83
Upstate, Downstate *versus*, 8, 21–22, 51, 98
urban women, 21–22
urban/rural dichotomy, 15–16

veteran scholarship, 38
vice chair of state parties, women as, 43, 58–59
voter block, view of women as, 39

Wagner, Robert, 130
Walker, Jimmy, 11
Wall Street Journal (newspaper), 128
Ward, William, 58–59
Watergate investigations, 102
Watson, James, 80
WCTU. *See* Women's Christian Temperance Union
Weinstein, Helene, 70, 85, 146, 165
Westchester Coalition for Legal Abortion, 152
Westchester County, New York, 5, 58, 78, 147–162
Westchester County Women's Republican Club, 58
"White Parents in New York Protest Plan to 'Pair' Schools" *(Wall Street Journal)*, 128
widows, of legislators, 37
Willard, Frances, 24, 25, 174n14
Willowbrook State School, 107–108
Wilson, David, 154
Wilson, Malcolm, 100

Wilson, Woodrow, 28
Winegarten, Ruth, 4
Winikow, Linda, 72, 76, 87
  death penalty and, 88
  newspapers funneling of funds to, 88–89
"Winikow Memorial Law," 88
WISH. *See* Women in the Senate and House
Witt, Linda, 149
WMCA v. Lomenzo, 18
WNRA. *See* Women's National Republican Association
woman legislator, as activist, 4, 66–67
woman legislator, as isolated figure, 52, 67
Woman Republican (newspaper), 54
Woman's Suffrage Party of Greater New York, 27
women elected to office, number of, 31, 36, 68, 149, 159–160
women in political parties, influence of, 29–31, 166–167
Women in the Senate and House (WISH), 149
Women Legislators from Westchester in 1992, 145t, *146*
Women's agenda, political
  issue abortion as, 5, 104, 119, 135–143
  issue advocacy general, 27, 62, 93, 165
  issue education as, 123
  issue family concerns as, 164–165
  issue mental health as, 107
  issue tension with party loyalty, 61
  issues broadening of concerns, 164–165
  Westchester changing nature of, 157
Women's Bureau of the Department of Labor, 23

women's caucuses, 110, 116, 117, 142, 161, 165
Women's Christian Temperance Union (WCTU), 23–24, 123, 174n12, 175n26
Women's Crusade, 174n12
Women's Division, of national party committees, 28
Women's Joint Legislative Conference (WILC), 41, 176n56
Women's League for Equal Opportunity, 41
Women's Legislative Caucus in Albany, 158–159
women's movement, 80–81, 103, 116–117, 122, 135
Women's Municipal League, 26
Women's National Republican Association (WNRA), 28
Women's political identity
  ambition political, 88
  authority as mothers, 21, 154
  civic activities, 68, 70–71
  conflicting gender standards, 40
  family obligations and, 31, 37, 153
  fighters for constituents as, 56–57, 83, 91
  gender stereotypes, 30–31, 61, 164, 166, 178n29
  as lawyers, 69–70
  party service and, 88, 166
  pre-suffrage political consciousness of, 24–25
  proteges of males as, 89–90, 146
  teaching background and, 123
  widowhood and, 37–38
  womanhood ideas about, 23
Women's Trade Union League (WTUL), 26, 41
Women's West End Republican Association, 29
working class women, NYSWSA and, 26
work-life balance, of women legislators, 164
Wright, Samuel, 89, 117
WTUL. *See* Women's Trade Union League

Yeakel, Lynn, 149–150
Year of the Woman, 147–162
Yoswein, Joni, 146, 160

Zaretsky, Joseph, *81*, 101

www.ingramcontent.com/pod-product-compliance
Lightning Source LLC
Chambersburg PA
CBHW030646230426
43665CB00011B/974